Charles James Wood

Survivals in Christianity, Studies in the Theology of the Divine immanence

special lectures delivered before the Episcopal theological school at Cambridge,

1892

Charles James Wood

Survivals in Christianity, Studies in the Theology of the Divine immanence
special lectures delivered before the Episcopal theological school at Cambridge, 1892

ISBN/EAN: 9783337815691

Printed in Europe, USA, Canada, Australia, Japan

Cover: Foto ©Andreas Hilbeck / pixelio.de

More available books at **www.hansebooks.com**

SURVIVALS IN CHRISTIANITY

SURVIVALS IN CHRISTIANITY

STUDIES IN THE THEOLOGY OF
DIVINE IMMANENCE

SPECIAL LECTURES

DELIVERED BEFORE THE EPISCOPAL THEOLOGICAL
SCHOOL AT CAMBRIDGE, MASS., IN 1892

BY

CHARLES JAMES WOOD

New York
MACMILLAN AND CO.
AND LONDON
1893

All rights reserved

COPYRIGHT, 1893,
BY MACMILLAN AND CO.

Norwood Press:
J. S. Cushing & Co. — Berwick & Smith.
Boston, Mass., U.S.A.

v

TO

𝔗𝔥𝔢 𝔕𝔢𝔳𝔢𝔯𝔢𝔫𝔡 𝔖𝔞𝔪𝔲𝔢𝔩 𝔇. 𝔐𝔠𝔒𝔬𝔫𝔫𝔢𝔩𝔩, 𝔇.𝔇.

WHOSE LOYAL HEART AND QUICKENING

MIND HAVE BEEN FOR ME A

STAY AND A STIMULUS

PREFACE.

This preface is merely explanatory. If an author thinks he ought to apologise for his book, then he ought never to publish that book. Besides, the Cerberus of literary criticism is not mollified by sops of apology.

My purpose in sending forth this book is to help honest and earnest truth-seekers both to find what is real and true in the realm of religious thought, and to accept with equal honesty and intelligence the Evangel of Jesus the Christ. Whenever men thus find and accept the truth as it is in Jesus, they will also realise and rejoice in the organic unity of the Church, for which I hopefully pray.

In citing the Scriptures of the New Covenant I have followed Tischendorf's Greek text. I have made my own translation in order to draw attention to points which our familiarity with the received versions causes us to overlook. The notes were added for the same reason that a short bibliography was prepared,— to assist those desirous of studying further into the subject.

Genuine criticism, from "those who know," I do not deprecate, but welcome. Truth is all, and I am naught, save only as I yield myself an utterance of the Living Truth Who abides in the heart of things.

I am glad that I am under obligations to my friend Mr. E. M. Kingsbury for revising for me the proof-sheets of this book.

St. Paul's Rectory, Lock Haven, Pa., U.S.A.
St. Matthias' Day, 1893.

CONTENTS.

LECTURE I.
The Introduction 5

LECTURE II.
The Idea of God 31

LECTURE III.
The Church 83

LECTURE IV.
The Forgiveness of Sins 143

LECTURE V.
The Resurrection 199

LECTURE VI.
Eternal Life 249

Bibliography 293

Index 301

THE INTRODUCTION.

Hooker. I know my poor weak intellects, most noble Lord, and how scantily they have profited by my hard painstaking. Comprehending few things, and those imperfectly, I say only what others have said before, wise men and holy; and if by passing through my heart into the wide world around me, it pleaseth God that this little treasure shall have lost nothing of its weight and pureness, my exultation is then the exultation of humility. Wisdom consisteth not in knowing many things, nor even in knowing them thoroughly; but in choosing and in following what conduces the most certainly to our lasting happiness and true glory. And this wisdom, my Lord of Verulam, cometh from above.

LANDOR, *Imaginary Conversations.*

Some men distinguish errour from truth by calling their Adversaries *new and of yesterday;* and certainly this is a good signe if it be rightly applied: for since all Christian doctrine is that which Christ taught his Church and the spirit enlarged, or expounded, and the Apostles delivered, we are to begin the Christian æra for our faith and parts of religion by the period of their preaching: our account begins then, and whatsoever is contrary to what they taught is new and false, and whatsoever is besides what they taught, is no part of our religion (and then no man can be prejudiced for believing it or not); and if it be adopted into the confessions of the Church, the proposition is always so uncertain, that it is not to be admitted into the faith, and therefore if it be old in respect of days, it is not necessary to be believed: if it be new, it may be received into opinion according to its probability, and no sects or interests are to be divided up on such accounts.

Bp. JEREMY TAYLOR, Sermon, *Of Christian Prudence.*
, Works, II. 275.

The idols and false notions which have already preoccupied the human understanding, and are deeply rooted in it, not only so beset men's minds, that they become difficult of access, but even when access is obtained, will again meet and trouble us in the instauration of the sciences, unless mankind, when forewarned, guard themselves with all possible care against them. Four species of idols beset the human mind, to which (for distinction's sake) we have assigned names: calling the first the Idols of the tribe; the second, the Idols of the den; the third, Idols of the market; the fourth, Idols of the theatre.

BACON, Novum Organum, I. 38, 39.

St. Clement of Alexandria, referring to the philosopher Herakleitos, wrote, *Strom.* V. 14 : " If you wish to trace out that saying, ' He that hath ears to hear, let him hear,' you will find it expressed by the Ephesian in this manner: 'Those who hear and do not understand are like the deaf,' and, 'eyes and ears are bad witnesses to men having rude souls.' "

What we call Christianity is a vast ocean, into which flow a number of spiritual currents of distant and various origin: certain religions, that is to say, of Asia and of Europe, the great ideas of Greek wisdom, and especially those of Platonism. Neither its doctrine nor its morality, as they have been historically developed, are new or spontaneous. What is essential and original in it is the practical demonstration that the human and the divine nature may coexist, may become fused into one sublime flame; that holiness and pity, justice and mercy, may meet together and become one in man and in God. What is specific in Christianity is Jesus — the religious consciousness of Jesus.

AMIEL, Journal.

SYNOPSIS.

1. A new method in the study of Theology is demanded by the conditions of the present day, in order to eliminate from popular religious thought some pagan survivals.

2. Illustration of the mixture of ethnic religious notions with Christianity in the early centuries of this era.

3. An attempt to give some of the causes of the incomplete reception of Christianity: Among the Apostles, post-apostolic Christians, ante-Nicene and mediæval theologians.

4. This accounts for a survival in Christian Theology of some incongruous and alien elements which contradict the very essence of the revelation of Jesus, and enfeeble it as an instrument for the Salvation of the World.

5. Therefore we should eliminate these Survivals as elements which are practically injurious. For this purpose a method of Theological study is here suggested and the outline given.

6. The Subjects are to be treated in five lectures.

7. There is no authority competent to release us from the demands of a comparative, historico-genetic study of Theology. All Theology thus examined is seen to be the growth of the religious receptiveness of mankind, the growth of the God-consciousness. In this sense alone is Christianity an evolution.

THE INTRODUCTION.

Gentlemen : —

If the crudities which may appear in these lectures were due solely to my own limitations of knowledge and thought, I should not advert to them, but, with confidence and tranquillity, leave that task to my critics. There is, however, a defectiveness due to the exigencies of the days in which we live.

1. It is easy to call any age a transition period, because time is always rushing forward, a resistless current, but surely it is plain enough to any observer that in an especial and marked way this age is a transition period in Theology. The cuneiform clay epistles of Tel-el-Amarna, the slabs of the great Babylonian epic, antiquities of the Nile and Euphrates valleys, the critical analysis of the Hebrew and Greek scriptures, and the comparative study of religions are casting upon Theology a light to which we cannot and ought not to shut our eyes. The old is passing away, and behold, all things are becoming new. The meaning of the higher criticism is manifestly the removing of those things that are shaken, as of things

that are made, that those things which cannot be shaken may remain. We are standing in the brightness of the early sunrise of a new day in methods of Theological study, and these methods are still too new to escape unripeness. Enough for us if our new forms of thought have a reality, have a vivid and vivifying force, and adjust themselves to the new shapes which the problems of our day assume.

Two props stay my mind in beginning these lectures, assuring me that it is worth your while to hear them, and my while to give them. The first is the substantial truth of the points taken, but the second, and all-important matter, is the method which I use. It is to this method that I bespeak your especial attention.

2. In order to point out the importance of this method in the study of Christian doctrine, let me premise an illustration. There stands to-day in the city of Constantinople the blasted, blackened stump of an ancient pillar. It is called the Burnt Column, and it is now about eighty feet high. An unknown Byzantine writer[1] in the reign of the emperors Arcadius and Honorius, tells us that the Emperor Constantine the Great erected this porphyry column one hundred and fifty feet high. He wound about it a spiral ribbon of bas-relief like Trajan's Column. He brought from Delphi the ancient bronze image of Apollo, and

[1] *Incertus Scriptor*, in Orelli's edition of Hesychius Milesius, 295.

on the pedestal of this image had inscribed, as if it were a portrait statue of himself, his own illustrious name. To the top of this column was then elevated this sacred image of Apollo-Constantine, and to make perfectly clear that the old god had been converted into a Christian numen, about his head they put a nimbus of darting rays *made from nails of the true cross.* Underneath the foundation of this porphyry column were placed the ancient palladium of the Roman Empire, that image which fell down from Heaven, and which Æneas through so many tribulations brought from Troy, and together with it the *twelve baskets of the miracle of the loaves and fishes!*

Strange conglomeration, apt symbol of the mass of our popular religious notions and Theology! Christian and heathen elements are mingled together! The task of the Christian student in Theology is therefore clearly indicated. He must try the oracles, whether they be indeed of God.

3. How came about this mixture of foreign elements with Christian Theology? Consider a moment, and it will be clear to you. The extent of the knowledge of divine truth in the world of men is a matter which is measured by revelation and receptiveness. Receptiveness is gradual, growing, or progressive. The divine method in the world is not revolutionary, but evolutionary. The Bible is a record of the progressive reception of divine truth. The Gospel grows into men's minds as the world grows old. This

condition of religious knowledge we discover at the very origins of Christianity. The teachings of Jesus were not fully understood, if understood at all, even by His most sympathetic disciples, therefore He was accustomed to say,[1] "I have yet many things to say unto you, but ye cannot bear them now." Even after the Pentecostal enlightenment the apostles were obviously not inerrant. Witness the Chiliastic expectations of the epistle-writers[2] of the New Testament. If such were the limitations of the receptiveness of the teachers whom Jesus chose to deliver His doctrine, how far more contracted probably were those limitations in the case of their hearers.

Several causes have helped to an imperfect reception by mankind of the religion of Jesus. The first is its rapid spread. It is estimated that there were at the end of the first century five hundred thousand Christians; at the end of the second, two millions; and at the end of the third century, from seven millions to ten millions. When we reflect how ingrained and slow to eradicate are the habits and convictions of a lifetime, yes, of the lifetimes of the generations of our ancestors, inbred, fixed, and generated into the

---

[1] St. John xiii. 7; xvi. 12, 17; St. Mark iv. 33.

[2] Weiss, *Biblical Theology*, I. 305 ff. Jewish Apocalyptic literature, the Books of Enoch, Moses, Isaiah, Solomon, etc., could not but have been known to Jesus and His apostles. There are not a few allusions to them in the New Testament, and some quotations, *e.g.* Jude 14.

very fibre of our character, is it wonderful that with all their sincerity, many of those early converts to the religion of Christ carried over into Christianity the notions and convictions of their past? It was inevitable.

Let me say, however, at this point, in order to guard while passing, that Gibbon did not in his fifteenth chapter offer this conglomerateness of early Christian doctrine as one of the causes of the rapid growth of the Church. Should the difficulty occur to your mind, recollect that Montanism had all the characteristics pointed out by Gibbon and this adaptability also, and yet Montanism was not a success. Nevertheless sound still are Gibbon's words of caution: "The great law of impartiality too often obliges us to reveal the imperfections of uninspired teachers and believers of the Gospel: and to a careless observer *their* faults may seem to cast a shadow on the faith which they professed. But the scandal of the pious Christian, and the fallacious triumph of the infidel, should cease as soon as they recollect not only *by whom*, but likewise *to whom*, the divine revelation was given."

The artists of the Christian Catacombs felt no scruple at using the figure of Hermes, of Bacchus, of Orpheus, as a symbol of the Saviour. And the ancient custom of representing a labyrinth upon the pavement was continued in Christian churches, and suggested the devotion of the Stations of the Cross.

No one can with an impartial mind read the pages of the isapostolic fathers, and not discern the influence over their thought of pagan terminology, and the persistence in their unconscious convictions of pagan folk-faith. Then, when Constantine became a quasi-Christian, he cursed the Church, not with the fabled "Donation," but with an imperial favour which made it fashionable to profess the Christian religion. Here again was a cause of an influx of many pagan ideas into Christian thought. Not at once, when such was the stuff out of which Christians were made, could the old pagan idea that religion consisted in the right performance of ceremonies be done away. Hence arose the complexities of ritual observance in the Church, reaching high-water mark in the monastic churches of Europe of the fourteenth century, and finding expression in the works of Durandus, Vincentius of Beauvais, Gavantus, Buffaldi, Martini, and the decisions of the Sacred Congregations of Rites; in short, in the idea of religious "function." In western Europe, Karl the Great determined that the Saxons must be Christians. When the Rhine was frozen over, he crossed, and forced them all to be baptised, and then he went back home. The next summer the Saxons openly returned to their idols. The next winter Karl returned and made them all be baptised again; and so on, year after year, till the Saxons got to be fixedly Christians.[1] Moreover, this

[1] *Annales Petaviani, Einhardi, etc.*, in Pertz' *Monumenta Germanica*.

great Christian emperor in his laws allowed monetary compensation for any crime except that of evading Christian baptism. For that alone the absolute penalty was death. How far do you think those Saxons entered into the religion of Christ? Read that letter [1] of St. Gregory the Great, where he advises the missionaries not to destroy the Saxon rites and Saxon sanctuaries, but to consecrate them to a Christian use and meaning. In this way the pagan customs of Christmas and of St. John's day, corresponding in date to the two Saxon solar festivals, have long lingered in Christendom, and have given rise to many Christian legends, invented to account for survivals [2] whose true origin had been forgotten. What wonder that Christians have retained many an idol of the den and of the market! If even the acute mind of the Greek Christian did not develop the thought of the eternal birth of Christ, before the day of Origen [3] from whom Athanasius received it, should we be surprised that the *Nibelungenlied*, written at the close of the twelfth century, reveals Teutonic Christendom almost unaffected in social life and personal character by the religion of Jesus?

[1] *Epistolæ S. Greg. Pap.*, XI. 71.

[2] Picart, *Cérémonies Religeuses*, Tome 9; Hospinianus, *De Origine Progressu Ceremoniis et Ritibus Festorum, etc.*; Du Cange, *Glossarium, passim*.

[3] Irenæus' doctrine of the dual nature of Christ was gnostic in form. Harnack, *Dogmengeschichte*, I. 516; Karl Bartsch, *Einleitung d. Nibelungenlied*.

Again, Christian reception of the teaching of Jesus, and the development of the same, were modified by the clericalism of the Church. In the first centuries of our era clericalism was inevitable from the very constitution of society. In all ages, clericalism is a passionate, blind protest against worldliness. It resulted then, as always, from that antagonism to the world which from the beginning arose between Christendom and heathendom. For that idyllic "Peace of the Church," where the noblest ideals of heathendom insensibly merged themselves into Christianity, as Mr. Pater has so exquisitely suggested in *Marius the Epicurean*, if ever a historic fact must have been limited and momentary, a lull between tempests. Never can reforming ages be tolerant; the Church and the world were then hostile. There could be no compromise, no recognition of half-truths, no general appreciation in the Church of the dignity and earnestness of the old culture. Necessarily, therefore, ecclesiasticism arose, as phariseeism and the caste systems had arisen before it, and it went about moulding Theology to suit its purpose; for a system of Theology, and a casuistry with copious index, it must have. Free thought is its foe. At the demand of the Church, the Emperor Justinian closed the schools of Neoplatonism. Yet St. Justin Martyr had reasoned in the new school of Plato, and Origen was a pupil of Ammonius of the Bag. Neoplatonism has, in spite of Justinian, always persisted as an element of Christian

Theology. It brought Augustine into the Church, and helped him to formulate opinions which finally generated Calvin and Calvinistic Protestantism. Also, the schools of Athens closed, Neoplatonism travelled eastward and took up its abode in the tents of Shem. Having allied itself with Arabian philosophy, it went in that guise westward as far as to Spain, and thence through Averrhoës and Avicebron,[1] gave an impulse to Meister Eckehart, to Tauler, to Henry of Suso, to the author of *Theologia Germanica*, and to the mystics in general of the fourteenth century,[2] and so helped on Protestantism and free religious thought on the Lutheran side. In the Roman communion, Cardinal Cusa was an eminent exponent of the same tendency.

4. The survival of early ideas is one of the most important subjects in the rational study of Christian Theology. Such persistence has been commonly ignored by Christian teachers, yet, under Christian name, dress, and rite, religious ideas of primitive culture often obstinately survive. A quaint example of this was given me by a clerical friend, who for a few years was connected with our Church Mission to the Sioux Indians at Yankton, Dakota. A chapel had been built there, and named "The Holy Comforter." Notwithstanding all teachings, catechism, Bible readings, and explanations, it was found that the common

---

[1] Ad. Franck, *Études Orientales*, 367.
[2] Harnack, *Dogmengeschichte*, I. 93–110.

Indian idea of the Holy Spirit was that of an indefinitely large and warm quilt, — comforter. Wide reaching in past ages has been the splendid cultus of fire, at least among the Aryan peoples; from the Vedas with Agni of the holy fire to the Latin Vesta of the household hearth. Among the Semites were the sacred fire-menhirs of Moab,[1] and the brazen cressets[2] which Solomon set before the temple. There was the fire of the gods, which darts from heaven upon the Soma,[3] leaving its fruit to be thereafter a vehicle of the divine substance, and to be adored also as a god — *teste*, hymns of the *Rig Veda;* the altar flame of Manoah,[4] which became a messenger to God; and the fire which, coming down from heaven upon Solomon's altar, afterwards burned perpetually, and remained during the seventy years of Babylonish captivity unextinguished, though hidden in a pit of water. Of this august and splendid paganism, I can think of only these survivals in official Christianity of to-day: the descent of the holy fire at the Church of the Holy Sepulchre at Jerusalem on each Good Friday, the ceremony of obtaining the new or Paschal fire, the church altars blazing with lights, and the never-dying flame of the sanctuary lamp.

---

[1] 2 Sam. xxiii. 20.

[2] W. Robertson Smith, *Religion of the Semites*, 469.

[3] Hillebrandt, *Vedische Mythologie. Soma und Verwandte Götter*, I. 117–266.

[4] Judges xiii.

Let me give another instance of what I think is a survival of primitive folk-faith. Primitive[1] man anywhere in the world venerates a boulder, a great rock, and particularly a meteoric stone. Beside such a rock as he has selected he puts offerings[2] of fruit, meat, oil, and wine, and then kindles a fire to consume them, pouring thereon oil and distilled liquor. To this custom we owe the standing stones, menhirs, scattered over the face of the earth, Carnac in Brittany, the Syrian menhirs, the Stonehenge, and finally the obelisk and the spire. On top the menhirs a little hollow was made, to receive the offerings to the stone-spirit. This is the earliest form of an altar. Nowadays a Mohammedan gravestone has a cup surmounting it which receives offerings of food to the ghost of the dead. A menhir Joshua set up;[3] at such a great stone human sacrifice[4] was offered. Samuel erected[5] a menhir. Religion, which is always conservative, long tried to preserve these stones uncut.[6] A curious religious observance came to be related to these pillars. In front of the mysterious temple of Dea Syria, on the site of the old Hittite capitol of Carchemish, there stood two lofty towers, or obelisks, resembling perhaps our Washington, or Bunker Hill, monument. To the summit of these pillars of Dea

---

[1] By *primitive* man I do not mean primeval man.
[2] 1 Kings i. 9. [3] Josh. xxiv. 26 ff.
[4] 2 Sam. xx. 8–10. [5] 1 Sam. vii. 11.
[6] Ex. xx. 25; Josh. viii. 31; Deut. xxvii. 5. Cf. Ex. iv. 25.

Syria went up her chosen priests, and remained there seven days in communion with the goddess. Now it is a matter to note that not far from this spot, and about four hundred years afterwards, St. Simeon ascended his pillar, and there remained the rest of his life rapt in the contemplation of God. After his example came thousands of stylites, pillar-saints, and to this day single columns are found scattered over the Syrian land. It was a menhir that Jacob set up, pouring oil upon it, and legend tells us how this same stone had been originally in the altar which Adam built after his expulsion from Paradise. Upon it Abel offered his sacrifice. It fell into ruin, but after the deluge was rebuilt by Noah. Again it fell into ruin, and again was erected by Abraham. Jacob gathered the scattered stones of it and put them under his head for a pillow; by a miracle these stones were melted into one. By the Phœnicians this sacred stone is supposed to have found its way to Spain and thence to Ireland, where Conn one morning, as he was going up Tara Hill, stepped upon it. The stone, as the legend goes on to say, screamed, and out came a fairy prince who revealed to Conn the future of Ireland; hence to the Irish the stone was known as Lia Fail,—the stone of destiny. Kings were crowned sitting upon it. Thence somehow it got to Scotland, because the Stuarts traced their line to Conn of Tara. At present this stone is underneath the seat of the coronation chair in Westminster Abbey.

I have told this legend in brief, because it admirably illustrates the manner in which Christian people invented myths or legends to account for customs whose origin they had forgotten. In the Church, however, the chief survival of stone-worship is detected in the demand for a stone altar duly anointed and consecrated, or at least a stone mensa, or slab, so prepared, and laid upon the altar for the offering of the holy sacrifice. Another reason why so many eccentric doctrines entered the Western Church is that Latin Christianity set itself to the organisation of European society, somewhat to the neglect of Christian thought. The Church of Rome, agreeable to the conditions of her early environment, became deeply impressed with the imperial idea of government, and has never since been able to divest herself of the conviction that universal sovereignty is hers by right.

5. In any adequate study of theology we must first of all examine the religious opinions which were already existent in the mental soil when the seed of Christian doctrine came to be sown broadcast in it. Thus we may be in the way to discover what early ideas survived in those nations that embraced the Christian profession. The correct method of studying Christian theology is the historic and comparative; likewise, the right method of studying religions is the comparative method. Folk-faith, the faith of the common people, belongs fundamentally to a right

study of Christian Theology, because the day has surely arrived when we must be able to compare without fear Christianity with the ethnic religions, thereby to demonstrate the supreme truth and unique divineness of the Christian religion. We need this method also in order to understand the dispensation of God to all His children, and, lastly, we need it in order that in our missionary teaching the true and the false may be discreetly sundered. Therefore the first part of my method is an examination of the environment into which Christianity was projected. In this examination I have, for the present, been obliged to neglect two important factors which should be calculated in any complete consideration of the reception and subsequent development of the gospel message; namely, Philosophy and Law. Consideration of those factors would extend these lectures beyond practical limits. The student may, however, be referred to Hatch's and Renan's Hibbert Lectures, to Maine, *Ancient Law*, Harnack, *Dogmengeschichte*, Baur, *Die Christliche Gnosis*, Erdmann's and Schwegler's Histories of Philosophy.

The next point is to determine, as far as possible, precisely what was the teaching of Jesus and of the New Testament writers. This is to be attempted by means of an unbiassed Biblical theology and exegesis. I would then trace the development of the seed in the traditional theology of the Church, pointing out from time to time some modifications of dogma which have occurred by reason of surviving folk-faith. This should finally bring us to a true state of the doctrine as it exists for my consciousness, perhaps also for yours. But this is not merely a matter of intellectual speculation. Life is making imperious demands upon theology that she be a factor as well as a fact. For example, the monism of Lotze and the Christian Scientists confronts us. To me they represent a metaphysical extreme which is false. It is logical enough if only we could be quite confident that a Jevons' syllogistic machine inside the skull works unerringly when it gets at conclusions beyond the gauge of consciousness. When ciphering with infinities, it is easy to make mistakes. Theology ought, therefore, to stand the test of present consciousness, if it is to be proven. It ought to answer to the actual requisitions of life, not necessarily to metaphysical and to traditional authority. The Vincentian canon has never met with fulfilment in the whole history of dogma, unless, perhaps, with the exception of that of the doctrine of the Trinity. It is inept, also, to try to force an exact conformity of the *lex credendi* with the *lex orandi*. It is not so attempted in the *Rituale Romanum;* it should not be in a *Rituale Anglicanum*. It has been said with some truth that every Roman Catholic becomes a solifidian Lutheran before he dies. The Book of Common Prayer is not a body of divinity, but a manual of devotion. It is a mistake to turn phraseology of prayer into creeds and dogmas. The one object before us, gentlemen, is the salvation of souls, the proclamation of the gospel, good news. Jesus came not to propound a theory of things, even of human nature, but to save a world. This, says the author of the book of the Acts, He began to do before His ascension; this work of salvation He continues through His followers. Theology has always forgotten herself when she has tried to construct a theory, coherent and logical though it be, and to substitute it for real life and actual character. Metaphysical consistency is impossible. God is too great for my brain. I am ambitious to be neither a Calvinist nor an Arminian. What we desire is that which is true, and from truth we demand no countersign. The world is full of antinomies which never have been solved. Both absolute freedom and absolute fate are *reductiones ad absurdum*. Nevertheless, human consciousness hymns in distinct tones the high laws of duty, of righteousness, and of holy love. Strenuously, therefore, must we strive to set forth the principles of Christ's teaching, and of the developed ideas of the gospel in such a manner that they may be saving, that they may be ethical, as well as intellectual, forces, because in these last days "the sober majesties of settled, sweet, epicurean life" are detected as a false element in Christianity.

6. For your convenience I have chosen the theological articles of the Creed to which to apply the

method of the theological study that I have so earnestly recommended. What I wish to make clear may be stated somewhat as follows: —

A. God is not dependent upon revelation, but revelation upon God.
B. The Church of the living God is a living Church.
C. Forgiveness of sins, and not of their results alone, is God's forgiveness.
D. The rise from the dead, which is of Christian teaching, is not a resuscitation nor a revivification, but a resurrection.
E. Eternal life is potentially a present fact, and we have no reason to believe that it will be a future fact unless it shall have been previously of this present world.

I desire the teachings of these lectures to be considered by you in their ethical rather than in their speculative outcome. If you cannot see their saving value, reject them. Let us not, at all events, sit idly with Dürer's Melancholia, pondering in pessimistic dejection, while the night cometh, wherein no man can work. Study Theology, not to make your pulpit a professor's chair, but that you may be a true teacher. Heed not those who in these days are saying that the study of Theology is useless. The foundation of a house may remain hidden from sight, and yet be none the less necessary for the superstructure. Let your Theology be the foundation of your Sociology.

Study Theology, and that seriously, not that you may bolster up an opinion, or defend an accepted notion, or persist in being impervious to all new ideas, but study to find the truth: to systematise somewhat correlated truths in order that you may observe their bearing one upon another, but especially that you may know how to console the grieving, strengthen the weak and faint, answer the questioner, and furnish genuine and healthful moral impulses. Let us be heedful not to incur the reproach that,

> "We teach and teach,
> Until like droning pedagogues we lose
> The thought that what we teach has higher ends
> Than being taught and learned."

At this time of the world no longer can any new ideas be brought forward. This the student of the history of religious opinion knows. Neither shall I hope to define all things clearly. If such is what constructive or positive teaching signifies, then it does not understand itself. That age which can definitely plan out a "Scheme of Salvation" has spoken its last word. There is no possibility of a final Theology. Yet Theology should none the less be positive and upbuilding. I do not come here to deny, but to affirm, yet not at all to deliver myself of a dogma. All that I desire to emphasise is the method of the study of doctrines which I here present, and illustrate with such an array of facts and data as my time, my space, and my limitations allow.

7. I know that there is a craving for clearness, for positive, definite teaching. But, gentlemen, understand well, that for living religious teachers this is not a day for dogma. When a religious idea becomes a dogma, it is because that idea has spent its force, it is no longer a living and a growing thought. If any one of you absolutely must have a neat and coherent system of Theology, *teres atque rotundus*, an irresistible authority, an infallible guide that he cannot mistake, whether Church, Bible, Creed, Reason, Sacraments, or Pope, I do not know where in this life he can find them. The boasted infallibility of each has in its turn yielded to the stress of life's demands. No, divine realities cannot be brought under the rule of three or under the regimen of Aristotle's categories, as the Council of Trent brought the dogma of justification. Whenever this has been attempted, one of two results has come to pass: either we are, as by Rome, asked to believe the incredible, or as by Geneva, what, though credible, ought never to be believed. In Theology there is no short and easy way, no cut and dried truth. All truth is from a living, self-revealing God, to a living, growing humanity.

> "But, more than man, God yet is perfect Man,
>   And, making men, said, 'Let us fashion them
>   In Our own Image.'
>   He, since time began,
>   Has been the Soul of man's soul, manhood's Sire,
>   Of all humanity the Light and Fire,
>   Passing imagination and desire,

>   Kindling each spark
> Of vital will that's flashed upon the dark
> Of this world's night, and ever blazing still
>   With a fierce purity of Love that will
> Consume all evil, offering up love's pain
> On the great altar where men's sins are slain."

So the apprehension of the truth is a progress and a development; for lo, God is with men unto the consummation of Time, ἕως τῆς συντελείας τοῦ αἰῶνος. Therefore, "the thoughts of men are widened with the process of the suns"; in this sense alone is it true that Christianity is an evolution.

THE IDEA OF GOD.

God bears Himself out of Himself into Himself; the more perfect the birth, the more is born. I say, God is at all times one. He takes cognition of nothing beyond Himself. Yet God in taking cognition of Himself must take cognition of all creatures.

MEISTER ECKEHART, Pfeiffer, *Deutsche Mystiker*, II. 254.

Deus est in Rebus, sicut continens res.

S. THOM. AQ., *Summa Theol.*, I. 1ª. 1. 8.

In tutte parti impera, e quivi regge,
Quivi è la sua città, e l' alto seggio.

DANTE, *Inferno*, I. 127.

Raise thyself to the height of religion, and all veils are removed; the world and its dead principle pass away from thee, the very Godhead enters thee anew in its first and original form, as Life, as thine own life which thou shalt and oughtest to live.

FICHTE, *Anweisung*.

The conception of sin, it is sometimes said, is at the root of Christianity. That is a false statement of a truth. For sin only becomes sin, and is only known to us *as sin*, in the light of that which is the heart and centre of Christianity, the belief in a Personal God, Who is a God of Infinite Love. All other truths of Christianity grow out of and gather around that central truth — the doctrine of the Trinity, which safeguards the eternal truth that God is Love.

AUBREY L. MOORE, *From Advent to Advent*.

Was wär' ein Gott, der nur von aussen stiesse,
Im Kreis das All am Finger laufen liesse!
Ihm ziemt's, die Welt im Innern zu bewegen,
Natur in Sich, Sich in Natur zu hegen,
So dass, was in Ihm lebt und webt und ist,
Nie Seine Kraft, nie Seinen Geist vermisst.
GOETHE.

For so the light of the world in the morning of the Creation was spread abroad like a curtain, and dwelt no where, but filled the *expansum* with a dissemination great as the unfoldings of the air's looser garment, or the wilder fringes of the fire, without knots, or order, or combination ; but God gathered the beams in His hand, and united them into a globe of fire, and all the light of the world became the body of the sun, and he lent some to his weaker sister that walks in the night, and guides a traveler and teaches him to distinguish a house from a river, or a rock from plain field ; so is the mercy of God ; a vast *expansum* and a huge Ocean, from eternall ages it dwelt round about the throne of God, and it filled all that infinite distance and space, that hath no measures but the will of God. And the mercy which dwelt in an infinite circle, became confirm'd to a little ring and dwelt here below, and here shall dwell below, till it hath carried all God's portion up to Heaven, where it shall reigne and glory upon our crowned heads for ever and ever.

Bp. JEREMY TAYLOR, Sermon, *The Miracles of the Divine Mercy.* Works, II. 314.

SYNOPSIS.

INTRODUCTION:

I. — 1. The Idea of God is innate in its form, but not in content.
    2. Its Content determines the character of Theology and of Religion.
    3. Evolution in folk-faith of the content of the Idea of God.

COMPARATIVE RELIGION:

    a. In the Animistic stage.
    b. In the Fetishistic and Shamanistic.
    c. The Polytheistic.
    d. Monotheism, not a result of evolution; in its bare form, not a fixed concept, — in Islam, Brahminism, Buddhism, Judaism, Modern Deism, . . . nor is
    e. Pantheism, a fixed concept of God in ancient and in modern times.

BIBLICAL THEOLOGY:

II. — The Revelation of the true content of the Idea of God is in and by Jesus Christ.
    a. Neither Jesus nor His religion a result of evolution.
    b. Jesus, Himself, the Revelation of the Unseen God.
    c. God thus revealed as essential Love.
    d. The identity of Love, Sacrifice, and Life in God.
    e. This obscured by survivals of folk-faith,
    f. Which have given rise to Sectarianism,
    g. And itself has arisen through various degrees of receptiveness;
    h. Yet receptiveness is the condition of the endless progress of man, and is conditioned by personal righteousness.
    i. This implies that humanity is a medium of revelation of the Unseen God,

  j. Who is immanent, explicitly,
  k. According to the New Testament Theology
    of St. John,
    of St. Paul,
  l. And implicitly, according to Old Testament Theology.

TRADITIONAL THEOLOGY:

 III. — Survivals of Folk-faith in development of the revealed Idea of God.
  a. The tardy reception of the Idea of the Trinity,
  b. Which nevertheless is rationally true,
  c. As is also the traditional Theology of the personality of the Holy Spirit.
  d. The rational Theology of God as Immanent is not wholly without traditional testimony;
  e. But survivals from Folk-faith have hindered the general acceptance of this truth.
 IV. — The practical import of the true Idea of God as the Immanent Triune.

THE IDEA OF GOD.

GENTLEMEN: —

God and Life in the world are final facts. Between the two, as between a dark dome of skies above, pierced with palpitating points of vivid light, and below, an ocean fathomless, inscrutable, sails that conscious entity we call the soul. The soul frames no syllogism to prove that sea and sky exist: not with the assertion "God is," does the Bible begin. Of the existence of God it spreads out no formal proofs, ontological, psychological, cosmological, or teleological. God is. This the Holy Writings assume as the foundation of all else. The starting-point of Revelation is the infinite and eternal I AM. Before Revelation is He who reveals.

I. 1. Not with the Idea of God to acquire does humanity begin life in the sphere of time.

> "Dwelt no power divine within us,
> How could God's divineness win us?"[1]

[1] *Wär' nicht das Auge sonnenhaft,*
Wie könnten wir zur Sonne blicken?
Wär' nicht in uns des Göttes eigne Kraft,
Wie könnt uns Göttliches entzücken?
                                        GOETHE.

By nature man is possessed of the Idea of God, by intuition and observation it is developed; for man is in the image of God. We sons of few days are not forced by searching to find out God. Not with the lens, not with problem, must we needs go up to the heights of the flaming suns and whirling stars, nor with deep-sea dredgings and with inspection of eozoic strata, down to the deep places of the earth, neither need we cross the ocean of Time and Space to some primeval truth unveiled for a brief season in the dawn of the years, somewhere in the mystic morning-land. The word is very nigh unto us, even in our heart and in our mouth.

The Idea of God is innate.[1] Not an abstract generalisation of the perfections of the world, for we have no notions of partial perfection, save as we derive them from an absolute Perfection; not a concept of what is contrary to the evil existence, for the contrary of that which is must be that which is not. If the Idea of God be ours by immediate perception or by intuition, why is not it unvarying and invariable like mathematical actions? This question does not follow. My life is to me a matter of immediate perception, and yet I cannot express it by, say,

---

[1] Bishop Beveridge, Sermon, *Omnipresence of God the Best Safeguard against Sin*. Works, V. 89. Were there not danger of misconstruction I should boldly state after Thomassin, *Dogmatum Theologicorum, de Deo*, I. 1, 1, that this innate idea is really God Himself immanent in the soul and present to consciousness.

$\cos a = \cos b \cos c + \sin b \sin c \cos A$. The idea is variant because it is a thought form, which is filled in, informed, and develops by means of observation, intuition, personal righteousness, and revelation. Truth flourishes out of the earth, and righteousness looks down from Heaven. The pure in heart, said Jesus, are in Heaven and behold God. The growth or evolution of the Idea of God is conditioned by the revelation of God, the receptiveness of man.

> "Man knows partly, but conceives beside,
>   Creeps ever on from fancies to the fact,
>   And in this striving, this converting air
>   Into a solid, he may grasp and use,
>   Finds progress."

2. I begin what I have to say with some words about the Idea of God, because that Idea is the keynote of all Theology. To begin with Sin, or with the Church, or with the Incarnation, or with the Atonement, or with the Eucharist, is to pull out a strand from the middle, and to tangle the skein of theologic order. Not without significance do Bible and Creed begin with God Who is the Origin and Beginning of all. The Idea of God, in its content, is absolutely the article by which the Church stands or falls, because in that Idea is all Theology implied, and by it the explicit doctrines are shaped and coloured.

3. In order to account for some singular religious notions that alloy the teachings of Christ, as they are

sometimes delivered in the temples and market-places in this nineteenth century of salvation, I ask you to turn your attention to divergent developments of the universal Idea of God.

a. In a primitive state, man feels that the world is alive.[1] He may be able, it is true, to distinguish between his own life and that of tree and horse, but in fact he does not always do so. For him there is present in all things a mysterious living force, impersonal, perhaps, but sentient. For the more part he suspects that the river, the tree, and the sun have life as he has, a soul like his own, claiming of his dim intelligence some sort of recognition and service. His

> "Untutor'd mind
> Sees God in clouds or hears Him in the wind."

With the spirit of the water-flood and of the oak tree he shares what most he values, food and drink, clothing and fire. He sets a calabash of wine at the foot of the tree, and oil and maize he sprinkles on the surface of the river. From this stage of thought to the vow of Jeptha and the sacrifice of Iphigenia by the seaside, the way is long, but the idea which developed is one. To primitive man it seems that if he should shoot an arrow up into the sky,

---

[1] I pass over the theory of the concept of luck as the precedent of the concept of the supernal. This notion has after a fashion been worked out in *The Supernatural, Its Origin, Nature, and Evolution*, by John S. King, 2 vols., 1892.

some drops of blood would fall; if he tear up by the root a mandragora, or any other plant, it will groan in pain. Should he, like Midas, whisper his secret to the river, the reeds will blab. The Kaffir and the North American Indian understand the language of birds and beasts,[1] but other less fortunate folk must drink the blood of a Fafnir, or possess Solomon's pentagraph seal. With St. Francis of Assisi, the child-man loves his "Sir brother, the sun," *Messer lo frate sole*, and praises God for "his sister the moon," and is wont to preach to the beasts, birds, and fishes. Like the Wandering Jew in Doré's famous pictures, the world about him is alive, sentient, intelligent, and sympathetic or antipathetic, look where he will, on rock, tree, and grass blades. Every plant is a sensitive plant. This sentiment revives in some of our best poetry, Wordsworth's *Rhyme of Peter Bell*, Coleridge's *Ancient Mariner*, Shelley's *Sensitive Plant*, and Swinburne's *Forsaken Garden*. The idea is pretty in poetry, but makes mischief in Theology. This stage of God-consciousness has been called Animism.

At this point of the growth of the Idea of God, man does not yet dream of the great Spirit as able to exist apart from the world, or without food and drink. The great Spirit is never absent, being, so to say, *adscriptus glebæ*, but, as the soul of the world, he may,

---

[1] *Kaffir Folk Lore*, by G. M. Thel, *passim;* Reports U. S. Bureau of Ethnology.

conceivably, fall asleep. If offended, he curses the ground, and it becomes stony; briars and nettles grow, the sun scorches, the wind flagellates, and, as an extreme, the thunder-bolt smites dead. Now what straightway occurs to the simple mind is to keep the Spirit in a good humour by giving him the best to eat and drink. Out of this thought develops the custom of sacrifice. The Levitical code nowhere explains the significance of sacrifice, but its symbolism, both in the priestly code and in the rest of the Old Testament, is clearly founded upon the notion of a gift of food and drink, *mincha* and *nesek*. The blood, wherein is the life, was especially due to Jehovah. Against defrauding the altar by offerings not fit for food the later prophets protest.[1] Micah assigns even to Balaam a doctrine which is more spiritual.[2]

b. The Animistic stage of primitive culture is from its very character not permanent. Men come to notice distinctions, and consequently, to their fancy, life or spirit then appears to ebb away from water and rock. It still remains in beast and man. So the great Spirit is moved a little way off from the extremities of the nerve fibres. Nevertheless at any occasion when an object is particularly considered it may be regarded as a focus of the spiritual presence, be that object a man, a phial of oil, an image, a bone, a coat,

---

[1] Zech. vii. 6; Mal. i. 7, 10; *Religion of the Semites*, by W. Robertson Smith, Lect. VI.; Wellhausen, *Prolegomena*, c. ii.
[2] Micah vi. 6, 7.

a cup of blood or of wine, or a cake of bread. This is fetishism, and here God is supposed to manifest Himself by chosen men, priests, prophets, and kings, and to speak through them, or to dwell in them, giving them peculiar powers of consecration so that they can cause Him to be specially present in a stone, or a rag, an image,[1] or in the sacrificial food. Upon such a chosen person it was conceived that the welfare of the people depended, for he was the tribe's representative,[2] the vicar of the god, the gentile-man, forerunner of our modern gentleman. Like the Dalai Llama of Lassa, like the former Mikado of Japan, and like the Pope in his Vatican, these divine vicegerents must live in seclusion. *Omne ignotum pro mirifico.* If these divinely possessed persons turn the head incautiously, misfortune will certainly occur. Their word is infallible; they control the wind and the rain; they are the media of communication between the god and men. They have a twofold power; they possess the two swords, and "sword is under sword," as saith the Bull, *Unam Sanctam.*

c. This mental attitude removes still farther away the great Spirit of life; nevertheless he is yet supposed to dwell in chosen objects, images, remote adyta of temples, and on the tops of high mountains like Meru, Olympus, Mauna Loa, and Fuji. Every race has its sacred mountain. With a withdrawal from

[1] *Records of the Past,* Second Series, III. 42, 43.
[2] Frazer, *Golden Bough,* I. 214.

the sense of near presence, the concept arising from the primitive, vague feeling of an omnipresent vital force takes upon itself human traits and limitations, and becomes differentiated. The great God of all continues to be borne in memory, but as afar off in some dark background, where, like Brahm, he slumbers through the ages. Gods many lord it over the races of men. The sun, each star, each water spring, each domestic hearth, and every one of the familiar uses of life is thought to have its resident manes, genius, djin, god, or spirit. Wine has its indwelling spirit, and corn, also, for people of this stage of culture. Each man, too, has his indwelling manes, or genius, or spirit, as Socrates has his daimonion. The genius of the Roman Emperor became the protecting spirit of the State. Every act of life, every moral trait, every conceivable thing and combination of things, had an indwelling spirit, a patron god. Ancient Rome alone had sixty thousand gods, and no Bollandists. Victor Hugo remarks,[1] with delicate satire, "Singular is the parallelism of the destinies of Rome; after a Senate which made gods comes a Conclave which makes saints." According to polytheistic notions of this sort, when a man died, his manes went to join the gods, and therefore deserved divine honours. Hence arose ancestor-worship and placation. The next step in the evolution was the cultus of the saints. Another notable survival of manes worship is

[1] *Pensées Mêlées.*

the doctrine of immediate sanctification after death. Were we to trust to the ordinary epitaph, we must infer that the article of death is plenary absolution, viaticum, sanctification, and canonisation, all in one.

As Animism had its truth, in that it perceived the immanence of God, so Polytheism had truth, and that which we particularly note was its truth that God is not merely some subtle, inexplicable, pervasive force, or some substance which is impersonal, but that He is a moral person, who is to be thought of as possessing in His relation with Humanity all humane qualities. Polytheism is a forward-reaching sense of the Incarnation. However, to this stage of religious culture belongs one mischievous influence; namely, the notion of God's wrath, jealousy, rigour, and avarice. For in Polytheism men think the gods such as themselves, and to this error the limitations of language have contributed. Thence arose the customs of gifts to the gods to keep them in good humour, of votive offerings or bribes, of propitiations, of barter and evasion, of the fear of the vengeance or wrath of gods, here and hereafter, which might be escaped by cajoling with flattery and gift the supernal powers. In this way the divine potencies, *Göttes eigene Kraft*, of man's sacred sonship became frustrate, and life in religion took the form of an ignoble scramble to save self.

Only slowly has the world outgrown the bondage of these crude ideas. Notwithstanding our Lord said, "He who findeth his life shall lose it," some there are who still think of godliness as at best a means of placating God and getting something from Him, and who live as if righteousness consisted chiefly, if not altogether, in avoiding what might anger God. If any man's receptiveness in these last days is so rudimentary that the secret of Jesus' deep unselfishness cannot get borne in upon his understanding, I would suggest for his consideration the following stanzas of the singularly evangelical hymn of St. François Xavier: —

> "My God, I love Thee — not because
>   I hope for heaven thereby;
> Nor yet because, if I love not
>   I must forever die.
>
> "Then why, O blessèd Jesus Christ,
>   Should I not love Thee well?
> Not for the hope of winning heaven,
>   Nor of escaping hell;
>
> "Not with the hope of gaining aught;
>   Not seeking a reward;
> But as Thyself hast lovèd me,
>   O ever-loving Lord!
>
> "E'en so I love Thee, and will love,
>   And in Thy praise will sing;
> Solely because Thou art my God,
>   And my eternal King."

d. When a truer Idea of God presented itself as it did to Abraham, the first Monotheist mentioned in the Bible, it gained prevalence slowly; but wherever it did obtain, history has demonstrated that there was invariably a superior development, both ethical and spiritual. This led Mr. Matthew Arnold to say that the Hebrews had a genius for righteousness. That Monotheism was not solely a product of natural development, the study of comparative religion goes to prove. The Folk-faith of the Aryan races, notwithstanding centuries of acute and profound metaphysic in India, never developed into Monotheism. Outside the Abrahamic tribes, nowhere was the religion of the Semites permanently a pure Monotheism. Even Israel hardly reached the ideal before 500 B.C. Till Aryan peoples accepted its goodly heritage, pure Monotheism had seldom been established in a stable form. Even at Sinai the Jews fell away, and their long history is but a chronicle of lapses into forms of Folk-faith. Has Islam had a cleaner record? No sooner had the breath of life left the body of Mahomet,[1] than a desperate effort was made to fix his deathlessness as a dogma or to canonise him as a god. Although for the moment this was averted, yet, says Kuenen,[2] Islam degenerated in a few years after the death of the Prophet into saint worship and pantheistic Sufism. Even for the

[1] Sir William Muir, *The Caliphate*, c. i.
[2] Kuenen, *Hibbert Lectures*, 41 ff.

rigidly orthodox, Mahomet is now their mediator, ever pleading with Allah. The bare monotheistic idea of God, while eliminating from religion grosser notions of Animism, Fetishism, and Polytheism, ran to the opposite error of reducing God to remote and contrahuman power, El, or a blind will, or an *Être Suprême*, which is an empty abstraction, or worse, — *Le bon Dieu*, an easy, indulgent *roi d'Yvetot*, exalted to the throne of the Universe. Or He remains vested in the more austere and terrific traits of the polytheistic idea, and these crystallised by an infinite power and a holiness which must not be questioned. Does not this Idea of God appear to be that of the Genevan school? Is God a law unto Himself and unto the world?[1] Not only in the long reaches of antiquity, but in modern times bare Monotheism has again and again traded its birthright for the pottage of agnosticism. Brahminism says of the Supreme God that before creation, — before logically, not temporally, — "before creation there was neither entity

---

[1] Does God do a thing because it is right, or is it right because He does it? The latter term of the dilemma obviously implies that He is arbitrary and non-moral, that in Him might is right; on the other hand we should be forced to admit that there is something outside God, right external to Him, conditioning His existence and determining His acts. This was the dilemma of the ancient Monotheist, which modern philosophy solves, by pointing out that right is not hypostatic, that it has no substance save in the mind of the divine Being. This reconciles the antinomies by uniting them, and the former is left as a statement to be used.

nor non-entity." Buddhism of to-day theoretically finds that infinite perfection is realised in total extinction of individual thought and volition. Jewish rationalism in the book Zohar attained in the middle ages to the idea of God as EN, nothing.[1] The Persian Sufis teach to-day that God is unlimited naught. Spinoza's definition of God as Substance is virtually a negation. In Germany since the Aufklärung, in England since Deism, and in France since the Voltairian cycle, the fruit of those gospels of naked Monotheism has visibly ripened into Agnosticism and Nihilism. John Milton, in bitter blindness of soul and body, developed Calvinistic Monotheism to its logical result, Deism, and ceased to attend any house of Christian worship. After two centuries other men have reached Milton's conclusions, and we are able to see that the Idea of God as a single person — for that is what I mean in this place by bare Monotheism — neutralises or negates itself in the processes of the human intellect. Plato is justified in saying that the absolute Unit is unthinkable; and with this assertion Sts. Basil and Gregory Nazianzen agree.[2]

e. A further form of the divine Idea, which arises in human consciousness out of the ancient Animism, will forever remain a fascination to the poet and to

---

[1] Ad. Franck, *La Kabbale*, 142; S. L. M. Mathers, *Kabbalah Unveiled*, 16 ff.; D'Herbelot, *Bibliothèque Orientale*.
[2] *Apol. ad Cæsarianos*, 619, c.

the mystic. In its more spiritual aspect the Idea has been nobly expressed in our own day:—

> "The sun, the moon, the stars, the seas, the hills and the plains—
> Are not these, O Soul, the vision of Him who reigns?
> Earth, these solid stars, this weight of body and limb,
> Are they not sign and symbol of thy division from Him?
> Glory about thee, without thee; and thou fulfillest thy doom,
> Making Him broken gleams and a stifled splendour and gloom.
> Speak to Him thou, for He hears, and Spirit with Spirit can meet—
> Closer is He than breathing, and nearer than hands and feet."

There belongs to the doctrine of God as the ONE and the ALL, τὸ Ἓν καὶ τὸ Πᾶν, a wealth of bravely beautiful suggestions; the opulence of the Oriental life with its ecstatic reveries, and the clear flame of Greek philosophy which burnt through the intensity of Neoplatonism into the "divine dark" of Dionysius the Areopagite.

As a matter of fact Pantheism always goes to seed. The degeneration of the Egyptian religion, which originally was profoundly Pantheistic, might be taken as a clear type of the development and decay of the Pantheistic Idea of God. That development is thus summarised:—

    1. God is conceived to be the God *of* Nature; then
    2. God is thought of as *in* Nature; then
    3. Nature is regarded as God; then
    4. It is concluded there is no God, only Nature.[1]

[1] See Renouf, Hibbert Lectures.

It seems probable that the Idea of God went through the same historical process among the Sumero-Akkadians and their Semitic successors the Chaldeans. Indeed, among every Pantheistic people this seems always to be the process, and in the German philosophy of our day from Schelling to Von Hartmann, it has been repeated. Nevertheless the truth of Pantheism remains — God is in His world.

> "The One Spirit's plastic stress
> Sweeps through the dull, dense world; compelling there
> All new succession to the forms they wear;
> Torturing the unwilling dross that checks its flight,
> To its own likeness, as each mass may bear;
> And bursting in its beauty and its might
> From trees and beasts and men into the heaven's light."

I think that in these lines Shelley is reaching out and groping after God, as after One of Whom the cosmos is a theophany.

II. *a.* Different from all these theories, different both in kind and degree, is the manifestation of God in Jesus Christ. Absurd is the conjecture of Renan, that Jesus, a child of the people, could construct an eclectic system out of all the theories of the world.[1] That should be sought at the hand of the sages of the Serapeum of Alexandria, or of the dilettante period of imperial Rome, and not from a peasant of Palestine. For one in the rugged stretches of Galilee, where the

---

[1] *Vie de Jésus*, cc. 1, 2.

ribs of the earth are bare, and anathema is laid upon the man who keeps swine and teaches his son Greek, small is the opportunity to combine Mosaism and Hellenism[1] in order to make a new religion.

b. Free yourselves forever from the notion that Jesus was a *doctrinaire*, and that Christianity is a literary religion, a set of final opinions about truth,[2] and life.[3] The heart of the Christian religion is the fact of a particular personal life. When Philip said unto Jesus, "Lord, show us the Father," the answer came straightway,[4] "Have I been so long time with you, and yet thou hast not known me, Philip? He that hath seen Me hath seen the Father." When our Lord standing before Pilate was asked, "What is truth?" He replied not in words, because He was the answer in fact. The author of the Epistle to the Hebrews gathers into one statement the whole significance of the Incarnation, relative to ethnic religions and Folk-faith, when he begins his homily with saying, "God having in so many fragments and many fashions[5] formerly spoken in prophets to the forefathers, at the latest of these days has spoken to us in His Son."

---

[1] Keim, *Jesus of Nazara*, VI. 426; M. Arnold, *Culture and Anarchy*, c. iv.

[2] ἀλήθεια.

[3] πράξεις.

[4] St. John xiv. 9. Cf. v. 17–19, 26; xii. 45; xiii. 20.

[5] πολυμερῶς καὶ πολυτρόπως, Heb. i. 1, 2.

"And so the Word had breath and wrought
  With human hands the creed of creeds,
  In loveliness of perfect deeds
More strong than all poetic thought."

The Incarnation was a revelation and manifestation of the nature of God. Unique is that revelation, where truths in manhood darkly join, deep seated in our mystic frame. In fervour the apostle exclaims, "Great is the revealed mystery of a Holy reverence Who was revealed in body, rectified in spirit."[1] This revealed mystery is the Logos, the Word of God, which had been "concealed before the ages and generations, but was in the present shown to His holy ones, to whom the Lord willed to make known what, among the Gentiles, is the wealth of the glory of this mystery, Who is Christ among you the hope of glory."[2]

c. This mystery of the nature and being of God was revealed to be LOVE. Oh, the vastness and depth of the mystery of love! For what is love? Is not it the essential action of out-yielding self, is it not fundamentally self-outgoing to another and for another? At the bottom this is what desire is, what

---

[1] μέγα ἐστὶν τὸ τῆς εὐσεβείας μυστήριον· ὃς ἐφανερώθη ἐν σαρκί, ἐδικαιώθη ἐν πνεύματι, κ.τ.λ., 1 Tim. iii. 16. Cf. Cremer's *Lex;* Winer, *Greek Gram. N. T.* 736.

[2] τὸ μυστήριον τὸ ἀποκεκρυμμένον ἀπὸ τῶν αἰώνων καὶ ἀπὸ τῶν γενεῶν, νῦν δὲ ἐφανερώθη τοῖς ἁγίοις αὐτοῦ, οἷς ἠθέλησεν ὁ Θεὸς γνωρίσαι τί τὸ πλοῦτος τῆς δόξης τοῦ μυστηρίου τούτου, κ.τ.λ., Col. i. 26 ff. Cf. Lightfoot, *Comm.* on the place.

appetite is, what life is. The significance of the Word-made-Flesh is precisely this, the manifestation of God as love, the substance and law of the Universe and of souls. Of this the world itself is a revealment, and the Nativity of Bethlehem a revelation. The Incarnation was the "Tear of Divine Compassion," the supreme manifestation of that process of Divine Existence which shall culminate in the glory of Christ in Humanity. Strange is it that Lucretius, in *De Naturâ Rerum*, should have come so near this true idea of Divine Love only to lose it in a myth unbelieved. Strange that Euripides, in the great passion play of *Bacchae*, should not have discerned that divine suffering is the ecstasy of God.

d. In itself substantial infinite Love, which God is, the outgoing of self for other, is sacrifice. That word sacrifice, I say, expresses the life of God, and of that life the Incarnation is utterance. The life of the Eternal is dynamic, not static. Therefore the Nativity was as much a part of the Passion of Jesus as His Crucifixion. The whole life, from Bethlehem to Golgotha, yes, to the Mount of Ascension, was the theophany of unseen Love. In this sense it may be truly asserted that the Incarnation is the centre of all Theology, the key of all the creeds. From this revealed mystery of Love, as being the operation or action of the life of God, we are given to understand what is the true Christian doctrine of sacrifice. That doctrine is, that sacrifice is not for propitiation, that it is not piacular, that it is not vicarious punishment, but that it is simply Love, the out-yielding of self, a law or process which is the savour of life unto life and not of death unto death. Of this, ancient artists were aware when they depicted the cross of Christ of living green, and Him upon it, erect, with arms outflung, as though to fold in embrace the worlds, erect as a King of love upon His throne, of whom it had been said in ancient records, "Tell it out among the nations that the Lord reigneth from the Tree."

e. Such is the glorious doctrine of the sacrifice of Christ. It is infinite, eternal love. True, "there is a gloom in deep love as in deep water," but modern Christianity, still under the spell of a crude Folk-faith, goes beyond gloom to horror, gives us doleful symbols of divine Love vanquished, of a dead God! Because Jesus is God, His infinite LOVE, manifested in the sphere of time, He must needs be crucified.[1]

Jesus became incarnate, not in order to propitiate a vindictive, and exacting, and wrathful Father, else Shakspere's *Merchant of Venice* were a nobler gospel. But He came, or became, in order to reveal to us Himself and the Father as one Infinite God, the Saviour,[2] saying, in flesh utterance, "That which may be known of God is manifest in men."[3] This heart of the Christian doctrine of God forms the basis of the

---

[1] Ἐρῶς ἐμοῦ ἐσταύρωται, sang the Greek hymn-writer.
[2] 1 Tim. i. 1; ii. 3; iv. 10.
[3] Rom. i. 19.

Epistle to the Romans, is especially the theme of the Johannine writings, and incidentally an evidence of the unity and authenticity of their origin.

f. I am persuaded that if Christian teaching be adjusted to this revelation of the mystery of Divine Love, the questions which vex our days, concerning inspiration, and atonement, and justification, and sacraments, and sanctification immediate or progressive, on this or the other side of death, all social and ethical problems, and resurrection, and retribution, and Church unity — all would vanish. To this, praise God, the Spirit is guiding us. "It is the historical task of Christianity to assume with every succeeding age a fresh metamorphosis, and be forever spiritualising more and more her understanding of the Christ and of salvation."[1]

g. Because God is perfect love He gives up Self completely; that is, in one aspect, reveals Himself entirely. The apostles and early fathers perceived this. Justin Martyr declares[2] that men of every race, that Socrates, Heraclitus, and others were Christians, because they lived according to reason, which is the divine Word immanent in the world. If the self-revelation be entire, then it must be that it is man's Idea of God which is limited in its content[3] by his conscious receptiveness, and that history is the annals of the education of humanity in the quickening of the

[1] Amiel's *Journal*, 3. [2] *Apol.* II. 83.
[3] St. John xiv. 10, 17.

God-consciousness. The diversity of forms of the Idea of God is due to the differences of degree of receptiveness, as through the "soul's east window of divine surprise," stained and figured, the light enters coloured and shaped, while outside abideth always the pure white Light.

> "The One remains, the many change and pass;
> Heaven's light forever shines, earth's shadows fly;
> Life, like a dome of many-coloured glass,
> Stains the white radiance of eternity."

h. Now this very receptiveness in its incompleteness of growth is the condition of endless development, for receptivity of the Infinite implies infinite receptivity. So it is a God-like potency in man, the potency of an endless growth, of an approximation unto the measure of the stature of the fulness of Christ, of sanctification, and of the dominance of the spirit unto eternal life. For God-consciousness is this, — first of all, — to know[1] the true God; not to know about God, but to know Him without intervention of a minor premise, to know Him also because He is (if I may use the phrase) lived. A holy life is a Catholic Creed, and orthodox theology is the intuition of the pure in heart. Perhaps perfect receptiveness implies apotheosis. This bold corollary Athanasius dared to accept, saying,[2] "He (the

---

[1] St. John xvii. 3.   [2] *De Incarn.* c. liv.

Word of God) became humanified in order that we might become deified." The end is by and by.

i. A survey of the growth of the religious idea in human consciousness makes us aware of another syllable, so to say, of the Word-made-Flesh; another thought, which is of deep and wide import. There is revelation and there is revealment. God reveals Himself to man in man. God in man as in the world external to man, God in man, a life ever pressing against the soul's barriers, crying, "Lift up your heads, oh ye gates, and be ye lift up, ye everlasting doors, and the King of Glory shall come in." Or, as our Lord Himself says, "Behold I stand at the door [of the heart] and knock, if any will hear my voice, and open the door[1] . . . my Father will love him and we will come unto him and make our abode with him."[2] God in man, Emmanuel, a light ever shining and waxing brighter and brighter through the earthen vase, in divers rites, customs, folk-faith and myths, as in the liturgic drama of history the Self-revelation of God outrolls.

j. The advent of our Lord Jesus Christ was not an arrival from a journey,[3] but a manifestation of the

---

[1] Rev. iii. 20.   [2] St. John xiv. 23.

[3] When Jesus is called ὁ ἐρχόμενος, it is always in the sense which the Rabbinic schools gave the idiom, *i.e.* the Messiah. The coming age, the world to come, meant the epoch of the Messiah. For the use of φανέρωσις, παρουσία, αἰὼν ὁ μέλλων, ἀποκάλυψις, see Weiss, *Bibl. Theol.*

Presence in which we had always been, a *parousia*, as Blake symbolises the nearness of that Presence in his wonderful Inventions to the Book of Job. When Jesus *appeared* He made apparent God.[1] He was God, personally acting as man, enabling us to

> " Correct the portrait by the living face;
> Man's God, by God's God in the mind of man."

I do not feel called upon to enter into an examination of the Biblical Theology of the Idea of the Triune God, and of the expansion of human receptiveness in relation to that Idea. The manner in which that has already been done by one of your own Faculty[2] leaves nothing further for you to desire. The doctrine of the Trinity now belongs to the content of Christian thought and life, however much the Aufklärung may be flippant over "a celestial committee of Three." Into the Biblical Theology of the Immanence of the Triune God we ought to attempt some little inquiry, for the reason that it is a doctrine which Christian consciousness has not fully and universally accepted.

k. Take first the Johannine writings. In Revelation[3] the writer takes up the symbol of the ancient tabernacle of Israel, and shows its fulfilment in the lives of God's saints. Upon their spirits, says he,

---

[1] ἡ Ζωὴ ἐφανερώθη, 1 St. John i. 2.
[2] P. H. Steenstra, D.D., *The Being of God as Unity and Trinity.*
[3] vii. 15, σκηνώσει ἐπ' αὐτούς.

God shall rest as He rested upon the Mercy-seat; and in the same book [1] there cries a voice from the unseen realm, "Behold the tabernacle of God is with men, and He shall tabernacle with them, and God shall be with them, and they shall be His people, and God Himself shall be with them." As a result of the erosion of metaphysics and poetry, the word Truth has come to correspond to a vague abstraction. To the average mind it connotes little that is clear. But translate ἀλήθεια by actuality or reality, and therewith read the first Epistle to St. John, and you will find that the fact of the divine indwelling will come to be sharply and distinctly focussed out to your mental vision.[2] In the Fourth Gospel it is seen that the thought is clearly consonant with the teachings of Jesus. For therein our Lord is recorded as saying that while on earth He remained in Heaven,[3] because He is in the Father and the Father in Him. As the Father dwelleth in Him,[4] so shall the Christians have God, the Spirit, dwell in them and be in them,[5] and as a result Christian consciousness will know that Christ is in the Father, and He in Christ, and Christ in us.[6] In consequence, a perfect divine-human unity will come to pass.[7] From this divine-

---

[1] xxi. 3.
[2] M. Arnold, *Literature and Dogma*, 179.
[3] iii. 13.   [4] St. John xiv. 10.
[5] St. John v. 17.   [6] St. John xiv. 20.
[7] St. John xvii. 21–24.

human unity and indwelling of God the Father, Son, and Holy Spirit, the prologue of the Fourth Gospel passes to the further thought of the cosmic indwelling. "That which was made was life in Him,"[1] we find in the best reading, signifying that through the immanence of the Logos the universe is alive.

In a word the Johannine thought is that Life (1) is the manifestation of Rational (2) Will (3); Life (1) is the Spirit, Reason (2) is the Son, and Will (3) is the Father, and in cosmic relation, Life (1) is the *condition* of the world, Reason (2) is the *form* of the world, and Will (3) is the *substance* of the world. Harmonious was this Idea of God with the gnosis of St. Paul. We are not surprised, therefore, to find in his Areopagite Sermon,[2] "God is not far from every one of us"; or to put the matter in very literal language, "Even though God be subsistent, not distant (or apart) from each one of us, for it is in Him that we live and move and exist."[3] In that most wonderfully profound letter to the Romans, St. Paul expounds on this basis the philosophy of the world, guarding against the Buddhist myth of the Veil of Maya, the world as an illusion, which, nursed in the cell of the Nitrian monk, and by the mystics of the Abbey of St. Victor, still survives in many a staunch Protestant hymn, "This world's a vain and fleeting show," and other words to like effect. Against such

---

[1] St. John i. 4. [2] Acts xxvii. 27, 28.
[3] Cf. Rom. xi. 36; 2 Cor. vi. 18; Eph. i. 23; iv. 6.

unreality of pietism and metaphysical vagary, St. Paul asserts, "The unseen things of God," *i.e.* His nature and character, "are discerned as thinkable (*noumena*) from an observation of the universe of an ordered world, by means of things made,"[1] which a poet of our day has paraphrased, —

> "The Somewhat which we name but cannot know,
> Ev'n as we name a star and only see
> His quenchless flashings forth, which ever show
> And ever hide Him and which are not He."

In the same strain follow those words from the homily to the Hebrews, where it is asserted that religious consciousness recognises the indwelling of God in the world by the manifestation of Him in the process of history: "By faith we are aware that the ages (eras) were fitted together by the utterance of God, so that out from that which is not apparent has come into existence what we look upon."[2]

This is nothing less than the enunciation of the principle of the divine significance and continuity of history and of the evolution of the world in life and thought. But there is an element which belongs before this, and we find it in the Epistle to the Colos-

---

[1] τὰ γὰρ ἀόρατα αὐτοῦ ἀπὸ κτίσεως κόσμου τοῖς ποιήμασιν νοούμενα καθορᾶται, ἥ τε ἀΐδιος αὐτοῦ δύναμις καὶ θειότης, κ.τ.λ., Rom. i. 20. Cf. Vaughan on Romans.

[2] Heb. xi. 3, πίστει νοοῦμεν κατηρτίσθαι τοὺς αἰῶνας ῥήματι Θεοῦ, εἰς τὸ μὴ ἐκ φαινομένων τὸ βλεπόμενον γεγονέναι.

sians,[1] where it is asserted against the false gnosis that the Son of God *is*, before[2] all things, and in Him all things cohere[3] as the particles cohere in the living organism. The Logos is the bond of the universe,[4] and is the Wisdom who, reaching from one end to the other, sweetly orders all things.[5] Because of this orderliness, the Greeks called the universe the kosmos, the beautiful order. This order, the Pauline gnosis goes on to say, in development of the idea, is not stereotyped, is not rigid in death. The Living One, who is the life of the world, lives, and the world grows. Hope is the drive-wheel of that growth which has been called evolution. The destiny of the universe is to become incorruptible[6] through the mediation of sons of God, who have thrown off "the brute inheritance," and have attained unto God-consciousness. At present there is going on in nature a fierce struggle for existence, the contest with environing forces which make for disorganisation,[7] and the universe groans in agony, and in the mounting upward of life and in the strife before the soul receives its new birth into the environment of God and righteousness, suffers birth-pangs.[8] Magnificent is the revelation of this cosmic passion, that upon its obverse is

---

[1] i. 17.

[2] πρό, not πρίν, before, as the sun is before its light, substance is in front of phenomena.

[3] συνέστηκεν.   [4] Heb. i. 3.   [5] Wis. viii. 1.

[6] Rom. viii. 21, ἐλευθερωθήσεται ἀπὸ τῆς δουλίας τῆς φθορᾶς.

[7] φθόρα.   [8] συνωδίνει.

a palingenesis (St. Matt. xix. 28), an everlasting birth-process, *êwige Gebârt*, as Meister Eckehart taught it, where the world finds its resurrection and eternal life only in spiritualised humanity. Of this world-process Calvary was an epitome, and the first Easter a prophecy of its outcome. Nature is the divine tragedy prolonged. Now all this is brought, in the mind of the apostle, back to personal life, wherein continues the redemptive process. "We have one God, the Father, out of Whom are all things, and we unto Him tend, and one Lord, Jesus Christ, through Whom are all things, and we through Him."[1] Without being further tedious, I think we may clearly conclude from this much of the Theology of the New Testament, that the world is in God, and God is in the world, and that God is the God triune.

1. The immanence of God was not wholly hidden from the religious consciousness of Israel; this I am far from asserting. Witness —

"Whither shall I go then from Thy Spirit? or whither shall I go then from Thy presence?

"If I climb up into heaven, Thou art there; if I go down to hell, Thou art there also.

"If I take the wings of the morning, and remain in the uttermost parts of the sea;

"Even there also shall Thy hand lead me, and Thy right hand shall hold me."[2]

---

[1] 1 Cor. viii. 6, note, ἐξ οὗ τὰ πάντα, — εἰς — δι' οὗ — δι' αὐτοῦ.
[2] Ps. xxxix. 6 ff.

"Am I a God at hand, saith the Lord, and not a God afar off? Can any hide himself in secret places that I shall not see him? saith the Lord.

"Do not I fill heaven and earth? saith the Lord.

"I have heard what the prophets said, that prophecy lies in my name, saying, I have dreamed, I have dreamed.

"How long shall this be in the heart of the prophets that prophecy lies? yea, they are prophets of the deceit of their own heart." [1]

But the tendency of the Israelites to revert to animistic and fetishistic ideas of God forbade emphasis and development of the idea. The heaven of heavens cannot contain God. The universe where He abides does not hold Him.[2] He transcends all limitations. He is in the world, yet more than it. Do not associate mass or size with the idea of the greatness of God. A point, position without extension, is as adequate a symbol of Him as unlimited space of four dimensions. Quantity is not a category of the Infinite.

III. We have thus far examined the soil and the seed which was cast into the soil; it remains for us to find out how it grew. It is true that, in a sense, the New Testament teaching of the immanent Triune is synthetic of all the various forms of Folk-faith which grouped themselves under the head of monotheism, polytheism, and pantheism. The Idea of the Father,

[1] Jer. xviii. 25 ff.
[2] Bp. Butler, Fourth Letter to Dr. Clark. Works, Vol. II.

God in His transcendence, is the truth of monotheism; the Idea of the Son, God dwelling in man, is the truth of polytheism; and the Idea of the Spirit, God pervading the worlds, is the truth of pantheism. Separate, these truths are false, because partial; united, they are the salvation of life. Therefore the Lord Jesus sent forth His apostles to baptise all nations in the name of the Father, and the Son, and the Holy Ghost.

a. The elementary proclamations of the New Testament develop themselves in the human intellect by the unavoidable logic into the dogma of the Holy Trinity. Jesus Christ taught that the Father is God, the Son is God, the Holy Ghost is God, and yet there are not three Gods, but one God. It took more than two centuries, however, for Christian thought to solve this paradox.[1] That greatest of the ancient rational theologians, Athanasius, convinced the world that the Idea of the Triune God was a truth of other than speculative import, and that it was rigidly logical; and for his position the aged fathers of the Nicene Council gave testimony that such had been the teaching of the apostles of the Lord.

---

[1] Not till the fourth century did the Church receive the accurate formula of the eternal generation of the Logos; there never was when He was not, οὐκ ἦν ποτε ὅτε οὐκ ἦν. Chrystal, *Six World-Councils*, 101 ff. St. Irenæus' doctrine of the dual nature of Jesus was gnostic in form. Harnack, *Dogmengesch.* I. 516. Fulton, *Index Canonum.*

b. God is the eternal Subject who knows the eternal Object who is known, and the Love who unites the two. Endeavour to eliminate from your life all faith in the Father, or in the Son, or in the Holy Ghost, and you will find your life distinctly poorer and less charged with motive, clearness, and hope. God conceived of as love, is energy, action. Action must result in somewhat, and of eternal action the result is eternal. What is that eternal result? Philosophy from Hellas to Hindustan responded that it was the world. But observation denied that a finite and changing world could be eternal. Consequently, God as love must love *someone* instead of *somewhat*. In one there can be no circulation of that love which is the life, which is the being and substance of God. Nothing without an object can become manifest itself, because it would proceed out from self forever. It is because of this fact that mathematical monotheism invariably becomes either pantheism or atheism, worship of the divine nothing. Action within one, I say, is impossible. That is why Brahm appears to be sunken in a slumber. Action in two is incomplete. That is why Ormuzd and Ahriman appear in the firmament of a Persian dualism, engaged in a struggle which can never end. Action in three is complete circulation; the infinite turn and return of that Life which is Love. Fitly with this idea ends the high strain of Dante's mediæval miracle of song, at the summit of celestial paradise, in the deep heart of the aureole rose of the elect saints and angelic hierarchy. Through the radiant medium of the Divine Humanity, he says: —

> "In the profound and clear subsistence
> Of the lofty light appeared to me three gyres
> Of colours three and single continuity;
> And one from other seemed to be reflected,
> As rainbow is from rainbow,
> While the third appeared a fire
> Which from the one and from the other equally
> is exhaled."[1]

Let me put this thought again: the Eternal Mind, conscious to Himself, eternally produces a Logos like Himself. Because of this likeness the Logos conscious to Himself and the originating Mind together produce also a Principle which is imperfect[2] like Himself, but because the being of the Logos is derived, what He together with Mind originates is a procession, which is a process, always going on, but since it is infinite, always complete. Why, asks one, should not the third divine principle produce a fourth, and so on? This was the crux of Gnosticism, and it

---

[1] *Nella profonda e chiara sussistenza*
Dell' alto lume parvemi tre giri
Di tre colori e d' una continenza;
E l' un dall' altro, come Iri da Iri,
Parea riflesso, e il terzo parea fuoco
Che quinci e quindi egualmente si spiri.
                                           Paradiso, xxxiii. 115-121.

[2] Not having what theologians term *aseity*.

produced the theory of emanations. The right answer is that the third principle does not produce a fourth, because the subject and object being linked, the three are complete in one subsistence and "continuity," as Dante suggests. The Holy Ghost is the life of the world, and the return of imperfection to perfection through the Church.[1] It is by this doctrine of the double procession that the Latin Church preserved itself from the vagaries of a Gnosticism, with its endless processions of æons from a father god and a mother god, which modern Mormonism has revived, making them with Adam to constitute the Trinity. The tendency in early ages towards this speculation was strong. In the Old Testament the Wisdom is feminine. Origen speaks of the Holy Ghost as a woman.[2] To the mind of the early Church the Holy Spirit was the feminine principle in God, but a desire to cut away the ground from under the Gnostics and to remove from religion that which always imports into life moral degradation, suppressed the development of this idea. Nevertheless, as Goethe says in his Chorus Mysticus at the close of *Faust*, "It is the deathless ideal of womanhood which is always uplifting humanity," —

"*Das Ewig Weibliche
Zieht uns hinan,*"

[1] W. T. Harris, *Hegel's Logic*, 14.

[2] ἄρτι ἔλαβε με ἡ μήτηρ μου τὸ ἅγιον Πνεῦμα ἐν μιᾷ τῶν τριχῶν μου κ.τ.λ., Comm. St. John, II. 7. 58. Cf. Bigg, *Christian Platonists of Alexandria*, 15. n. 1.

and to supply the want of such an ideal in old days they had Montanistic incarnation of the Holy Ghost in a woman, and in modern days we have the pious opinion of the Assumption and enthronisation of St. Mary the Virgin, "Our tainted nature's solitary boast"; to whom, Wordsworth believed that perhaps, "Not unforgiven the suppliant knee might bend."[1]

c. Traditional Theology is right when, upon the basis of the New Testament, it insists that the Holy Ghost is person. That which substantially proceeds forth from out of person is person.[2] We, as conscious persons, argue thence that God, our Source or Cause, the All-Father, is person. Thus the circle of reasoning is completed. Spiritual existence is found to imply personality as inseparable from it. The Holy Ghost is more than a pervasive spiritual current, or atmosphere, or aura, or subtle substance of some imaginary sort. He is something more than an effluence from God, a stream from the fountain-head of Deity; something more than the influence of Jesus, either as personally near us by His ascension into the plane of omnipresence, or by reason of the effect of the example of His historic career. The

---

[1] Feuerbach, *Essence of Christianity*, c. vi., sees in human nature necessity for the divine motherhood.

[2] The notion that the term *persona*, person, signifies in theology a *rôle* is an error arisen from not considering that the ancient theologians were not etymologists; they employed words in their actual sense. *Persona* = ὑπόστασις in Greek Theology.

Holy Spirit is not a *zeitgeist*, nor a stream of tendency, nor the psychic course of nature. Or if He be these, He is something more. He is a Person, the Lord of personal spirits. If God the Father be immanent in the souls of men, then by virtue of the circuminsession of the Persons of the Holy Trinity the Holy Ghost is also immanent. Therefore there must be some sense in which the Holy Ghost is personally and substantially the human soul's indwelling source of life and thought. An apocalypse of this came to prophet Ezekiel in the Vision of the Holy Waters. Through the personal Spirit the reason of the eternal Logos is imparted to men, as Jesus said, " He shall receive of Mine and shall show it unto you," and as St. John commented, " The Life was the light of men."

Somehow thus the Christian consciousness conceives of God as triune in His subsistence. His life and existence are complete within Himself. Consequently creation is not necessary to His consciousness and life. Therefore He is not the ground of evil. Thus at one and the same time, in removing a necessity of an eternal world, the dilemma, atheism, — no God, or pantheism, no world, — is avoided. God still remains absolute and yet personal, since His limitations are within Himself. I regret the necessity of appearing in this lecture somewhat transcendental. The topic is profound. Thus much on the rational Theology of the Idea of God. In order to indicate the extent to which traditional Theology received the revelation of the Triune Love in Christ and in the world, the brief catena which follows is all my time will allow.

d. I think that it should be said that in each created thing are the ineffable sacraments of the Divine dispensation. — ORIGEN, *Comm. St. John* xxiii. 3.

The omnipotent Logos pervades the universe, manifesting His energy throughout it and enlightening beings both visible and invisible; them He holds together and unifies by His powers, giving life and preserving life for all which exists. — ST. ATHANASIUS, *Against Gentiles*, c. xlii.

God is within everything; He is without it; above and beneath, and His substance is not divided. It is entire and the same throughout. It pervades beings, dwells around them, dwells alongside and penetrates them. — ST. GREGORY THE GREAT, *Morals*, Bk. II. c. 12.

God is the fountain of being for all that exists, the source of life for all things which have vital energy, and the principal reason for all rational creatures. He is the limitless Ocean where life exults in fulness of being and vastness of extent, — a shoreless Sea which sole contains itself. — ST. JOHN OF DAMASCUS, *Orth. Faith*, I. 8, title 1.

All creatures are a theophany. — JOHN SCOTUS ERIGENA, *Comm. on St. John.*

All things we see should, in relation to God, who alone truly is, be called accidents.— CARD. CUSA, *Exerc.* VII.

Reason is the inner light in which God speaks to us.— ST. THOMAS AQUINAS, *Ad. Magis. Joan. Vercell.* II. a. 1.

Reason is in man as God is in the World.— IDEM, *De Reg. Princ.* Lib. I. c. xii.

God is in all things, not indeed as a part of the essence or as an accident, but as doing is in that which does.— IDEM, *Summa,* I^a., VIII. 1, Resp.

God after a common way, by presence, by power, and by substance, is present in all things; in some sense, however, He is said to be present in a way more intimate, by grace.— IDEM, I^a., I., VIII. 3 contra.

e. From this catena you may see that the Idea of God as the immanent Triune did to some extent enter the consciousness of Christian theologians, but against its full acceptance both folk-faith and philosophy combined, and to this day a veil is upon the heart of many Christian teachers. The old gods, driven away, linger still upon the frontiers of Christendom, or return masked. Venus and her crew sallied forth from the Horselberg to ensnare Christian knights. The valkyrie of Odin became the witches of Christian Europe. Minucius Felix says that the gods of the nations were devils, and Milton assists the permanence of this revival in contemporary religious thought by making the old gods of classic paganism the lords of a Christian hell. St. Paul said: an idol is nothing, and even the Hebrew poet,[1] at a moment of deeper insight, perceived that the false gods were non-existent. Arianism, which St. Athanasius and the Nicene fathers feared would bring back polytheism, did in fact develop in an opposite direction. The children of Arius and of Ulfilas have merged into congenial Islam. The notion of bare transcendence of God in relation to the world, a pagan element, still survives in the common acceptance of Socinian and Zwinglian systems. In former times it was this notion which gave character to the Antiochine school of exegesis, and suggested to Nestorius his eccentric position. One form of the notion of bare transcendence is the expansion of the concept of divine sovereignty by a disproportionate extension of the principle of absolute foreordination, and by that notion of divine government, which is known as "preëstablished harmony,"[2]

[1] Ps. xcvi. 5, *elilim*, Heb., lit. *nothings*. Vulgate translates it *dæmonia*.

[2] Bouillier, *Philosophie Cartésienne*, II. 451 ff. Much to answer for has Leibnitzian speculation with its preëstablished harmony, and that "best of all possible worlds," which used poor Candide so roughly; because the theory of Leibnitz and his school brought in that sterile deism of Voltaire and of Hobbes, which chilled the life of the Anglican Church of the eighteenth century, till warmed by the piety of Venn, Newton, Cooper, Walker, Cecil, Simeon, and the other early evangelicals, together with the fervour of the first Methodists.

as though God had wound up the circling universe as a watch is wound up, or set it spinning like a top.

Common in our childhood were the ideas of God, as of one sitting afar off beyond the clouds upon a white marble seat, looking down upon the revolving suns and planets, and the busy ant-hill of this world; or as in the ancient epic, where it was said that Zeus had gone away for a twelve-days feast among the blameless Ethiopians; or as when Elijah with immeasurable sarcasm mocks the priests of Baal,— "Cry aloud: for he is a god; either he is talking, or he is pursuing, or he is in a journey, or peradventure he sleepeth, and must be awaked."[1] When the notion of the solitary transcendence of God survives or revives in Christianity, the idea of the trinity of the Divine Being is implicitly contradicted; the Father and Son are put in opposition, as the Manichees and Albigensians (and high Calvinists virtually) conceived of them. An expiatory and propitiatory theory of sacrifice, a theory distinctly heathen, survives from folk-faith; all teaching of divine omnipresence becomes irrational, incomprehensible, and futile; grace becomes a substantial efflux to bridge over the chasm between God and His world; consequently the Church assumes a sacerdotal, and the grace of the sacraments a material, nature. The object of religion is, upon this premise, supposed to be the soothing of divine wrath, and an

[1] 1 Kings xviii. 27.

evasion of the penalty of sin, the resurrection to be a corporeal resuscitation, and everlasting life a combination of precious metals, precious stones, and endless psalm-singing.

The inexorable verdict of history is that the concept of the Trinity is the only permanent form of the Idea of God; it is the only rational form. It is the Christian doctrine of God. "It was through the Christian religion that the absolute Idea of God, in its true conception, attained consciousness. Here man, too, finds himself comprehended in his true nature, given in the specific concept of *the Son*."[1] It is the only basis for the teaching of foreign missions. Clear away from this idea in the minds of the people accretions of survivals of primitive folk-faith.

In pagan days of Rome, a temple was erected to Romulus, and his aid and protection for young and sick children were invoked by the memory of his own arduous infancy. That same temple is now standing, converted into the church of St. Theodorus,[2] and in that church at the present day may be seen Italian mothers with their infants, in prayer before the high altar, or making votive offerings, invoking the aid and intercession of St. Theodorus. Here cultus of the saints is clearly seen to be a survival of ancestor-worship, and an ancient god is still worshipped in the

---

[1] Hegel, *Phil. of Hist.* III. 3.
[2] Tylor, *Primitive Cult.* II. 121.

guise of a Christian modern saint. Likewise in the popular religion of the Greeks of the present, that mountain which was anciently held sacred to the sun, Ἥλιος, is now reverenced as Mount St. Elias. Every one knows that St. George of Nicomedia never existed. His legendary contest with the dragon is a survival of the myth of Horus and Typhon, belonging to Egyptian mythology, the mythos of a never-ending victorious contest of good over evil, which is the solution of the riddle of pain and sorrow. Art was the bridge over which many religious ideas of heathendom crossed to Christendom. Especially Gnostic art.[1] Notwithstanding St. Paul exhorted the Galatai of his day to abandon belief and worship of "poor and powerless elementary spirits,"[2] contrasting them with the real and vitalising energy of Christ, nevertheless to this day the Christianised descendants of these Galatians offer religious service to the elementary spirits of mountains, trees, and waters, calling them, as their ancestors did, stoicheia.[3] A survival of Animism is evident in modern spiritism and occultism. Also it lies at the foundation of "Christian

---

[1] Cf. Theodoret, *Eccles. Hist.* I. 15. Didron, *Christian Iconography*, passim. J. P. Lundy, *Monumental Christianity*. G. W. King, *The Gnostics and their Remains*.

[2] στοιχεῖα, Gal. iv. 9.

[3] L. M. J. Garnett, *The Women of Turkey and their Folk-Lore*, I. 130.

Science," which is not Christian, and is not Science. Fetishism is too obviously the characteristic of some theories of the sacraments and of their operation, to demand particular illustration. A curious instance of the development towards polytheism is to be found in Père Lacordaire's Letters from Italy, where, having adopted a "special devotion" to the "Madonna of the Oak," he writes back to a friend in France whose cult is the Madonna of some other title, " My Madonna salutes your Madonna." Extraordinary! Yet there is but one Madonna. In the faith of the common people Our Lady of Loretto is as distinctly another individual from Our Lady of Sorrows as the Greek Here was another person from Aphrodite.

In a somewhat like spirit the Provençal Christians, the Albigensians, and others, thought of the Eternal Father as wrathful, hateful. Jesus, whom they loved and worshipped as mild and merciful, they set over against the Father. This dualism is a survival of Gnostic and Manichee influence. The stained windows in South French cathedrals have preserved evidence of the survival of this oriental dualism.[1] Modern Romanism has not wholly freed itself from this dualistic survival; the cultus of Mary tends to present her as more benignant than her son. This is all due to the primitive notion of a divine mediator. For example, the Christ in the Last Judgment of Michael Angelo is far from being as lovable as Mary

[1] Didron, *Christian Iconography*, I. 180-191.

in Fra Angelico's Coronation of the Virgin and in the Madonnas of Botticelli and Luini.

IV. What is the task of Christian teachers on this standing point? I shall not answer after the manner of Dr. Bushnell in his famous lectures, when he advised his hearers to stick close to the old terminology, while they privately meant his new interpretation of the Atonement. I grant that it is indeed a serious question whether we can immediately remove the mythical and pagan elements which survive in Christian Theology and in popular religion, without the risk of impairing their ethical force and moral sanction for the average man. But have we not had enough of the evils of accommodation? Modern thought is already careless of an absentee God. Wordsworth in despair at the empty deism of his day, in anguish cries out: —

"Great God! I'd rather be
    A Pagan, suckled in a creed outworn:
So might I, standing on this pleasant lea,
    Have glimpses that would make me less forlorn."

For my part I accept heartily the thought of Amiel recorded over forty years ago: "Our century wants a new Theology; that is to say, a new and more profound explanation of the nature of Christ and of the light which it flashes on Heaven and humanity." Too long, gentlemen, have we been in bondage to a philosophy which, since Bacon, has put a chasm between God and His word; too long have the faiths of the childhood of humanity alloyed the pure gold of the teaching of Christ, and by an extension of the Vincentian canon have been constituted *the* orthodoxy. We have halted between two opinions, the God revealed in Jesus, and the Baalim. At this vacillation the world is becoming impatient. When Plotinus was dying he said, "I am striving to bring the God which is within me into harmony with the God of the Universe." This suggests the task of Christian teachers in the premise. Quicken the God-consciousness in each soul. Teach men that there is no truth for any man until he lives it, that only in so far as men make truth and life, creed and deed, identical, can they know truth. To know God, do good.

A need of our new age is a profound and ever-wakeful sense of the presence of God. This can be received intellectually only as we comprehend with mind and heart that significance of the Incarnation expressed in the name Emmanuel, and that significance is first the sure and real presence of God in the world and in men, and consequently that manhood is eternal because of the abiding of an eternal element in it; that pain and sorrow, the agony of the world, are evidences not of death, but of the immanent Life. If any one thinks that he hears the ebb of faith's ocean, —

> "Its melancholy, long, withdrawing roar,
>   Retreating, to the breath
> Of the night-wind, down the vast edges drear
> And naked shingles of the world," —

let him not dream that love of truth, of righteousness, that self-control, all merely for their own sake, that unselfishness, that assent to " a Power outside us not ourselves that makes for righteousness," — these alone, can in this nineteenth century take the room of Father God. No; God is something more than a stream of tendency, more than qualities, wisdom and goodness. So it is high time that we men should definitely decide whether Mr. Arnold and Mr. Moody are the voice of the Zeitgeist in the wilderness of these latter days. It is high time that we should confess our divine sonship, in virtue of which alone we are able from the ground of the heart to say, "Our Father"; that from Jesus instead of from metaphysics we should seek the true content of the Idea of God, and like St. Ignatius to the Romans, confess, "I am Theophoros, the God-bearer, for I carry Christ within me." This alone is the basis of that human brotherhood which arouses the undying enthusiasm of humanity. Only thus can we come into that temper wherein we are able rightly to consider the importunate social problems which press upon us at this end of the century. This alone is the ground of a reasonably religious and holy hope. Rest assured that when brought to the test of the needs of life it will be found that while the speculative idea of the Holy Trinity may vex the non-philosophical mind, nevertheless practical life cannot eliminate from thought, from ideal, from motive, from action, the idea of God as love infinite and immanent, of God the Father, God the Son, and God the Holy Ghost. Finally, it is the ground of that personal devoutness to the immanent triune Love which can make its prayer —

> "Oh, Hidden Love, who now art loving me;
>   Oh, wounded Love, who once was slain for me;
>   Oh, sun-crowned Love, who art alive for me;
>   Oh, patient Love, who weariest not of me, —
>   Alone of all Thou weariest not of me.
>   Oh, bear with me till I am lost in Thee,
>   Oh, bear with me till I am found in Thee."

THE CHURCH.

Nam et Ecclesia proprie et principaliter ipse est Spiritus Sanctus in quo est Trinitas unius Divinitatis. — Atque ita exinde etiam numerus omnis, qui in hanc fidem conspiraverit, Ecclesia ab auctore et consecratore censetur. Et ideo Ecclesia quidem delicta condonabit, sed Ecclesia Spiritus per Spiritalem hominem, non Ecclesia numerus Episcoporum, domini enim non famuli, est jus et arbitrum; Dei ipsius non sacerdotis.

TERTULLIAN, de *Pud.* XXI.

It is evident unto all men, diligently reading Holy Scripture and ancient Authors, that from the Apostles' time there have been these Orders of Ministers in Christ's Church, — Bishops, Priests, and Deacons. Which offices were ever more had in such reverend Estimation, that no man might presume to execute any of them, except he were first called, tried, examined, and known to have such qualities as are requisite for the same; and also by public Prayer, with Imposition of Hands, were approved and admitted thereunto by lawful Authority. And therefore, to the intent that these orders may be continued, and reverently used and esteemed in this Church, no man shall be accounted nor taken to be a lawful Bishop, Priest, or Deacon, in this Church, or suffered to execute any of the said Functions, except he be called, tried, examined, and admitted thereunto, according to the form hereafter following, or hath had Episcopal Consecration or Ordination.

Preface to the Ordinal, Book of Common Prayer.

If any Man therefore shall affirm, either that during the continuance of the Old Testament, the Merits of Christ's Death actually to come, were not sufficient to save all true Believers; or that there was then no *Catholick Church;* or that at any time there was any other Rock but *Jesus Christ,* the blessed Seed upon whom the *Catholick Church* was then built; or that many of the gentiles were not always (for aught that is known to the contrary) true members of the *Catholick Church;* or that Christ Himself was not the sole Head or Monarch all that while of the whole *Catholick Church;* or, that the said *Catholick Church,* after the members of it were dispersed into all the places of the World, was otherwise visible than *per partes ;* or, that Noah did appoint any man to be the visible Head of the said *Catholick Church ;* or, that the *High Priest* among the *Jews* had any more authority over the *Catholick Church* of God, than *King David* had over the Universal Kingdom of God ; or, that the said *High Priest* had not greatly sinn'd, if he had taken upon him, or usurped any such infinite Authority ; he doth greatly Erre.

  Bp. OVERALL's *Convocation Book,* Canon xxxvi., A.D. 1606.

 I believe that this holy Church is Catholic, that is to say that it cannot be coarcted or restrained within the limits of any one city, town, province, region or country, but that it is dispersed and spread universally throughout all the whole world. Insomuch that in what part soever of the world, be it Africa, Asia or Europe, there may be found any number of people of what sort, state or condition soever they be, which do believe in one God, the Father, Creator of all things and in one Lord Jesus Christ His Son, and in one Holy Ghost, and do always profess and have all one faith, one hope, one charity, according as it is prescribed in Holy Scripture ; and do all consent in one true interpretation of the same Scripture and in the right use of the Sacraments of Christ, we may boldly pronounce and say that there is this Holy Church, the very Espouse and Body of Christ, the very Kingdom of Christ and the very temple of God.

      Institution of a Christian Man, 1537.

 Le christianisme historique s'est affirmé de tout temps comme la religion absolue. L'Histoire de ses dogmes n'autorise point une semblable prétention. Elle nous montre ses docteurs de tous les âges, depuis les apôtres jusqu'aux réformateurs, variant souvent dans leurs opinions, se contredisant, se combattant sans trêve, affirmant un jour ce qu'ils nieront le lendemain, et construisant ainsi, pièce à pièce, au milieu des luttes les plus vives, l'imposant édifice de ses doctrines.

     HAAG, *Histoire des Dogmes Chrétiens.*

SYNOPSIS.

INTRODUCTION:

    Nothing in folk-religions closely analogous to the Christian Church.

COMPARATIVE RELIGION:

    I. — The nearest approaches in primitive culture to a Church.
        a. Shamanism.
        b. Mysteries of Eleusis.
        c. Roman Imperialism *vs.* Protestant Individualism.

BIBLICAL THEOLOGY:

    II. — The New Testament doctrine of the Church.
        a. The teachings of Jesus.
        b. The acts of Jesus. He constitutes simultaneously and together the Church and its ministry.
        c. The Church, as such, is visible.
        d. Function of Baptism, place of repentance.

TRADITIONAL THEOLOGY:

    III. — Some traditional opinions about the Church. The slow development of the "four notes" of the article of the creeds.

    IV. — The utter indefiniteness of primitive and early Christian consciousness as to the nature and essence of the Church. Christian theologians, however, agree that the Church is necessary for salvation.

PRESENT PROBLEM:

    V. — Critical examination of the "four notes" of the Church to determine their value and real existence.
        a. ONE — not two or more — communion an outward sign; uniformity not requisite; view of the several forms of Church government in their relation to organic unity of Christendom; their relation to God as immanent; unity of Christendom cannot arrive till we have abandoned literalism in Theology and Biblical interpretation.

 b. HOLY. The witness of History. Holiness of the Church realised in her individual members, but not alone in assent to dogma. Holiness then a *terminus ad quem* of the Church in Time. Relation of Sacraments to holiness. The Church the highest exponent of that redemptive operation which is discerned in the cosmic process.

 c. CATHOLIC does not denote extension, or exclusive possession of divine truth, or the life of the world arising into consciousness; but does suggest that Church is living, and that Christian consciousness of the present is to be accepted as the nearest approximation to reality. The true place of tradition. Catholicity is intensive, not extensive, in the Church.

 d. APOSTOLIC. This does not forbid living development of Theology. What is Apostolic Succession? Will it support the "Sacramental System"? It is a fact and witness to historic continuity. Conclusion, that the "four notes" of the Church are goals or ideals towards which the Church tends.

PRACTICAL TEACHING:

VI. — Practical import of this idea of the Church; its relation to various organisations, religious and secular, and to the realisation of Corporate Unity. The Unity of the Spirit and the bond of peace.

THE CHURCH.

GENTLEMEN: —

The Church is the unique creation of our Lord Jesus Christ. Nothing in all ancient heathendom answers to it in constitution or in institution. Such a thing as a congregation of faithful men was not known. Only the telesterion,[1] the hall of the initiation of the mystai at Eleusis, corresponded to a modern church building. The ancient temple was a shrine, *naos*, for the abiding divinity, or a precinct marked off on ground and sky, *temenos* and *templum*, for the observation of auspices, or simply a sacred spot, *hieron*. It was not for the people. The Parthenon could in its entirety have been set down inside the nave of Cologne Cathedral. A single boulder or isolated rock in Hindustan often served to carve out a complete temple. The vast temples of Egypt were for priests, pomps, and sacred beasts, and not for the laity. But the Stoic sects in the West, and northern Buddhism in the East, were at an early date so impressed with the methods of

---

[1] Dyer, *Gods in Greece*, 189.

organisation of the Christian Church, that they adopted some of its external features. Every attempt at tracing the evolution of the Christian Church from the synagogue and theocracy of Israel will have to be abandoned; for the inner principle of the Church, as I expect to show, is distinctly different from the *kahal* of Israel [1] and from the Levitical hierarchy. While the origin of the Christian Church may not be discovered in ancient folk-faith and customs, it is nevertheless evident that precedent conditions did at the beginning limit the reception of the Church-idea and shape the development thereof.

I. *a.* In primitive culture the church is the priesthood, the shamans or medicine men of the tribes; and religion consists in performing ceremonial acts.[2] Thence flow down, glacier-like, into later civilisation, two streams of survival,—religious functions in the domain of Christian worship and magic, whether sanctioned for our credence by Pierre d'Aban, Cornelius Agrippa, and that painful and godly man the Rev. Cotton Mather, or implied in *ex opere operato* doctrines of the Atonement and of the Sacraments. Also, according to the faith of primitive folk, the priest or the chief priest is the representative of his tribe or gens. He is the *per-*

---

[1] As the school of Vitringa assumes; cf. Killen, *Framework of the Church.*

[2] Note, *sacrifice,* from *sacrum facere,* to do a sacred thing, and to do it *rite,* correctly. Tylor, *Primitive Culture, passim.*

sona gentis, the parson, and because he must, in this office and capacity, act with careful consideration for others, he is the prototype of our modern gentleman. In him is bound up the welfare of his people, for he is something of a corporation soul of the tribe; through him the gods speak, his word is god's-spel, gospel, and, as such, is infallible. Because he alone can direct the layman how to appease divine wrath, to offer acceptable gifts, and to believe right things, the shaman is regarded as a vicar of the gods and a mediator between gods and men.[1] In many cases he is held to be the son of the god, and is not allowed to grow old or to die in weakness or disease,[2] lest the life of the tribe should thereby wane with him. He is therefore slain while in his full vigour, and is thought to carry away with him to the ghost-world the sins of the tribe. In another sense he the representative of the corporate life of the tribe; in a word, the corporation soul, by fiction said never to die. O King, live forever; the King is dead; long live the King; the King never dies. What divine or singular powers belong to the priesthood, the primitive priest

---

[1] Clergymen in Cornwall are supposed to be able to drive out evil spirits. A woman asked one to walk around her and read some passages of the Bible in order to exorcise the ghost of her dead sister, who, in the form of a fly, persistently worried her. *Folk-Lore Journal*, v. 27. George Fox also was convinced that he had the power of exorcising the devil. See "Journal." Cf. Reports of the U. S. Bureau of Ethnology, *passim*.

[2] Frazer, *Golden Bough*, c. 3.

transmits to his successors through touch or by the transmission of the sacerdotal insignia of masks, cloaks, costume, and conjuring apparatus. According to the survival of this folk-faith the priesthood is the Church; that is to say, the fifth essence of it.

b. The subtle and spiritualising intellect of the Hellenic peoples took up these crude elements of earlier thought, and transmuted them into a profound mythos of the Eleusinian mysteries, where the story of Dionysus and of Demeter set forth the highest pagan idea of the divine Soul of the world and of the secret of sorrow as revealed in the redemptive issues of life. But the Eleusinian mysteries were for the select, the mystai, the initiated, and the adept. Their high doctrines were strictly esoteric.[1] Who cannot perceive the survival of this conception in parts of Christendom of to-day, in the Abyssinian Church, with fold upon fold of curtains surrounding the altar; in the Greek Church, with its veiled altars shut in by lofty iconastases, from behind which the voice of the priest is heard muffled, in the proclamation, "Holy things for the holy,"[2] and in the solemn bidding, twice repeated, "Let the catechumens depart?" Almost we catch the echo of the herald of the ancient pagan mysteries, *Procul, o procul, este profani!* Not even modern Protestantism, Genevan or Anglican, has thoroughly relinquished this notion that the Church of the Lord Jesus is for adepts only.

---

[1] Dyer, *Gods in Greece*, c. v.   [2] τὰ ἅγια τοῖς ἁγίοις.

c. Another powerful factor in shaping the development of the Church has been the tradition of Roman imperialism. Rome was the inverse of the Jewish theocracy, and yet by its genius for organisation and centralisation, Rome has perpetuated in Christendom the theocratic system of Israel in a Christian form. Imperial Rome had no Church and no dogma. The State took the place, and the emperor was Pontifex Maximus. The civil law prescribed beliefs. Dante, through a strict imperialist, bewails in one place the secular survival of Roman imperialism: —

"Ah, Constantine, of how great evil was the mother, not thy conversion, but that dower, the first rich pope from thee did capture." [1]

It was, however, not by a fabled *dôt*, that Constantine, the first Christian emperor, corrupted the Church, but by impressing it into the form of a monarchy, making the hierarchy the reverse of that coin whose obverse bore the image of Cæsar.[2] The parish and the diocese were in Constantine's time names of divisions of the Christian Church.[3] With the theory of

[1] *Ahi Constantin, di quanto mal fu matre,*
Non la tua conversion, ma quella dote
Che da te prese il primo ricco patre!
Inferno, xix. 115.

[2] Renan, Hibbert Lectures, *The Influence of Rome on Christianity and the Development of the Catholic Church.*

[3] Pelliccia, *Polity of the Christian Church*, Sec. iv. 1, 2 ; Moeller, *History of the Christian Church*, 329 ff. ; Fulton, *Index Canonum;* Guizot, *History of Civilisation.*

Roman imperialism that the State was the Church, both the Vedas of the Orient, and Plato in his *Republic* agree, but the bishops of Rome, by the logic of events more powerful than their own wills, reversed antiquity. The Holy Roman Empire, through bulls and interdicts and crusades, exactly inverted, for a while at least, the pagan imperial idea. Will Rothe's dream ever become realised, and the Church be merged in the State; or further, to adapt Browning's lines, —

> "That one Face, far from vanish rather grows,
> Or decomposes but to recompose,
> Becomes my Universe and feels and knows?"

But this is transcendental. Within the bosom of autocratic Rome there existed an adverse element, which in due time was to manifest itself in revolt against all traditional form of church organisation. I allude to the Roman Collegia, the Greek ἑταιρείαι, and their derivatives, the guilds and brotherhoods of the Teutonic nations. The principle of these societies was popular and democratic. They elected their own officers, whose powers derived from the society; their object was mutual benefit, charity and fellowship. Working under the surface of society and hidden from Church authorities, they finally emerged into the light of ecclesiastical history as the congregational forms of church organisation, such as have arisen in these latter days. These are our survivals from ancient Rome, — Papacy and Congregationalism. Between them lies Anglicanism, logically inconsistent, yet resting upon a foundation firmer than logic: these three forms are the only tenable shapes of ecclesiastical organisation.

II. Into such a field of the world the Divine Sower went forth to sow His seed. What precisely was the teaching of Jesus touching the Church?

a. The Lord came not to teach a new system of philosophy or of ethics. His purpose was not primarily humanitarian, nor ultimately mystical. He began with a proclamation[1] of the joyful message[2] of God. This is termed "the Gospel of the Kingdom,"[3] and its burden was, "The Kingdom of Heaven is at hand; repent ye,[4] and believe in the gospel.[5] From the parable of the sower, it is clear that at the time these words were spoken the Kingdom was within Jesus.[6] Jesus is the revealment of God; that is, God the Saviour self-revealing Himself in an individual of humanity. That which Jesus is, God is. Jesus is Saviour, because God in His eternal and essential character is Saviour. The significance of the words and deeds of Jesus is found in this, that He reveals. But to those who are blind, He cannot make Himself to be a revelation of God

---

[1] κηρύσσειν, St. Mark i. 14. [2] εὐαγγέλιον.
[3] St. Matt. iv. 23. [4] μετανοεῖτε. [5] St. Mark i. 15.
[6] Cf. St. Matt. xi. 27, "No man knoweth the Son but the Father; neither knoweth any man the Father, save the Son, and to whomsoever the Son will reveal Him."

the Eternal. There must be a receptive condition. For this reason, Jesus cried, "Repent," change your mental attitude,[1] your entire way of looking at life, and believe in the good message. This effected, God enters more fully into the life of man. It is not that the Eternal changes His attitude of favour toward men.[2] He is One, and changeless. In the three parables in St. Luke,[3] God as the Good Shepherd is searching for the sheep; as the woman, is diligently seeking the coin; and as the father of the prodigal He always loves and yearns after His child. Truly, the Triune God, the Kingdom of Heaven, is revealed to be near at hand, — God within His world, reconciling it unto Himself. This Kingdom is not, as the Jews hoped and supposed, a state with armies and thrones, and Zion exalted in the place of imperial Rome. No, the Kingdom of God cometh not with observation; it is a Kingdom of the poor in spirit. For the Kingdom of God is within; for God is within thee, immanent. Now it is, in truth, difficult sometimes to distinguish in the New Testament between the Kingdom of God, the Kingdom of Heaven, and the Church. The reason is sound, yet they are not synonymous. The Kingdom of God is as leaven which one took and hid in three measures of meal. Clearly the Kingdom of God is not disembodied. Perhaps in this it is true as Spenser sang, —

"For soule is forme, and doth the bodie make";

[1] μετανοεῖτε.   [2] Is. lix. 1, 2; James i. 17; Rom. xi. 29.   [3] xv.

the divine leaven generates the Church, for the Kingdom of God is originally God Himself, the immanent Triune, and the Church arises from the conscious union of souls with the God within. Our Lord sets forth His measures of meal; in plain words, His Church. At the beginning He says, "I will found My Church,"[1] and every word tells. St. Paul freely develops the thought, and something organic and external is undeniably implied. In another place [2] the teaching of Jesus repeats the same figure. This indicates distinctly that He instituted His Church. To His apostles or disciples He says, "Ye have not chosen Me, but I have chosen you."[3] The disciples did not therefore institute a *collegium*, or society, or voluntary club. The purpose of this institution is disclosed by the Founder, "As the Father hath sent Me, even so send I you." According to the implied premise, no mission could be more plenary in power and authority. In these days the first elements of the gospel of Christ are called sociology, so far have we lost the sense of a Saviour God, a saving Church and what it actually is to be saved.

b. How was this society constituted? Not much can be gained from the memorabilia of Jesus. St.

---

[1] οἰκοδομήσω μου τὴν ἐκκλησίαν, St. Matt. xvi. 18 — οἰκοδομή, 1 Cor. xiv. 12–26; οἰκοδομεῖν, xiv. 4; 2 Cor. x. 8, xiii. 10. Rom. xiv. 19, xv. 2; Eph. iv. 29, etc. The Church is built as the world is built, as a body is built.

[2] St. Luke vi. 48.   [3] St. John xvi. 16.

Matthew gives us to understand that upon the principle, or the consciousness, of divine Sonship the Church is founded. This means, as the words of this place show, vital relation with the Holy Spirit within. From St. John [1] we learn that the apostolate was constituted together with the Church. Upon this point I beg leave to insist. The Church, then, is called a net, which holds fishes, small and great, good and worthless. It is also a tree, because, as instinct with the Spirit of Life, it grows freely with the process of the years. It is distinctly obvious that Christ's religion in its organised form is not individual, but corporate. When on the cross, He declined the ministry of a single person, but accepted the same service, when offered by combined endeavour,[2] and His promise is to two who agree touching a petition, and where two or three are gathered together, there will He be. The Church, as we shall see, was instituted and constituted together. In St. Luke it is told how the two returned from Emmaus and found the eleven and those with them;[3] and while they were talking, Jesus appeared in the midst,[4] and breathed upon the assemblage, possibly over five hundred, and said, "Receive ye the Holy Ghost." From

---

[1] xv. 16.

[2] Cf. St. Matt. xxvii. 48 with St. John xix. 29; and Sewall, *Microscope of the New Testament*, 111 ff.

[3] xxiv. 33, τοὺς ἕνδεκα καὶ τοὺς σὺν αὐτοῖς.

[4] St. John xx. 19.

this, as well as from what has preceded, it is evident that our Lord founded His ministry together with the Church, and as a component part thereof:[1] not that it was evolved from the laity according to the congregational theory, or developed from the hierarchy according to prelatical imaginings. In the teachings of Jesus concerning His Church we have its two sides given together and unseparated, the Spirit and the organic structure, the invisible and the visible, the Kingdom of God and the Church. The Kingdom of God is the soul of the Church, God the Holy Spirit outgoing into the world. The Church is the special organon of God.

c. While the Kingdom is the inner substance of the Church, it is the procession and operation of the Holy Ghost within the individual souls, and within the corporate organism of the Church. As our Lord is the pattern of the perfect individual soul and character, so the Kingdom of God is the perfect ideal of human society. That this ideal might be realised in the world, the Church was instituted and constituted in the manner which we learn from the New Testament. The Nineteenth Article of Religion has a fairly good working definition of the Church suited to our times. "The visible Church of Christ is a congregation of faithful men, in the which the pure Word of God is preached, and the Sacraments be duly ministered according to Christ's ordinance, in

[1] Acts xi. 15.

all those things that of necessity are requisite to the same." Admirably vague! I do not like the phrase "Visible Church," for it is a pleonasm. The Church is by its institution and constitution visible, except where extending over those who depart thence in the Lord.

d. In the relation of the Kingdom and the Church, there is a double process from without to within, and from within to without. We are born into the Kingdom of God by metanoia,[1] repentance, conversion, change of heart, of mind, of character, of purpose, and the like. This puts us into vital union with God, who, in a final sense, is the Kingdom. The soul is open to the operation of the Holy Spirit. This begets obedience to Jesus in external acts, including His sacramental ordinances, and thus we come into that external or visible fellowship, which is the Church. On the other hand, we may, by baptism, be born into the Church, an environment of sacred and sanctifying influences which quicken the God-consciousness, so that we are brought into vital union with the holy God, which results in metanoia. The Church is fitly named in the apostles' prayer, "The fellowship of the Holy Ghost"; for its operation is to unite man with God, and men with one

---

[1] *Metanoia*, translated in New Testament by "repentance," connotes so much more than the word "repentance" to most minds that I shall here use the word in English. *Metanoia* signifies not only sorrow for sin and resolve for good, but a change of the whole mind and character.

another, until the Saviour's prayer shall be fulfilled, "That they all may be one even as we are one, I in them, and Thou in Me, that they may be made perfect in one."[1]

III. *a.* The Idea of One Holy and Apostolic Church, the Communion of Saints, was not early developed in the consciousness of Christendom. In the East this article of the Church does not occur in the creed of St. Ignatius, A.D. 107, nor in that of Origen at the middle of the third century, nor in the creed of Lucian of Antioch at the beginning of the fourth century. It first appears in the private creed of the arch-heretic Arius, 328. At the middle of the fourth century St. Cyril of Jerusalem taught his catechumens to profess faith "in One Holy Catholic Church"; and a quarter of a century later, Epiphanius, the Father of Orthodoxy, says, "We believe in One Catholic and Apostolic Church." The Nicene creed has no article of the Church, but in the Nicene-Constantinopolitan form it appears in all its fulness, "One Holy Catholic and Apostolic Church." This point was reached in the East toward the close of four hundred years of Christian thought.[2] In the West, owing to the accident of distance from the centre of living theological thought, tradition early came to be relied upon. St. Irenæus, at the close of the second century, begins his creed thus:

---

[1] St. John xvii. 23.
[2] Harnack, *Dogmengeschichte* II. 267, note 1.

"The Church, though scattered through the whole world to the ends of the earth, has received from the apostles and their disciples the faith." And again: "If the apostles had not left to us the Scriptures, would it not be necessary to follow the order of tradition which those to whom they committed the churches handed down?"[1] Upon this notion of Irenæus, which is nothing more than a question, has been based the theory of tradition. Nevertheless, Irenæus goes on to say what is utterly contrary to traditionalism. Indeed, it looks like rationalism or mysticism. "To this order," says he, "many nations of barbarians give assent, those who believe in Christ, having salvation written on their hearts by the Spirit, without paper and ink, and guarding diligently the ancient tradition." After all, Irenæus may be quoted for distinctly opposite sides; controversy drove him to lay much stress upon Church and tradition.

In this confusion of ideas we see the mingled tendencies of the Eastern and Western Churches. Let us examine more closely the development of the idea of the Church by the Latin theologians. Tertullian, at the beginning of the third century, inserts in his rehearsal of faith no article of the Church. Novatian, the dissenter, A.D. 230, alludes to the Church, but makes it no article of his creed. But St. Cyprian, who controverts the Novatians, asserts strongly, "I believe in the forgiveness of sins and eternal life through

[1] *Against Heresies*, iii. 4, 1.

Holy Church." "*Extra ecclesiam nulla salus.*" In the old Roman creed, A.D. 341, the article of "Holy Church" occurs, having crossed over from Carthage. Marcellus of Ancyra, Rufinus, and Augustine A.D. 400 know the article of "Holy Church." Nicetas, in the middle of the fifth century, inserts in his rehearsal of faith, "Holy Catholic Church." In the Sacramentary of Gaul, about the middle of the seventh century, we have "the Holy Catholic Church, the Communion of Saints"; but not until St. Pirmin, and the middle of the eighth century, do we find that the Latin Church generally arrived at the formula of the "Holy Catholic Church, the Communion of Saints," and at the Apostles' Creed as we now recite it.[1] The Eastern Church to this day has not yet reached a formulated permanent definition of the Church.[2] But the Greek Church did go so far as to condemn Cyril Lucar's doctrine that the elect alone constituted the Church of Christ.

IV. In the old days the question was, "What sign givest thou?" likewise in the present day the world requires marks of the Church. If this wonderful organisation, which is called the "Body of God," be in the world, how shall we recognise it should we meet it in the highways? Is the Christian Church the sum of those who acknowledge

[1] Schaff, *Creeds of Christendom*, II.
[2] Wiener, *Confessions of Christendom*, 332; Moeller, *Symbolik*, II. 7 ff.

Christ to be superior to all other men in wisdom, power, and goodness? Is it made up of those who are born of the water, or of the Spirit, or of both? Is it a compact, well-defined association with doctrines and worship completely uniform? Is it endowed with special and occult powers, and has it a hierarchy with peculiar gifts not personal but official? Are all the members of this society spotless in life, unerring in their ideas, and with eyes ever fixed on the golden domes of heaven? If the trumpet of the creeds gave forth an uncertain sound, we are prepared to find the early divines of Christendom also vague in their notion of the Church. In the Ignatian Epistle to the Smyrneans, A.D. 168 (?), we already find this strong expression, "Wherever Jesus Christ may be, there is the Catholic Church";[1] but this should not be hastily quoted for the confusion of ecclesiasticism by some Martin Marprelate, because in the same sentence, and just before these words, the writer had said, "Wherever the bishop may appear, there let the congregation be." Evidently this correspondent of the Smyrneans was not non-prelatical. The eucharistic prayer in the Didaché contains a petition that the Church may be "gathered into the kingdom" of God, in order that it may be "delivered from evil and perfected."[2] Nothing here of the theory of a

---

[1] Epistle of St. Ignatius to the Smyrneans, viii., Lightfoot, *Apostolic Fathers*, 129.

[2] The Teachings of the Apostles, cc. ix., x., Lightfoot, *ut sup.*, 221.

Church for the holy and worthy alone, for those alone who know by experience that they are washed and sanctified and accepted! St. Irenæus shows the effect of his Roman environment when he says, "Wherever the Church is, there is the Spirit of God."[1] Yet Irenæus goes on to say, "Where the Spirit of God is, there is the Church and every kind of grace; but the *Spirit is truth.*" This throws all again into confusion. Could any ecclesiasticism be more arrogant? Yet observe that in these citations there is nowhere a definition of the Church. Even the Alexandrine theologians were vigorous believers in the Church. The mild Clement writes positively, "As the will of God is His work and is named Kosmos, so also His purpose is the salvation of men, and this is called the Church."[2]

The taint of Shamanism must have survived strongly in the blood of the African churchmen, Tertullian, Cyprian, Donatus, and Augustine, who, all of them, define the Church, when they venture near any definition, as inhering in the clerical order. St. Cyprian in particular introduced the idea of Roman imperialism into the Church, in his effort to get at basis of unity. Personally St. Cyprian contradicted his doctrine of the unity of the Church as sitting in the chair of St. Peter at Rome, just so soon as the occupant of that chair did not think with Thascius Cæcilius Cyprianus. The Cyprianic idea

---

[1] *Against Heresies,* iii. 24.   [2] *Paidagogos,* 1, 6.

obtained. It was congenial to the conditions of its day. As heathen Rome had conquered heathen Carthage, so now Christian Carthage came to dominate and dictate the thought of Christian Rome. With it all, from St. Polycarp to St. Augustine, the most diligent examination discovers only this, the opinion of the absolute necessity of a Church outside which there is no salvation. In this opinion, by the irony of things, both Protestant and Romanist at the present agree. How any one is to determine clearly what constitutes this necessity of salvation, they never agree to say. St. Ignatius thinks that the necessary element is the Episcopate. Tertullian and St. Cyprian say it is the realm of Peter's throne till Peter's throne decides against them; then they think differently. Origen says the Church is made up of petrine people;[1] St. Clement, the Alexandrine, of knowing people,[2] but not making it clear whether these knowing ones were speculative or practical knowers of God. The Montanists, Donatists, Novatians, and the like, all emphasised the subjective side of the Church. They were lineal successors of the old collegia and mysteries. To them it seemed intolerable that any but the pure, the adepts, the initiated, should be reckoned in the Christian society. They, by generations of secret teaching and training, were utterly opposed to monarchial organisation in Church or out of it. Consequently an Episcopacy which was not a temporary

[1] πέτροι.   [2] γνωστικοί.

office seemed to them arrogant. More outrageous in their eyes was the extreme development of prelacy by St. Cyprian. Though we search as carefully as we can among ancient churchmen and separatists, nowhere do we find any clear or consistent consensus about the idea of the Church, consequently nowhere a Catholic definition. The practical solution of the question, each polemical theologian made for himself. St. Augustine called those who did not agree with him, "sort of Christians" (*quoquomodo Christiani*). And the custom inaugurated by such august authority is notoriously still far from obsolete.

V. It has come about in the run of years that Christendom confesses at length that there is one Holy and Catholic Apostolic Church. Where is it? When was it? Was it over in Palestine before Paul withstood Peter because the latter was to be blamed, and they twain, with their retainers, like Lot and Abram, set their faces in opposite directions? Was it when Athanasius stood against the world? Was it in the pusillanimous and ignoble compromise in the Council of Florence? Was it in Calvin's harsh regency of Geneva, or in the servile Convocation which dared not protest when Henry Tudor styled himself the Supreme Head of the Church? These four notes which Theology sounds with deep satisfaction are really the scorn of History. As external signs they have never been realised in all the chronicles of wasted Time. Yet we do well to believe them, for they are the potencies of the Church, the ways of the Spirit's outworking in the world, syllables of the word which God in humanity utters, the process of the operations of God-consciousness, the highest manifestation of God in the world, reconciling it unto Himself, and therefore the ideal, the goal of the evolution of the Church which our blessed Lord founded. As Jesus, by His kenosis,[1] subjected His divine knowledge and power to human limitations, a thing the apocryphal gospels convict themselves in not recognising, so the Church is another kenosis of God the Holy Ghost; but through the ages it increases in wisdom and in stature, and in favour with God and man.[2] The "four notes" are the marks of the high calling of the Church, the calling which shall be attained when the Leaven has leavened the whole of the measures of meal, and the Kingdom of God has come; *i.e.* is evidently manifested as identical with the Church. Then shall Humanity have become the word and the utterance of God to all the worlds.

a. The Church is one. The Donatist objection that distinction between visible and invisible, ideal and real, Churches sets up two or more Churches, still stands good.[3] The Church of Israel was bound together by kinship: this bond Jesus strongly and

---

[1] Phil. ii. 7, ἀλλὰ ἑαυτὸν ἐκένωσεν.
[2] Aquinas, *Summa*, III^a. 15.
[3] Bellarmin, *Eccles. Milit.* c. ii.

repeatedly rejects. In its place, taking the ancient and world-wide symbol of blood brotherhood esteemed closer than kinship, He — I will not exactly say substituted, because the soul, the life, the Kingdom of God, was at first alone His, — He began to generate the one Church. Because there is one God, one Lord Jesus Christ, one Spirit, there is one body. When in any measure that unity is realised in external signs, they are one Lord as the object of religion, one faith as the motive of life, and one baptism as the ceremonial sign of the same. Klee, the Roman Catholic theologian, tells us [1] that in the early Church unity was signified and maintained by (1) Letters of Communion, (2) by the Dyptichs, (3) by the Eulogia, portions of the eucharistic food sent and exchanged by bishops and presbyters far removed from one another, and (4) by the Agapæ or Love-Feasts.[2] Here, at all events, we have definite signs of a definite tangible thing. Unfortunately, however neat this statement looks, as a matter of fact its practical working served only to signify those who agreed together. As circumcision was a visible sign of membership in the congregation of Israel, it is reasonable to conclude that we are correct in our interpretation of the gospel story that baptism is the covenant

---

[1] *Histoire des Dogmes Chrétiens*, Vol. I. 82.

[2] Cf. with this custom of Love-Feast the ancient ἀνδρεῖα of the Spartans, Cretans, and Carthaginians, and the Charistia of the Romans.

sign of the Church. Therein shall we not recognise a form of unity, not perfect but inceptive? Every person baptised according to the manner and form dictated by Christ is a member of Christ's Church; yet since other things belong to the integrity of this organisation, such a membership of individuals does not make societies, sacred or secular, Mormon or Masonic, to which baptised persons may belong, unified into the Church. Unity is not necessarily uniformity in creed, ritual, or in Church government. Creeds pass because their language becomes obsolete; ceremonies vary, and should vary, according to the temper and culture of the worshippers. There still survives among us the taste for the sacred mask dances, which passed into the Dionysiac rites and gave birth to the deathless dramas of Æschylus, Sophocles, and Euripides, and then down through the Middle Ages in mystery, miracle, and passion plays, and in the dramatisation of the ceremonies of the Church, to represent before the eyes of simple people the divine tragedy of the cross. There is, indeed, no lack of manuals of devotion which for our edification point out when the celebrant represents Christ in His betrayal, and when in His trial before Pilate, and when He bowed the head and died. Now to say "these things shall not be" is simply to ignore that human culture and development have several degrees. To enforce such a law of uniformity would result in narrowing down the Church to the receptiveness of the "knowing ones," the heirs of all the ages in the foremost files of time. They are few; but if they are spiritually uplifted by the mystical, metaphysical devotion of a Friends' meeting, in God's name let them have it. At all events let us now determine nevermore to waste valuable hours in conventions, diocesan or general, over rubrics designed to secure minute and absolute uniformity. That can never be done so long as minds differ. So long as we are in bondage to the crudest literalism of Scripture, creed, and rubric, so long will there be diversity, disunion, and schism. The Spirit unites; the letter divides.

There are two broad types of Church organisation, the episcopal and the congregational. All others are modifications of one of these. Papacy is an extreme of prelacy. As an historical development it is quite intelligible; as an evolution from the teachings of Christ, it can offer no respectable claim. Of testimonies of the fathers for and against the Petrine Claims[1] I presume you are weary. I am. The great

---

[1] However, I append some fresh matter in this note. St. Chrysostom calls Peter the foremost of the apostles, the mouthpiece of the disciples, and the leader of the chorus or band.—*Com. on St. Matt.* xvi. 19.

In St. Augustine's Sermons, 76, we find this declaration: "Simon was the name of His foremost disciple before Christ gave him the name of Peter, the figurative signification of which name is the Church. *Petra*, or *rock*, represents Christ; *Petrus*, or the *disciple*, represents Christian people. *Petra*, or *rock*, is the principal designation, just as *Petrus* is from *Petra*, not *Petra* from *Petrus*.

obstacle to the unity of the Church inhering in the Papacy is the lapses of the Papacy, and present problematical validity of the Pope according to the canon

So in like manner *Christ* is not called from *Christian*, but *Christian* from *Christ*. Thou art Petrus, and on this petra which thou hast confessed, upon this rock which thou hast recognised in saying, 'Thou art Christ, the Son of the living God,' I will build My Church; that is, upon Myself as the Son of the living God, I will build My Church. Upon Myself I will build thee, not Me on thee. The Church is not built upon them, but upon Christ." — *Opera*, V. 479.

In Sermon 270, this doctrine is repeated: "Jesus said to His disciples, 'But whom say ye that I am?' Peter answered, one for the rest, one for all, 'Thou art the Christ, the Son of the living God.' 'Happy art thou, Simon Bar-Jona, etc.'; I say to thee because thou hast thus spoken of Me, thus confessed Me, receive a blessing: thou art Petrus, I am Petra; *Petra* is not from *Petrus*, but *Petrus* from *Petra*, just as *Christian* is not from *Christ*, but *Christ* from *Christian*; so upon this petra I will build My Church, not upon the Petrus which thou art, but upon the Petra which thou hast confessed. But I will build My Church; I will build thee, who by this confession bearest this figure of the Church, *i.e.* represents the Church." — *Opera*, V. 12, 38, 39.

Still again, in Sermon 295, we have this: "Upon this Petra which thou hast confessed, upon this which thou hast said, 'Thou art Christ, the Son of the living God,' I will build My Church, for thou art Petrus; but Petra is the rock, Christ, from which *Petrus* is derived." — *Opera*, V. 13, 48, 49.

Of a work extant, which St. Augustine wrote against an epistle of the heretic Donatus, once a Bishop at Carthage, the author says this: "In this work I said of the Apostle Peter, that upon him, as upon *Petra*, a rock, the Church was founded; which meaning is also proclaimed by the mouth of many in the verses of the most blessed Ambrose, where he speaks of the cock crowing thus: 'This is that rock of the Church crowing who removes sin.' But I

law of the Roman Church. The Presbyterial system of Church Organisation is a modified form of prelacy. *Presbyter*, as Milton perceived, is *priest* writ large. The Presbyterial invention mediates between Episcopacy and Congregationalism. Like all forms of Puritanism and Papacy, it is substantially a survival of Judaism. It appeals to the synagogue. One with as good reason could appeal from Shakspere's *Comedy of Errors* to Plautus' *Menæchmi*. For Scriptural authority this system has selected an adverb for its foundation.[1] Upon such a foundation can Jerusalem be built as a city that is at unity with itself? Method-

---

remember often afterwards I thus explained what the Lord said: 'Thou art Peter,' etc. Which is to be understood as upon that which Peter confessed, ' Thou art the Son of the living God,' and thus Peter, so called after that rock, or petra, representing the part of the Church which is built upon this rock, and received the key of the Kingdom of Heaven. For it is not said to him, Thou art Petra, but thou art Petrus. But Petra is Christ, whom Simon has confessed as the whole Church confesses Him, and was hence called Peter. But which of these two opinions is the more probable let the reader choose." — *Retractationes*, Lib. I. c. 21.

Enough of this dreary stuff. The principal presumption in favour of St. Peter having ever visited Rome is that St. Paul is so much more portentous a figure that there must have been some powerful cause why Roman tradition did not settle upon him, since also there is no question that he resided in Rome.

The most thorough and hitherto unanswered criticism of the pretension of the papal chair to the supremacy of the Church as the sole condition of Church unity, will be found in *Petrine Claims at the Bar of History*, by the Rev. Dr. R. F. Littledale.

[1] μάλιστα, in 1 Tim. v. 17.

ism adopts Episcopacy as a form of Church Government, administers it like the Papacy, and uses the Presbyterial form of ministry. For Episcopal Church Government the Protestant Episcopalians make no actual stand, although in theory they are stiff for it. We Protestant Episcopalians are practically Congregationalists slightly ameliorated by prelacy. Therefore I do not see in any of these forms of ecclesiastical organisation a ground promising for unity. Congregationalism is the despair of unity. In its logical extreme it becomes every man a church unto himself. That ultimate being reached, a fellowship between churches springs up, and a congregation is formed. The Congregationalist forgets that Christ in flesh and in Nature has a method of selection. For the cause of unity it must be acknowledged that Congregationalism excels the Papacy in speaking smooth things and easy to understand.

Shall we choose either autocracy or individualism? Ecclesiastical Cæsarism or the Zeitgeist? We must go further on before deciding, and we must take a retrospect of the road we have thus far travelled. While the soul of the Church is a kingdom, the Church is not an autocracy. Divine sovereignty and divine immanence imply for the Church elements both monarchic and democratic, and these are not contradictory the one of the other, any more than divine omnipotence and human freedom. For divine sovereignty does not necessarily imply divine separation. The Head of the Church is Jesus Christ, not a president God, as the Mormon doctrine says; nor does He reign by popular suffrage, as we sing in the hymn, "Bring forth the royal diadem, and crown Him Lord of all." This theory fits neatly in with that speculation about the universe, wherein Dr. Haeckel talks of citizen atoms diffused throughout space, and saying, "Go to, let us congregate and see if anything will come of it." A world came of it, and the atoms were stupefied. Nay, but in Church as in world laws of atoms do not account for collocation of atoms. These things convince me that Church union is not an accomplished fact. Because of schisms from the day of Sts. Peter and Paul, — because of varying ideas of God and survivals of old folk-faith, because of extreme bondage to the letter of Scripture and creeds, — never since Pentecost has the Church known an external unity. However, the article of the Creed is credible if we mean one Lord, one faith, one baptism, one God the Father of all, who is above all, through all, and in you all. And as your consciousness of Him grows more vivid you will attain unto the unity of the Spirit and the bond of peace. Therefore, I say the unity of the Church is the goal toward which it moves, the process of its existence until God shall be all in all. Higher criticism, textual criticism, rational theology, and theosophy are signs of a movement towards unity of the spirit which lies beneath the letter.

b. What age or region will render us a picture of the Church holy in the blameless lives of all its members? Was holiness realised in the Robber Synod, or in the brawls between the blues and greens in the streets of orthodox Byzantium? Was holiness resplendent in the Nitrian monks who with oyster-shells savagely slew the maiden Hypatia? Is holiness exemplified in the Albigensian anomia, and the crusade which exterminated it, or in the pornocracy of Rome? Shall we find it among the Anabaptists of Münster, or in the Huguenot craft of the Condés, or in the cold, pitiless righteousness of the Laudians, or in the brutality of Cromwell's men, or in the cruel intolerance of the Massachusetts Bay Colony? Were the Rev. John Wilson, shaking his fist and calling down the extreme vengeance of God upon misbelievers whom he had brought to the scaffold, and Mistress Anne Hutchinson, with her inner light and her ungovernable tongue, fruits of the holiness of the Church? The holiness of the Church was not more marked before the Great Schism than in later days. Between orthodoxy and holiness the connection is not clear; but I am far from sure that Protestantism, higher criticism, and progressive orthodoxy, are doing much for the realisation of this note of the Church. Perhaps. For in the present, the holiness of the Church is the life of the Kingdom of God within her, and the external holiness of the Church consists in the realisation of the Christ-life in her individual members. It lies also in the faith or propositions of truth which may be comprehended by individual members. But it does not lie in orthodoxy, for self-conscious orthodoxy is the eighth deadly sin. Holiness lies in the faith in personal righteousness of God and man, and in the common worship, in prayer, in the Word, and in the Sacraments. It is both outer and inner. The holiness of the Church is evidently rather a goal than a starting-point. She begins by saying, "Beloved, now are we the sons of God.[1] She seeks by worship, instruction, and sacraments to waken the sense of this divine sonship, in order that she may manifest to the world the holiness which is the love, which is the life, which is the power of God,— namely, God Himself, divine grace.[2] The realisation of the holiness of the Church and its actualisation is this: to serve as the highest expression of the Soul of the world, in the world of souls, and to the world of souls.

The process by which in the Church the individual soul is made vitally conscious has been called by various names, repentance, conversion, redemption, metanoia, justification, sanctification, salvation, and eternal life. The distinctions are not real; they belong to the method of scholastic theology. Fundamentally they are one, are but so many stages of the process of the soul in becoming Christ-like. It

---

[1] 1 John iii. 2.   [2] St. Thomas Aquinas, *Summa*, I^a. viii. 3.

is a process of growth, of development, and of evolution. Of this process, the Sacraments are signs and helps. " Covenant sign " does not exhaust the meaning of baptism as regeneration. The sign stands also for a growth in consciousness of holiness. Because holy baptism represents birth out of an old environment, the world of nature, where the law of life is self-interest, into a new environment, the Church, whose law is unself, it is therefore a baptism unto repentance, metanoia, a new point of view from which to survey life. We are baptised in the name of the Father, and of the Son, and of the Holy Ghost, not as by a magic formula. " In the name," means into the character. The term is a Hebrew idiom. Baptism " in the name " implies an intent to conform to the character of our Father, God, our Saviour, Christ, and our life-giving Spirit. But somehow a survival of a pre-Aryan disposition towards magic, which the Babylonians inherited from their Ugrian predecessors, we also have inherited, and we tend to use the divine name, the saving name, as a spell to conjure with,[1] notwithstanding that the Third Commandment expressly forbade such a use of the name of God.

" There must be in the outward sign of a sacrament that which properly represents the spiritual operation of the sacrament," says Aquinas in his reasonable

---

[1] Keim, *Jesus of Nazara*, V. 371, explains the Hebraism, "in the name."

fashion.¹ The sacrament of the Holy Communion, inasmuch as it is a meal in common, represents first of all the fellowship of the Spirit, which is the true and only feasible brotherhood of man.² The table of the Lord is a solution of many of the social difficulties of the present day. In that this sacrament shows forth the Lord's death, it stands also for the essential nature of righteousness or eternal life, which is self-sacrificing love. Of this the Lord's death was the supreme exponent in time, of the inner and eternal operation of the Living God, and therefore of godly life.³ In that the sacrament of the altar is food, it signifies first a gift of God, and next the assimilation and appropriation of the divine life by living it. In this last stage of significance the sacrament represents the union of the soul with God. The symbol ought not to be taken as the thing symbolised. In short, the holiness of the Church is realised in the measure that we accept the principle of unself as the law of life; of unself, I mean, not as the end, but for the sake of another. This is the foundation of the corporate character of the holiness which Christ requires. Unself as an end in itself is a survival or revival of Buddhistic and like pagan ideals.

By the Holiness is meant the visible manifestation of the result of the redemptive process, whereby the

---

[1] *Summa*, III. lx. 3.   [2] 1 John i. 7.
[3] Cf. Sup. p. 47, εὐσέβεια, 1 Tim. ii. 2.

kingdoms of this world shall become the Kingdom of God and of His Christ. To this far-off divine event the whole creation moves, and sin, and pain, and sorrow are spokes in the vast wheel of life. The Church is the ideal of the world in its evolution, as Jesus, God, is the ideal of the Church in its growth towards true unity. The Church, then, is the highest exponent of that stage we have reached in the forward, upward movement we call the cosmic process, the clearest development of God-consciousness in the mind of humanity.

c. It seems difficult in these days to get any definition of Catholicity upon which all Christians or any considerable majority of them agree.[1] Catholicity is in effect the password of some kinds of Orthodoxy.

---

[1] When Seymour was in Rome fifty years ago, the dignitaries of the Church thought surely he would become a convert, and every morning they met with him for conversations on the matter. Their questions and answers were conducted in writing. One morning he wrote this proposition: The Roman Church nowhere declares herself infallible. He met with vehement denial; but when he required an authoritative statement of the infallibility of the Roman Church, the cardinals and doctors could not, he tells us, produce it. Years after, one of these Roman dignitaries is said to have admitted (Capes, *To Rome and Back*) that they had always received unquestioned the infallibility of the Roman Church, and were astounded when after the carefullest investigation they could find no authoritative statement of it. I would add that this proposition had been formulated, and it is difficult to believe that the theologians who conversed with Seymour were not aware of the assertions of the Bulls of the Popes.

For of Orthodoxy there is more than one sort. Catholicity has been taken to mean that part of the Church which has "valid orders and valid sacraments," or that which adheres to the rule of Theology laid down by the first six or seven ecumenical councils, or that which holds a traditional theology, as for instance of St. Augustine, or that which is intellectually broad and tolerant, mystical or metaphysical, rational or sceptical. It might seem that we could accept some one of these positions, such is their variety, but turn the theologic tube on tube of lens critical and historical, and these fixed stars of hope are blurred to mist. It is not so easy as at first blush it seems, to say what are valid orders, and valid sacraments, and who have them, what councils were ecumenical, and what Augustine did really give as the residuum of his doctrine after his retractations. Indeed we cannot always understand just what the Pope means, or the General Assembly, or the General Convention. Duration of Time and extent of Space do not gauge the Church's Catholicity. They may in those years when the earth shall be full of the knowledge of the Lord as the waters cover the sea, but not yesterday and not to-day. It is fine to say, like the late Mr. Arnold, that "the infallible Church Catholic is really the prophetic Soul of the wide world dreaming of things to come, the whole human race in onward progress, discovering truth more complete than the parcel of truth any momentary individual man may seize." The charm is really in the ingenious adaptation of the beautiful phrase from Shakspere. The truth of the definition is in God's cosmical redemptive process, but the definition itself does not exactly express our Lord's doctrine of the Church. It is, however, true that the Church is living as the tree and the grain of mustard seed, because its soul is the Spirit Who maketh alive. It is the Church of the *Living* God, and there is no really assignable limit to the growth of His body and manifestation. Again, if by the infallible Church we mean the consciousness of Christendom, we mean a fact, not a dogma; and this is all there is of truth in the notion of the infallibility of the Church. It is the utterance of the God-consciousness. People who doubt the guiding of the Spirit of God, call Him Zeitgeist. They go back to ante-Nicene days to find evidences of the guidance of the Holy Ghost; for them He is now virtually asleep with Brahm, or passive in Nirvana. The appeal to antiquity has a side which is true, but when pressed as it has been, is like asking us into "a seed store to examine the beauty of a flower garden." Tertullian was right when he said, "Wherever are the Three, Father, Son, and Holy Ghost, there is the Church, which is the body of the Three."[1] So Catholicity is inclusive, not exclusive. It inheres in the Kingdom of God; that is, in the Infinite God, Who comprehends and includes all reality. There is this

[1] *De Baptismo,* quoted in Pearson on the Creed.

potency, this ultimate of the growth of the Church, not in the chair of Peter, nor in an Episcopacy, nor in an accurate form of doctrine, nor in the relation of the individual with Christ. A study of the history of dogma shows that any one of these propositions is a theory which could not stand the test of controversy. In one sense, present and visible, the Church might be called Catholic; that is, in its adaptability to all nations and all times. In so far as it has received the true Idea of God it is differentiated from all ethnic religions and therefore is universal.

d. The Church is apostolic if it continue in the doctrine of the apostles. By the doctrine of the apostles I do not exactly mean their limited statements or formulas of divine truth and their incompletely developed consciousness of God. As Hooker says, "We must note that he that affirmeth speech to be necessary among all men throughout the world doth not thereby import that all men must speak necessarily one kind of language. Even so, the necessity of polity and regiment in all churches may be held, without holding any one certain form to be necessary for them all."[1] No doubt the Holy Spirit is still guiding the Church; nor did He cease with the Church of the apostles, of the isapostolic fathers, with the Nicene Council, with the Second Council of Constantinople, with Augustine, with Aquinas, with Luther, or with Hooker or with Pusey or with Pearson

[1] Hooker, *Eccl. Pol.* III. 2.

on the Creed, or with Browne on the Articles. As God is a living God, the Church, His Body, lives, develops, differentiates in comprehension and in statement of truth. By the side of natural evolution in the world is supernatural evolution in the Church. The cosmical and ecclesiastical processes illustrate one another. What is developed from apostolic germinal idea belongs to the doctrine of the Apostolic Church, and the fundamental and grand all-embracing idea which we get from the apostolic writings is that of the immanent Triune.

Apostolicity has been made to inhere in Apostolic Succession. This theory, Hallam says, began to be urged about the end of Elizabeth's reign.[1] In one sense the theory is true, and in another it is false. Bishop Hall distinguished when he wrote, " How fain would you here find me in a contradiction. While I onewhere reckon Episcopacy among matters essential to the Church, and otherwhere deny it to be of the essence thereof! Wherein you willingly hide your eyes that you may not see the distinction which I make expressly between the being and well being of a Church. . . . No, brethren, to hold their discipline altogether essential to the very being of the Church, we dare not be so zealous."[2] Appeal has been made to the First Epistle of St. Clement to show the connecting link between the apostles and fathers on

---

[1] Cf. Sir Francis Bacon, Works, II. 5, 14.
[2] Bishop Hall, Works, IX. 690.

this subject. But Clement[1] says nothing more than that the apostles, foreseeing strife about the office of oversight in the Church, appointed whom they thought worthy to succeed them, and left instructions that when these died other approved men should succeed them in the ministry. Consequently, says he, our blame is great " if we eject from the Episcopate those who have blamelessly and holily fulfilled its duties." St. Clement says nothing of a tactual succession, nothing of the grace of Orders. He is speaking in the interest of orderliness and tranquillity, and of continuance in Episcopal office of men once placed therein. St. Irenæus also is invoked to give testimony in the same favour, but he speaks of the succession of the ministry only as being a witness to those doctrines of the Church which had from the apostles been handed down. The Apostolic Succession may be true as a fact in history — it cannot be disproved; but is a Scotch verdict in its favour enough to warrant the uprearing upon it of a vast sacramental system? The Assyrian when he would represent the grace of god in the sky towards men on earth, depicted ropes hanging down from the symbol of the god. This answers to a popular conception of grace, to a notion which is profoundly materialistic. A widely prevalent theory of the Sacraments is inhaled with the materialistic atmosphere which we breathe. A sceptical friend once asked

[1] I. 44.

me, "Why are the clergy so materialistic?" This cruder theory of grace and of the Sacraments will not lack traditional authority nor a long *catena patrum*, nor the pat simile of grace flowing through the Sacraments as gas through the gas-pipes, or, at any rate, as electricity along the wires.

The theory of transubstantiation is a survival of fetishism. I recognise that the dominant theological thought is consonant with the materialistic tone of the age, and every day it is becoming more popular; but is it true? Is not this whole theory of tactual Succession and sacramental system built thereon, like a vast pyramid resting upon its apex? To what did the bishops succeed from the apostles? You recollect how, when Aquinas went to Rome, the Pope showed to him all its splendour and opulence, and remarked, "Brother Thomas, if Peter was forced to say, Silver and gold have I none, his successors are not obliged to say so." — "No," answered Aquinas, "neither can his successors say, I say unto thee arise and walk."

I need not apologise for quoting in this place and at some length the words of the Bishop of Central New York. They represent a reasonable phase of present-day ecclesiastical opinion. Bishop Huntington we recognise as one of the most open-minded and thoughtful of our House of Bishops: "We have on hand two theories of the Episcopate as to its working. They should be discriminated, and each should be held in view in discussions about small dioceses and multiplied bishops. Otherwise, sentiment will take the place of wisdom, and mistakes may be made which it will not be easy to correct. On the one hand is the idea that the bishop is not only the chief pastor in some real sense, and *Pastor Pastorum*, of the diocese, but is in direct and intimate pastoral relations with the laity in all the congregations. This, or something like it, is loosely in the notions of many advocates of Episcopal multiplication. Two results would be unavoidable. Dioceses conducted in that way cannot include more than thirty or forty congregations, whether parishes or missions, at the utmost, unless human capacities and endowments are stretched beyond human precedent. Secondly, the prerogative, authority, official importance, and self-direction of the priest and pastor, whom we now call the rector, must be abridged and curtailed to whatever extent the theory which makes the diocese a modern *Parochia* is carried out. Then rectoral distinctions will be in large part transferred to the bishop. It is he who directs, leads, decides, in all parish affairs. Guilds, societies, choirs, plans of work for both sexes, young and old, services, ritual peculiarities, will be appointed and controlled by the bishop. Presbyters are his assistants or agents, and he entrusts them with more or less power and liberty, according to his disposition and views. Human nature is not to be made over to accommodate an ecclesiastical experiment. Where all this is understood and prepared for, where the clergy are trained and ordained and used to it, it may work admirably. That it would work without some friction and some strain in a generation accustomed to a different *régime* is not at all certain. Two heads are not a physiological or an administrative convenience. In time, the diocese would come to have a uniform ecclesiastical type and colour. Clergy not in agreement with the bishop ecclesiastically or theologically would find it agreeable to retire. Reliance upon official suasion or personal magnetism, in such a condition, would prove, at trying emergencies, a delusion and a snare. In ritual there would be in time diocesan 'Uses' sharply defined. I am not now arguing for or against this system, or conjecturing whether it is what the American Church desires, but am trying to state what, as it appears to me, this system would inevitably bring forth. It would enlarge the House of Bishops fourfold, and the control of the bishop over the rector in parochial details in much the same proportion.

" The other conception of this office is substantially that which has prevailed among us hitherto, and prevails now. I say substantially, because there is no fixed standard with which the varying notions about it, floating in divers minds, can be compared. The office itself admits of widely different degrees of activity and efficiency, according to the gifts, accomplishments, and energy of the man who holds it. Yet, on the whole, the range and limits of its proper functions are fairly understood. The bishop ordains and sometimes institutes the clergy, attends by letter or in person to their call, settlement, removal, and transfer; receives their requests, complaints, and inquiries, and other communications; visits them and their families pastorally; consults with them after their difficulties and necessities. He examines, receives, directs, and often assists candidates for Holy Orders, in many cases personally instructing them and providing for their expenses. He has to do with the erection and form of many church buildings, the care and title of the property, and sometimes the insurance, frequently assists in obtaining the means to build, is apt to lay the corner-stone, and consecrates or opens the edifice. He confirms candidates once a year in public and private, throughout the diocese. In special emergencies, or with the good-will of the rector, he sometimes renders the offices of baptism, marriage, and burial. He adjusts differences arising among parishes and ministers, he decides cases of disagreement by the interpretation of Church-law or by arbitration, acting judicially. He is called to organise or initiate general charities, guilds, societies, benevolent work in Church-houses, or to preach at their anniversaries. In our theory, whatever our practice, the three Orders are well defined, as well with respect to their rights as their duties."[1]

Such being the practical condition of things in this Church, shall we take up the words of Bishop Andrews, "Though our government be of divine right, it follows not that a church cannot stand without it. He must needs be stone-blind that sees not churches standing without it." Or the words of Hooker, "Unto the complete form of Church polity much may be requisite that the Scripture teacheth not, and much that it hath taught become unrequisite, sometime because we need not use it, sometime because we cannot. In which respect, for mine own part, although I see that certain Reformed Churches, the Scottish especially and the French, have not that which best agreeth with Sacred Scripture, I mean the Government that is by Bishops, inasmuch as both these Churches are fallen under a different kind of Regiment; which to remedy it is for the one altogether too late, and too soon for the other, during their present affliction and trouble: this their defect and imperfection I had rather lament in such case than exagitate, considering that men oftentimes, without any fault of their own, may be driven to want that kind of Politie or Regiment which is best; and to content themselves with that which either the irre-

---

[1] The Rt. Rev. Dr. Huntington, *Address to the Diocesan Convention of the Protestant Episcopal Church in the Diocese of Central New York*, 1880.

mediable error of former time, or the necessity of the present, hath cast upon them." [1]

If we cannot find any statement or assertion of a tactual succession in the Anglican Articles of Religion, if it was not held by the English reformers, nor insisted upon by Cosin, or Jewell, or Andrews, or Hall, or Whitgift, or even by Saravia, then shall we hold it to be essential to the being of a church? Nay, we should in that case out-herod Herod in our exactions, we should go beyond the Roman Church; for it is well known that in the reigns of Mary and Elizabeth, in the propositions which Rome made for the "reconciliation" of the English Church, there was no requirement that the clergy should be reordained,[2] and yet we know quite well, as Keble tells us,[3] that "numbers had been admitted into the ministry of the Church with no better than Presbyterian ordination." Since the Church was instituted and constituted together, the order of the ministry must be held as of its integrity rather than of its essence, and in this sense we

---

[1] Hooker, *Eccl. Pol.* III. 11. It should be recollected that the seventh book of the *Ecclesiastical Polity*, as we have it, was not written in full by Master Richard Hooker, but was written from notes some sixty years after his death. The seventh book should therefore be interpreted in conformity with the preceding part of the work, and not the first six books, so that they may agree with the seventh. Whoever manipulated the notes of the seventh book was not precisely of the mind of the judicious Hooker.

[2] Courayer, *Validity of English Ordinations*, 234 ff., 323.

[3] Introduction to Hooker's Works.

may understand the words of the seventh book of Hooker's *Ecclesiastical Polity :* " There may be sometimes very just and sufficient reason to allow ordination made without a bishop. The whole Church visible being the true original subject of all power, it hath not ordinarily allowed any other than bishops alone to ordain. Howbeit, as the ordinary course is ordinarily in all things to be observed, so it may be in some cases not unnecessary that we decline from the ordinary ways. — And therefore we are not simply to urge a lineal descent of power from the apostles, by continual succession of bishops, in every effectual ordination."

We may well ask what is taken as the sign of the apostolicity of this Episcopal Church. Surely the "greater works" are not visibly performed in these post-apostolic days. Do we lay the sick where the shadow of the Bishop of —— may fall upon them as he passes by? Do we bring handkerchiefs and napkins from the Bishop of —— to heal the sick? Has the Bishop of —— the unique power to deliver over one bound unto Satan? If, then, the tremendous assumption of such a succession of ministry as shall serve for an unbroken conduit for a substantial force called grace gives no sign of itself, in gifts of healing and tongues, in the immediate evangelisation of the world, and in the conviction of the human heart, or in any other mighty work, we may well ask ourselves if it be necessary to hold to tactual succession and substantial grace, and if we do, what is the practical outcome? These theories, it is true, have been held by good men, and I suppose still may be held, but no kite of a theological formula should draw theories from the upper air of speculation down into a statement of creed. The one theory, of the ministry, demands the other, of Sacraments,—and both are without a scrap of external testimony.[1] But Apostolic Succession, as a sign of the historic continuity of the Church and of its form of organisation, cannot be denied to be a matter of fact in history. No better method could be conceived of preserving this sign of continuity than by the ceremony of the laying on of hands. If the Church inheres in a hierarchy, presbyterial, episcopal, or papal, then Biblical Theology must be ignored, History must be ignored, the phenomena of deep spiritual life in the dissenting churches must be ignored. Finally, if this theory be true, the late Dr. Newman was perfectly consistent in transferring his allegiance from the Bishop of Oxford to the Bishop of Rome, the Bishop of Bishops; because a hierarchy instituted and constituted in and by itself as the head of the Church and the source of its religious life must be like shamanism, and the Roman hierarchy a survival of shamanism.

[1] Episcopacy cannot be set off by itself as an organisation or a conduit through which grace flows. If in any way the validity of the Sacraments depends upon Apostolic Succession, it is only secondarily, and because Episcopacy is of the integrity of the Church. I do not say of the essence. Of this integrity the laying on of hands is a visible sign.

This section I will conclude with weighty words from Professor Shields, of Princeton, writing on the relation of the Apostolicity to the Unity and Catholicity of the Church. "But what is the Historic Episcopate? It may mean very much or very little, according to its definition; and its definition will be full or meagre, according to our point of view. At present we can only view it in its external relations, as a Christian institution appearing among other Christian institutions and organisations. I do not here pretend to define it *per se* as an ecclesiastical dogma; much less to give an inside view of its powers and effects upon those who devoutly receive it. I shall aim at a little more than a verbal definition of the phrase itself. Christianity is historic. It has had organic life and growth from the beginning. It was more than mere sentiment or doctrine. It was a Church as well as a gospel. It has ever been visibly organised with fixed institutions pre-existing from age to age until the present time. Among these institutions is the historic Episcopate. Thus viewed, it may be defined negatively and then more positively. . . . As we pass to a positive definition or description we shall see still more clearly how comprehensive is this great Christian institution. Not only did its original structure involve congregational and presbyterial elements, synagogues, and elders, as well as bishops, but its historic growth has pervaded the whole Christian world. As instituted at first by our Lord Himself in the work of the apostles, they exemplified it in their acts and epistles, while planting and training the first parishes and presbyteries. Thenceforward, it extended over the entire Church, through the centuries before the Council of Nice. After the great schism it was continued in both the eastern and western sections of Christendom until the Reformation. At the present day on its Catholic side, as maintained in the Old World, it embraces the ecclesiastical principle of the Greek, the Roman, and the Anglican Churches; while on its Protestant side, as developed in the New World, it has also embraced the ecclesiastical principles of the Lutheran, the Reformed, the Presbyterian, the Methodist, the Congregational, the Baptist, churches. It has embraced them actually, if not consciously or avowedly. Without sacrificing the Episcopal principle, it has incorporated the Presbyterial principle in diocesan conventions and standing committees, and the Congregational principle in free parishes and vestries. As good Congregationalism and as sound Presbyterianism can be found inside the American Episcopate as outside it. And could our various congregational and presbyterial denominations now come together under the same stringent and elastic bond, through bishops of their own choice, with their creeds and usages untouched, they would do no violence to their respective missions in this new age and country. No other Church system is at once so large and cohesive.

Not the congregational, because of its localising tendency and inorganic state; not the presbyterial, because of its brittle fragments and lack of centralising force; not the episcopal alone without the congregational and presbyterial institutions, with which it must ever be in living connection. The three elements as fitly joined in one organism make an ideal unity; and it is a unity which might become actual. At the centre of our divided and distracted Christianity we have before our eyes the spectacle of Episcopalians, Presbyterians, and Congregationalists, in all but the name loyally held together in the catholic faith of Christendom."

Because the Church is living, is dynamic, not static, its characteristics, Unity, Catholicity, Sanctity, and Apostolicity are forces rather than aspects, are operations rather than results. They cannot be photographed, even in spirit pictures. They cannot be measured by rule or weighed in a balance. Life submits to none of these tests; they are forms of the Living One in His manifestation. If men endeavour to force one of these notes, invariably they silence another. Press Unity, and you destroy Catholicity; exact tests of Holiness, and you destroy Unity; require formal Apostolicity, and you run the risk of silencing the note of Holiness. They are notes of the tones which God sounds, not men. It is the persistence of the temper of primitive culture which demands mechanical means of union with God, which, conceiving of Him afar off in space, strives to construct for Him a substitute here on earth. It is not the doctrine of earliest Christianity, and though it were, it is not true.

VI. If we desire to teach the one Holy Catholic and Apostolic Church, I believe we shall do better to study the Christendom of the nineteenth century than that before the great schism. As that sound old seventeenth century divine, Jeremy Taylor, said in one of his sermons, "From every sect and community of Christians take anything that is good, that advances holy religion, and the divine honour; for one hath a better government, a second a better confession, a third hath excellent spiritual arts for the conduct of souls, a fourth hath fewer errours, and by what instrument soever a holy life is advantaged, use that though thou grindest thy spears and arrows at the forges of the Philistines; knowing thou hast no master but Christ, no religion but the Christian, no rule but the Scriptures, and the laws and right reason, other things that are helps are to be used accordingly."[1] The Unitarians stand for the principle of humaneness in Christianity, and this is the profoundest significance of the Incarnation. For the more part they dissent from our dogma, and not from faith in the Lord Jesus Christ. They also demand that their hope should be reasonable, religious, and holy. If we would break down the middle

---

[1] *Christian Prudence*, Works, II. 287.

wall of partition between us, we must emphasise this principle. The Presbyterians stand for the principle of personal righteousness. Let us heed their cry. The Baptists demand a reality of religious life and consciousness corresponding to the sacramental symbols. Be not heedless of their witness. The Methodists stand for the principle of a religion of the affections, and if they went out from us, it may be that we are lacking in this element of our teaching. The Congregationals, or Independents, stand for personal freedom in religious thought and ecclesiastical organisation, and this gift of God we may deny no man. We need also to regard the growth of Free Masonry and kindred orders, of Societies of Ethical Culture, of Secularism in all its shapes, of Socialism, and of the Press; and we should carefully consider and reflect whether their existence and influence be not due to something which the Church has left undone. I say again that the Theology which you here learn is necessary to your ministerial function, but you must digest it and reduce it to practice in religion and religious teaching. Convert your theology into sociology.

Thus far my purpose has been to demonstrate that the true idea of God is the idea of Infinite Immanent Love, that the Church is in some special way the manifestation or utterance of that Immanent Love, which is Life. At no time more than the present does the world demand that the Church shall fulfil truly her function as the organon of God. First of all, then, the utterance of the Church to the World is that human life in all its ways should be conformed to the Divine Life. Now clearly, in that life there is no room for the principle of self-interest however enlightened. There is no room for competition and covetousness as the law of trade; there is no room for social caste and separation. The social problems of the age call for your most earnest attention; the solution of them is to be found in your Theology. All the works of human life, even buying and selling, employment and labour, should be sacraments of human brotherhood. Nowhere in the life of God, as revealed in the earth-life of the Lord Jesus Christ, was there a single enunciation of the law of self-interest and of social separation, as a religious or economic motive. Nowhere in the Beatitudes is there a word concerning privileged classes and superior natures. If, then, there be one thing which the Church must take as its message from the very heart of God to the men of the world, it is the principle of love, self-sacrifice for the sake of another, as the very condition of political, economic, and personal righteousness. You are not to be ordained to get good parishes. The world to-day, if ever, demands moral heroism in the pulpit. In your hands is given the power of the keys. Whenever you console a grief, lessen a pain, elect a good magistrate, make a salutary law, or a good sewer, you open the kingdom of heaven to those in misery and pain. Shall the Church drop her keys of the kingdom into the hands of Henry George, Frances Willard, and General Booth? The Church needs men who submit themselves to be receptive of the Divine, and to fearlessly utter His message. It needs men who are willing, at the price of a momentary unpopularity, to rebuke greed, heartlessness, and self-will in the guise of Christianity. It needs men who are able to inspire our social and political conditions with the spirit of the Divine Life. It will be your duty to teach the world that the good Lord Jesus has not had His day, but that it is coming, as Tennyson truly says. Although it may seem little, yet we ought to be exultantly thankful that we can say it, Christianity, the Church, has up to the present time made a good beginning in this world. In general, the God-consciousness of Christian men is but just awakening, dogma is becoming ethical. When we learn to look beneath the letter to the spirit which is *veritas*, then schism will cease. When we recognise that all authority lies in truth, in reality, and not in Bible, tradition, hierarchy, or any standard external to itself, then will the Unity and the rest of the notes of the Church begin to be actualised in the world of Time. Then shall the Word of God be distinctly syllabled through and to humanity, and then shall we catch the first glimpse of the true "Peace of the Church."

" Peace beginning to be
  Deep as the sleep of the sea
  When the stars their faces glass
  In its blue tranquillity :
  Hearts of men upon earth,
  Never once still from their birth,
  To rest as the wild waters rest
  With the colours of Heaven on their breast!

" Love, which is sunlight of Peace,
  Age by age to increase
  Till angers and hatreds are dead,
  And sorrow and death shall cease :
  ' Peace on earth and good-will!'
  Souls that are gentle and still
  Hear the first music of this
  Far-off, infinite bliss!"

THE FORGIVENESS OF SINS.

He who has yielded to temptation may indeed, by the repentant feeling of which prayer is the expression, secure himself from further yielding; but the tendency toward loss of self-control, initiated by the first surrender, cannot be rendered non-existent by any *ex post facto* act of contrition, though its operation may be counteracted. And if the misdeed, as usually happens, has involved others than the agent, its evil consequences must endure and ramify, until they at last disappear through some natural process of equilibration. No amount of repentance for lying can deprive lies of their tendency to weaken the mutual confidence of men and thus to dissolve society. No penance or priestly absolution can do away with the persistence of force.

FISKE, Cosmic Philosophy, II. 464.

> I think this is the authentic sign and seal
> Of Godship, that it ever waxes glad,
> And more glad, until gladness blossoms, bursts
> Into a rage to suffer for mankind,
> And recommence at sorrow; drops like seed
> After the blossom, ultimate of all.
> Say, does the seed scorn earth and seek the sun?
> Surely it has no other end and aim
> Than to drop, once more into the ground,
> Taste cold and darkness and oblivion there:
> And thence rise, tree-like grow through pain to joy,
> More joy and most joy, — do man good again.

BROWNING, Balaustion's Adventure.

For God so pardoned us once, that we should need no more pardon. He pardoned us *by turning every one of us away from our iniquities.* That's the purpose of Christ, that He might safely pardon us before we sinned; and we might not sin upon the confidence of pardon. He pardoned us not only upon condition we should sin no more, but He took away our sin, cured our cursed inclinations, instructed our understanding, rectified our will, fortified us against temptation, and now every man whom He pardons He also sanctifies.

Bp. JEREMY TAYLOR, Sermon on Miracles of Divine Mercy,
Works, II. 348.

A dubious, strange, uncomprehended life,
A roll of riddles with no answer found,
A sea-like soul which plummet cannot sound,
Torn by belligerent winds at mutual strife.

The God in him hath taken unto wife
A daughter of the pit, and — strangely bound
By coils of snake-like hair about him wound —
Dies straining hard to raise the severing knife.

For such a sunken soul what room in Heaven?
For such a soaring soul what place in hell?
Can these desires be damned, the doings shriven,
Or in some lone mid-region must he dwell
Forever? Lo! God sitteth with the seven
Stars in His hand, and shall not He judge well?
JAMES ASHCRAFT NOBLE.

To the truly honourable man the Divine forgiveness of his sin is the most pressing of all necessities because it is the primary condition of real liberation from sin. . . . The act of forgiving consists in God's making the sinner conscious of His own gracious attitude toward him by actually realising it in his experience. The sinner experiences, realises, becomes conscious of it.
R. ROTHE, *The Still Hours*.

There is quackery in religion no less than in medicine, and multitudes give themselves over to it; in the foolish hope that by some merely outward application — some creed accepted, some prayer said, some penance endured, some action performed, some church obeyed — they can cure an inward disease. But nature is everywhere protesting against such self-deception: and no man who listens to her voice can abandon himself to such futile methods. What he requires is that his disease must be cured, and not merely covered up or condoned.
GEORGE HARWOOD, *From Within*.

I have heard my lord say — That no equivocation should be used either in Church or Law, for the one causes several Opinions to the disturbance of men's Consciences : the other, long and tedious suits to the disturbance of men's private Affairs : and both do oftentimes ruine and impoverish the State.

Life of Wm. Cavendish, Duke of Newcastle, by Margaret, Duchess of Newcastle, A.D. 1667.

SYNOPSIS.

INTRODUCTION:

The relation of the Forgiveness of Sins to the purpose of the Church. Actual *vs.* forensic forgiveness.

COMPARATIVE RELIGION:

I. — Theories of Forgiveness of Sins in folk-faith.

a. The appeasement of an angry, evil, or non-moral deity. Origin of commercial theories of forgiveness. The idea of fate and of fear as a religious motive.

b. The substitution of another to bear the penalty of sin: the scapegoat theory in its various forms; sin-eating; the worship of the sacrificial victim; the divine scapegoat in Jewish theory, in the Norse *Voluspa*, and in the *Prometheus Bound;* the bearing of this theory upon pessimism and the problem of Pain; the survivals of the scapegoat and substitutionary theory in modern Theology.

BIBLICAL THEOLOGY:

II. — An examination of the New Testament shows that the purpose and work of Jesus is to remove sins, consequently their penalty. Significance of the symbol of the lamb. The New Testament doctrine of ransom an ethical doctrine; its relation to the true idea of God and to the office of the Church. Was the death of Jesus a penal satisfaction, a commercial substitution?

TRADITIONAL THEOLOGY:

III. — In the evolution of Christian Theology survivals of folk-faith have hindered a full reception and free development of the teaching of Jesus concerning forgiveness. But Christian Theologians have not been altogether without moments of insight into this truth. The opinion of Irenæus, of Origen, of Justin Martyr, of Tertullian, and of Anselm. Ritschl's Criticism of the Anselmic Theory of the Atonement. Further criticisms of this theory; the utility of having a clearly defined system of the Atonement; the mistake of beginning Theology with the fall; survival of paganism.

PRACTICAL ASPECT:

IV. — *a.* Turning again to the constructive portion, teach not this doctrine with too much refinement of formal Theology and method.
  b. Further consideration of fear as a motive to righteousness leads us to believe that it belongs to a rudimentary stage of the development of human character.
  c. The true idea of pain, a coefficient of redemptive process.
  d. Evil rightly understood is perceived to be privative, and sin to be generated by the will; hence forgiveness is rectification of the will.
  e. The psychology of sin suggests the answer to the historic question, "Cur Deus Homo?" The essential union of God and man in sacrifice in the sphere of Christ's mediatorial work. This gives an ethical force which forensic theories lack.
  f. This teaching stands the test of psychological analysis,
  g. Of rational scrutiny and of
  h. Human experience. The relation of this actual forgiveness of sin to that fictitious forgiveness which, founded on legal phraseology, is powerless to answer the demands of life.

THE FORGIVENESS OF SINS.

Gentlemen: —

The final form of the ecumenical creed is precisely, "we confess one baptism for the purpose of removal of sins."[1] This is the Church's antiphon to the great commission of the Master. "As ye journey, make all nations learners, baptising them in the name of the Father, and of the Son, and of the Holy Ghost."[2] The Church of God is a school for learners; — perhaps it would be better to say with St. Ignatius, — of those who "hope to begin to learn." The Church is this because it is, as I have already stated, a special manifestation of the Triune Love in Whom we live, and move, and exist, Who is ceaselessly out-yielding Himself, that we may become one with Him. The process by which that union takes place is termed variously, Sanctification, Salvation, Forgiveness of Sins. Because in the Church is the distinctest consciousness of this redemptive operation

---

[1] εἰς ἄφεσιν ἁμαρτιῶν. We might translate this, "unto the end that there may be a removal of sins." The difference is inappreciable.

[2] πορευθέντες μαθητεύσατε πάντα τὰ ἔθνη, κ.τ.λ., St. Matt. xxviii. 19.

of God in His world, set forth by the Lord Jesus Christ, the function or office of the Church in a special way is the removal of the evil of the world, of society, and the forgiveness of sins. Has the Church forgotten that her mission is to heal the woes, and right the wrongs, of the children of men? Her mission is a social, because an individual, work. It is first of all individual. God speaks to humanity in speaking to each individual soul. Externally, baptism, as I have said, is a sign of the Christian covenant, and it is a sign of promise. It is the sacrament of regeneration, because it is the door of birth into a new environment of prayer, praise, and all sanctifying influences, of an attitude of receptiveness towards God, of removal of sins, which is the state of salvation, of deepening the sense of godliness, which is the beginning of the consciousness of God; the beginning, I say, for the Eternal is not a mere *Begriff* of rectitude. The Church is really a new environment, a supernatural world. The principle of life in the natural world is self-interest, the principle of the Church is unselfishness. The gospel of Jesus Christ is the only true sociology, and we as gospellers should study the questions of modern sociology that we may know how to apply the remedy of the gospel to the ills of the body politic.[1] The two worlds are there-

---

[1] I recommend all our younger clergy to enter the *Christian Social Union* of the United States. Particulars may be learned by addressing Prof. Richard T. Ely, Madison, Wis.

fore utterly different. We are born into the natural world, with its fierce struggle for existence, but this is a condition of temporary life. To attain endlessness, we must be born again, into a new environment, and must learn to conform ourselves to it. To this end, Baptism was ordained, that we might be born into a higher plane of action,[1] into a visible organisation which is an institution, Christ-founded and God-filled, of which the law is the giving up of self. This renunciation is a condition of the forgiveness of sins. I freely admit that this has not been the generally accepted interpretation of this Article of the Creed, or that doctrine of forgiveness most in vogue throughout all the nineteen centuries of Christendom. A magical and not a moral operation has been the notion of Catholicism and Calvinism

---

[1] The Gorham judgment settled nothing for the doctrine of baptism in the English Church, for the decision was based upon a statement which the Privy Council attributed to Mr. Gorham, but which he took special pains to deny. Mr. Gorham's real position was undoubtedly that of conditional regeneration, in the old traditional sense of regeneration. His bishop, Dr. Philpotts of Exeter, possessed of the same traditional idea, affirmed that baptismal regeneration is unconditional in the case of infants, but conditional in the case of adults, thus implicitly affirming two baptisms, which is contrary to the Creed. Proby, *Annals of the Low-Church Party in England*, II. c. 38. This confusion illustrates the untenability of the notion of substantial grace, imparted or infused, when brought to any scientific test, and it suggests to us the necessity of examining carefully the full significance of the baptismal covenant.

alike, and upon the Protestant Episcopal Church, including within it both these mental attitudes, a double portion of the spirit of this error has fallen. From the Euskarian predilection for magic and charms, from the mysteries of Eleusis, where "sea surges dash all sins away," from the Mithraic taurobolium, from the Norse wise woman, with her potent philter in a horn scratched with powerful runes, we have inherited the convictions that forgiveness of sins is a magical, non-ethical, purely objective wiping out of a score against us, and a settlement of our account in Heaven's great ledger, by a free cancellation of a debt which could never be liquidated, and charging the same to the account of another. In this way, salvation is made a commercial transaction, where still in the temple of Christian Theology, are the benches of the moneychangers, and the seats of those who sell doves. We ask those who press their proof-texts of commercial redemption, To whom was the price paid; to God or to the Devil? Indeed, we are bought with a price; but the price is paid to the souls of the redeemed. The Good Shepherd brings home the lamb upon his shoulders.

I. The evolution of Folk-faith reveals that it is the disposition of men to shift upon another the results of their sin. A résumé of the ruling ideas of sin and its remission is easily made. The theories of sin, outside the teaching of Christ, develop themselves in three or four main lines.

THE FORGIVENESS OF SINS. 147

a. In his primitive condition man attributes evil as well as good to one and the same divine power. He thinks that with God might makes right, supposing that God is altogether such an one as himself. He imagines that God arbitrarily makes one vessel for honour and another for dishonour; one human being for degradation here and eternal agonies hereafter; another for piety here and the reward of endless joy hereafter. As Mr. Browning's Caliban ruminates upon his god, Setebos : —

> "Making and marring clay at will? So He.
> 'Thinketh, such shows nor right nor wrong in Him,
> Nor kind, nor cruel: He is strong and Lord.
> 'Am strong myself compared to yonder crabs
> That march now from the mountain to the sea;
> 'Let twenty pass, and stone the twenty-first,
> Loving not, hating not, just choosing so . . .
> As it likes me each time, I do: so He . . .
> Conceiveth all things will continue thus,
> And we shall have to live in fear of Him
> So long as He lives, keeps His strength: no change,
> If He have done His best, make no new world
> To please Him more, so leave off watching this, —
> If He surprise not even the Quiet's self
> Some strange day, — or, suppose, grow into it
> As grubs grow butterflies: else, here are we,
> And there is He, and nowhere help at all."

Perhaps Jacob Grimm is right in saying, " The idea of the devil is foreign to all primitive religions for this reason, that in all primitive religions the idea of

God is the idea of the devil." The savage is dominated by fear, — of ferocious beasts, of malignant enemies, of growing old, of his medicine man and witchcraft, and, above all, of some awful unseen presence, and of vampires ravenous, and ghosts that gibber and squeak. Dr. Judson from Alaska,[1] and Mr. Robert Louis Stevenson,[2] from the South Seas, assure us that to-day primitive people are afraid of the dark, and of loneliness, of the sky, and of the forest, and most of all of something they know not what. Fear, said the Roman sceptic, made the gods, and it is an open secret that the concealed god of Rome, whose name it was death to reveal, was Fear. Fear must be the sentiment controlling man, when his idea of God is that of an austere justice up above the clouds, as an arbitrary, self-satisfying power beyond the furthest fixed star, who makes and mars by " the [3] eternal and most free purpose of His will," by "the unsearchable counsel of His own will, whereby He extendeth or withholdeth mercy as He pleaseth, for the glory of His sovereign power over His creatures." Arbitrariness is but another name for chance. Chance is the real devil of this world. Now, against this fundamental error of the idea of a self-satisfying, arbitrary God, the late Canon Liddon wrote :[4] " Sin does not contradict an arbitrary law made by God, but

---

[1] *Report of Bureau of Education.*   [2] *Ballads.*
[3] *Westminster Confession*, III. 6, 7.
[4] *Elements of Religion*, 156.

a law which is eternal as the nature of His Being. So old theologians said that were sin (*per impossibile*) exaggerated sufficiently it would annihilate God." Long has survived the appeal to fear to furnish a religious motive. Protestant revivalists and Roman Catholic "missioners" still find it useful. It is still the short and easy method of making men professing Christians. There is, however, in it this serious defect, that it is not the principle of the doctrine of Christ. His teaching is that the conditions of future bliss and woe are within the soul, that they belong to its character. If through character we may be lost then through character we may be saved. This is not the same as to assert salvation by character. The truth is fairly well expressed when old Omar Khayyám sings through Fitzgerald's verse:—

> "I sent my Soul through the Invisible,
>   Some letter of that After-life to spell:
> And by and by my Soul return'd to me,
>   And answer'd 'I, Myself, am Heav'n and Hell:
>
> "'Heav'n but the Vision of fulfill'd Desire,
>   And Hell the Shadow from a Soul on fire,
> Cast on the Darkness into which Ourselves,
>   So late emerg'd from, shall so soon expire.'"

The notion of God as an arbitrary, that is to say non-moral, Power has been preserved in the ancient symbol of the Divine Potter, which Egyptologists from Sir Gardner Wilkinson to the late Miss Edwards have noticed and made note of. In the mural pictures belonging to the early dynasties, we see Knum, the Divine Potter, shaping man upon a common potter's wheel. Carlyle abundantly ridiculed this pot-theism, as he named it, in Christian Theology, and confessedly the notion does look like a survival from primitive culture. Prof. Shedd, of Union Theological Seminary, pointed out that in the Epistle to the Romans[1] the proof-text of fatalistic pot-theists, the figure of the Potter and the pots, is of God as a Saviour, not as a Creator, and that St. Paul is stating the liberty of God to save some and ignore others, not from consequences of His creative and causative act, but of their own self-determination. Also, Dr. Hodge says: "In the sovereignty here asserted, it is of God as a moral governor and not as a creator." Though we be not willing to go with these reverend professors even thus far in their theory of the arbitrariness of God, yet we cannot but rejoice that supralapsarianism hath experienced the lifting up of a heel, and that Jacob Böhmen has been elected to a professorial chair.

"Ay, note that Potter's wheel,
 That metaphor! and feel
  Why time spins fast, why passive lies our clay, —
 Thou to whom fools propound
 When the wine makes its round,
  'Since life fleets all is change; the Past gone, seize to-day.'

[1] ix. 21.

"Fool! All that is at all
  Lasts ever, past recall;
    Earth changes, but thy soul and God stand sure:
  What entered into thee,
  That was, is, and shall be:
    Time's wheel runs back or stops: Potter and clay endure.

"He fixed thee mid this dance
  Of plastic circumstance,
    This present, thou, forsooth, wouldst fain arrest:
  Machinery just meant
  To give thy soul its bent,
    Try thee and turn thee forth, sufficiently impressed."

With this interpretation of professors and poet, will, I hope, vanish this proof-text of a devil-worshipping element of absolute predestination from the realm of Christian Theology. I cannot, although I have already quoted so much, refrain from citing also these words of good old Jeremy Taylor: "What is the secret of the Mysterie, that the eternal Son of God should take upon Him our nature, and die our death, and suffer for our sins and do our work, and enable us to do our own? He that did this is God: Who *thought it no robbery to be equal with God*. He came to satisfy Himself, to pay for Himself the price for His own creatures; and when He did this for us that He might pardon us, was He at that instant angry with us? Was this an effect of His anger or of His love, that God sent His Son to work our pardon and salvation? Indeed, we were angry with God, at enmity with the

Prince of Life: but He was reconciled to us so far, as that He then did the greatest thing in the world for us: for nothing could be greater than that God, Son of God, should die for us: here was reconciliation before pardon: and God that came to die for us did love us first before He came: this was hasty love."[1] Further discussion of the subject of divine decrees may be left to those individuals who, if Milton[2] may be trusted, make this their chief topic of conversation. Humanity in its childhood, supposing that God is the Author of evil as well as of good, makes it a matter of the highest import; and his chief duty in life to soothe the wrath and the evil disposition of God. At first, whatever might be his real opinion, man in the piety of his heart says what he thinks he ought to say, — "whatever this God does is good." The Yezidee, or devil-worshipper, will not allow the devil's name to be uttered. Pretence is made that he is good, is God, lest he should take revenge upon men. The Greeks also from a sense of self-protection, flatteringly called the Furies, the Eumenides, well disposed. In a similar way a crude notion of divine sovereignty has attempted to persuade itself that the evils of life are not evil. This shallow optimism, however pious its motive, justly provoked the derision of Voltaire.

If a primitive man has had some pleasure, he is

---

[1] *Miracles of the Divine Mercy*, Works, II. 347.
[2] *Paradise Lost*, II. 555 ff.

afraid lest he may have thereby aroused the envy of the gods, and, consequently, he hastens to undergo voluntarily some pain as an expiation. To avert the vindictiveness of these malicious supernal beings he will devote what he most values in order to placate them. His fundamental idea of human life is that it has no right to pleasure or joy. Just here we perceive the fountain-head of theories of satisfaction in sacrifice and atonement, of puritanism and the ascetic life, of purgatory and indulgences, and, in short, of the whole theological system of a commercial salvation: as though to God some equivalent must be given for human happiness, and He must be continually propitiated, and His anger soothed.

b. The next step, after shifting moral responsibility to another, is to transfer the guilt and penalty of sin. Just here we believe that we can detect the beginning of the idea of substitutionary sacrifice and vicarious punishment, which in subsequent days has played so large a rôle in Christian Theology. The ante-Nicene Church[1] held the doctrine of vicarious suffering, not of vicarious satisfaction. Now vicarious suffering is an obvious fact of life. Whence, then, came into Christian Theology the large element of vicarious satisfaction? The historian, Gibbon, delivers one of his sneers at Christianity when, speaking of Alboin's invasion of Italy, he adds in a note[2]

---

[1] Hagenbach, *History of Doctrines*, I. 262. [2] C. xlv. n. 14.

that the goat which the Lombards sacrificed they first worshipped, and he adds, "I know of but one religion in which the god and the victim are the same." In point of fact, Gibbon convicts himself of knowing very little about any religion whatever, for the idea which appears to him singular is wellnigh universal, although in highly developed religions it has been somewhat obscured. In Mexico they made an image of God out of maize or of dough, and after this had been adored, it was distributed among the people.

In the parish of King's Teignton, on each Whitsun-Monday, a lamb is drawn about in a cart and is gaily decked. The next day it is killed, roasted whole in the middle of the village, and all the villagers partake. The origin of the custom having been forgotten, a legend about a spring of water has been invented to account for it.[1] The singular aptness of this survival in the Eastern Church deserves our particular attention. In the "Order of the Holy Prothesis, as performed in the Great Church and in the Holy Mountain," the loaf of the Eucharistic oblation is set forth, made with a square projection, "seal," on the top, called the Holy Lamb. The rite proceeds: *Then the Priest takes in his left hand the oblations, and in his right the holy spear.* In remembrance of our Lord, and God, and Saviour, Jesus Christ. (*This he saith thrice.*) *He then thrusts the spear into the right side of the seal and saith, as he cuts,* "He was

[1] *Ethnology in Folklore*, by G. L. Gomme, 30, 125.

led as a sheep to the slaughter." *Into the left, saying,* "and as a blameless lamb." ... *And the priest, thrusting the holy spear obliquely into the right side of the oblation, raises up the holy Bread, saying,* "for His life is taken away from the earth." *The deacon saith,* "Sir, sacrifice." *The Priest saith, while he cuts crosswise,* "the Lamb of God is sacrificed." ... *Then they both adore reverently three times.* Again, in the proanaphora (before the consecration) of the liturgy of St. Chrysostom, there is an adoration of the Sacramental Oblation, and these words occur in the prayer, "For thou art He that offerest, and art offered, and receivest, and art distributed, Christ our God, and to thee we ascribe," etc.[1] But the Latin Church adores the Eucharistic food not until after the words of consecration. Among English, Scotch, and Welsh peasants, sin-eating, which was once a universal custom, still in remote localities is occasionally observed.[2] Though no longer anywhere in Christendom, so far as I know, is any one baptised for the dead, yet at the funerals of these peasants to whom I have just referred, poor people are hired to eat a "sin-loaf," and thus to take upon themselves the sins of the dead. The same custom of sin-eating for the dead obtains in Turkestan.[3] This sin-eating[4] was an

---

[1] *The Primitive Liturgies*, by Neale and Littledale, 106, 180.
[2] *Ethnology and Folklore*, 117.   [3] *Golden Bough*, II. 155.
[4] Cf. Hos. iv. 8., and references below; also *Water of Jealousy*, Num. v. 11-31.

important element in the rationale of the sacrificial meal of the priests, according to the Levitical code. By the eating of the sacrifice over which the sins had been confessed, and to which, by imposition of hands, the sins had been transferred, the priest was supposed to have taken into himself the sin or the guilt of it. The theory was that the holiness of the priesthood in this manner neutralised the virus of the substance of sin. If, however, by the defective holiness of the priest, or from any other cause, some sin remained unneutralised, it passed up to the high priest, who once a year transferred it by imposition of hands to a scapegoat.[1] An American theologian has extended this idea of pardon through sin-eating by asserting that the Eucharist is the Sacrament of Absolution. In this ancient theory and practice of sacrifices do we rightly discern the beginning of the origin of the revelation of a mediator and redeemer.[2]

The transference of guilt to a sin-bearer is a common element of Folk-faith. When a Moor has a headache he will sometimes take a lamb or goat and beat it till it falls down, and he believes that the headache has then been transferred to the animal.[3]

---

[1] Willis, *Worship of the Old Covenant*, I. 43.

[2] Professor Robertson Smith, who to me is not perfectly clear, seems (*Religion of the Semites*, 330 ff.) to dissent from this explanation of sin offering.

[3] *Golden Bough*, II. 149. Cf. Lev. xiv. 7, where a bird is let fly to carry away a taboo.

In Travancore, when the Rajah is very ill, a Brahmin is brought in who embraces him and voluntarily assumes the guilt of the Rajah's sin, saying, " Oh, King, I undertake to bear away all your sins and diseases; may your Highness live long and reign happily." The Brahmin sin-bearer is then thrust forth from the country, to which he may never return. Superstitious sailors in order to ease their ship of misfortune will maroon one of their fellows. Jonah's crew cast him overboard to save themselves, by offering him a sacrifice to the angry god.

This custom of sin-bearing prevails throughout all races in various forms. It has among Christian peoples often been relegated to the realm of witchcraft. In 1615, Catherine Bigland[1] was tried for having transferred by magic arts a disease from herself to a man. The Scotch Baron of Fowlis, being very ill, in 1588, sent for a witch, who told him that he could not recover unless the principal man of his blood should die in his place. At midnight, at a place near high-water mark, a grave was dug and the sick man placed in it; the grave was then covered with green turf, and the witch was asked who should die in place of the baron. She replied that his brother George should die for him. After this ceremony the sick man was removed from the grave to his bed. He recovered, but his brother George died. In the Highlands it has been customary to wash a cat in

[1] Gomme, *Ethnology in Folklore*, 142 ff.

water which has been used for washing the body of a sick person, and then the cat is set free to carry off the disease. A further development of this thought of sin-bearing led to the saining torch used by the border troopers at the funeral of one of their fellows. This torch was made from the fat of a slaughtered enemy, or at least of a murdered man. Another vehicle for the expulsion of evils, moral and physical, between which primitive man does not clearly distinguish, is a little boat. This is the favourite among the islanders of the Archipelago. In China a kite bears away sins to Shang-ti, the sky-god; in Malacca an ox is driven off into the forest for a tiger to kill; in Lhása, the holy city of Thibet, the sin-bearer is a man driven forth from the city with such rough treatment that seldom he survives.[1] Annually was sent from the sanctuary of Israel a goat devoted to Azazel. Upon him were concentrated the sins of the sons of Jacob. That Azazel was in early times a personification of evil, we may learn from an older document in the Book of Enoch,[2] where Azazel appears as the most malicious of the fallen angels, the demon who taught men the sins of lust and sorcery. By the archangel Raphael this wicked spirit was bound and cast forth into a deserted region. From the Book of Enoch it appears also that Azazel filled in early Hebrew folk-faith and myth the place occupied after the exile by Satan. To Azazel in desolate regions the high priest

---

[1] *Golden Bough*, II. 199.   [2] Book of Enoch vii-xi.

sent forth the scapegoat laden with the sins of the people. The Talmud gives us to understand that the scapegoat's death was caused by being pushed over a precipice. This reminds us that yearly at the Thargelia, the Athenians threw from the Acropolis a man and a woman, that they might bear the sins of the City of the Violet Crown back to the source of sin. In a like manner victims were hurled from the Tarpeian rock in Rome, and the legend of Tarpeia was a subsequent invention when the true origin of the custom in piacular substitution had been forgotten.[1] The idea which originally was connected with this form of sacrifice was the freeing of the tribe from an impious member. After the original thought had been forgotten, the doctrine of substitutionary death entered into the religions of both Aryans and Semites. In ancient Babylon a young man was selected, and for a season treated as a god, and afterwards scourged and crucified, to bear away the sins of the nation.[2] In Mexico of ancient days, exactly the same sacrifice of a human scapegoat was offered yearly. This widespread theory of pacifying an angry god by a gift was evolved from the earlier notion of feeding the god, a notion which held in its heart the essence of all effectual sacrifice; namely, self-sacrifice. But the

---

[1] Cf. 2 Chron. xxv. 12; Hosea x. 14. It has been stated that the late Professor Palmer of Oxford was slain by the Arabs for a like sacrificial purpose.

[2] *Golden Bough*, I. 226; *Dio Chrysostom*, Orat. 469.

ethical notion was almost universally obscured, and then supplanted, by the ceremonial rite.

When the Jewish high priest suggested that it was expedient that one man should die that the whole nation perish not, he simply proposed to make of Jesus a human scapegoat, a propitiatory sacrifice, and a piacular substitution for the nation. This ancient folk-faith of primitive peoples has survived in Christian Theology to our own day, darkening the counsel of God, and overshadowing the precious and profound significance of the sacrifice of Calvary, degrading it from a revelation of God's character into the ignoble pacification of an irritated God, according to some bargain made in the midst of Trinal Unity, at "Heaven's high council-table," where the Eternal Son agreed to assume all the guilt and punishment for sins He had never committed, and by a cruel death to bear them away in accepting vicarious punishment. Some of the ante-Nicene Christians [1] invented another, but scarcely more spiritual theory, which is, that Jesus, by being sacrificed as a scapegoat to Satan, deceived the arch-fiend, who thereby lost his power over all men. This common belief appears in a spirited and picturesque passage of the Apocryphal Gospel of Nicodemus, a passage which has been imitated by Milton in his description of Satan quarrelling with sin.

[1] Cf. Hagenbach, *History of Doctrines*, I. 260; Haag, II. 159 ff.

All these scattered forms of folk-faith and myth came, in course of time, to concentrate in a great and splendid mythos of the woe of the world. In the Norse Edda,[1] Odin the high god sings: "I mind me hanging on the gallows-tree nine whole nights, wounded with a spear, offered to Odin, myself to myself, on the tree whose roots no man knoweth [Yggdrasil, the Cosmic Tree symbol]. They gave me no loaf, they held no horn to me. I peered down, I caught the mysteries up with a cry, then I descended. I learned nine songs of might, ... I got a draught of the precious mead blent with Odreari [Inspiration]. Then I became fruitful and wise, and waxed great, and flourished. Word followed fast upon word, and work followed fast upon work, with me." Now, even if it be suspected that somehow the tragedy of the Christian Gospels had travelled North, and entered into this myth, just as in some mysterious way the life of Buddha has got itself enshrined in the *Legenda Aurea*,[2] in the chapter about Sts. Barlaam and Josaphat, it is clear that the Gospel could have in no way had the shaping of Æschylus' great tragedy of *Prometheus Bound*. The inner idea belongs to what had been felicitously termed the Eternal Consciousness, for the ethos which was there upheld for an ideal is that of the son of a god bound with outstretched limbs upon the

---

[1] *Háva-mál*, Vigfusson and Powell, *Corpus Poeticum Boreale*, I. 25.   [2] Ch. clxxx.

jagged rocks of the world, and beaten with hot sunrays and scourged with icy winds; and the mythos, ancient as the Summero-Akkadian days, when the epic of Izdubar first came to birth; and the ethos is as far travelled, if you will have it so, as Dsilyi· Neyáni, the culture hero of the Navajo sacred dance.[1]

A modern poet makes much in his pessimistic verse of this mythos of humanity, crucified by god, or by fate, or by force, or by chance : —

> "As once the high God bound
> With many rivet round,
>   Man's saviour, and with iron nailed him through,
>   *   *   *   *
> So the strong god, the Chance
> Central of Circumstance,
>   Still shows him exile who will not be slave."

But God crucifies man never. In sin it is man who crucifies God ever afresh, by barring out the operation of the Holy Spirit within the soul, grieving the Holy Spirit of God whereby we are sealed unto the day of redemption. There is the whole world's width between the tragedy of Prometheus in the Dionysiac mysteries, and the Divine tragedy of Calvary. It is a mistake common to many students of comparative religion to confuse the ethos, or ethical content, of a religious custom or myth with its external moral teaching, and to lose the mythos, or the fundamental

---

[1] *U. S. Reports, Bureau of Ethnology,* 1884; Sayce, Hibbert Lectures.

mythical content, in the details of subsequent developments of the myth in the minds of those who had lost its original *motif;* in a word, to lose the spirit in the letter. In the study of Christian Theology, the application of comparative religion, as well as of the historical development of Christian Doctrines themselves, calls for careful recollection of these distinctions. With no more reason can we trace the programme of the Divine death of the Gospels to the Promethean myth, than the origin of Corregio's painting of the Nativity at Bethlehem to that other divine nativity which the master hand of Phidias carved on the pediment of the Parthenon. A noble Athenian believed that after witnessing the drama of Prometheus he should be ashamed to go home and nurse his own petty griefs and vexations. Shall we in the shadow of the Cross have no higher idea than that another pays the price for us, another suffers in our stead, another is our scapegoat? Jesus in His life-long passion wrought a redemption, but published no theology of redemption. Nor did He, as Strauss suggests, set Himself to fulfil in a spectacular way the programme of the twenty-second Psalm. All this is an ancient error which has come down to us from the highlands of History, confusing and confounding sin and pain, assuming that pain is the substitute and recompense for sin, and thereby generating a vast labyrinth of satisfaction, and merits, and justification, and indulgences, and of purgatory doctrines from the pilgrimage of the Hindu Yama to Dante's Vision and St. Patrick's Purgatory in Ireland, and suggesting gross and grotesque notions [1] of soul's torment for sin in this world and beyond it. One observation alone is here necessary. If the true Christian idea of sin be that it is wrong, is what is intrinsically unholy, immoral, an offence against an absolute principle of right, then clearly no such idea existed in primitive culture. Primitive man has no sense of sin; he has only fear of penalty. His idea of forgiveness, based upon this crude notion, has survived in Christianity to so wide an extent as to have well-nigh obscured the whole Christian idea of sin and its forgiveness. Of one thing the idea of the divine immanence assures us: pain and sorrow are not the manifestation of a wrathful Deity, and therefore not a satisfaction in sacrifice. Sorrow is not sorrow's fruit. Pain is joy seen on the wrong side; for it is the signal of life, of that Life which strives within the world, within the consciousness of each soul with groanings too large for utterance. Pain, whether of body or of soul, is

[1] Every religion which has evolved beyond the stage of fetishism has its story of purgatory. The Rajah Judsishtar and Yama in India, the Egyptian land of Amenti, the descent of the Assyrian Ishtar, the Norse myth of the descent of Baldr, Odysseus, Er the son of Armenius, Æneas, Perpetua, and Felicitas, the Monk of Evesham, Alberic of Monte Casino, Hildergarde, St. Bridget, Drihthelm in Neoght, Dante, Swedenborg, and Mrs. Oliphant's Little Pilgrim are of the more familiar visitors to the world of the dead.

the symbol of redemption. Nightly looks down upon the lands and waters of the earth a dead world; upon this side, at any rate, of the moon, life is extinct; *there* is no pain. We turn to the Cross, the supreme symbol of agony; *here* is life. Never forget that this is the significance of the Cross. In the lands of the Eastern Church you would not be allowed to forget it, because the Greek Christians always place a slanting bar across the base of the cross whenever they set it up in city streets, country roads, or on church domes. This bar placed slantwise represents the foot-rest of the Cross, which was displaced by Jesus in the stress of his extreme agony. Every pain is a step by which we mount to a higher plane of life where existence burns more intensely. If this step be not taken the soul falls back into disorganisation and death.

II. I do not feel myself called to embark upon the shoreless ocean of atonement and justification doctrines. It will be enough to examine the teaching of Jesus about the Forgiveness of Sins. That this removal was His purpose and work is evident from the very name given to Him.[1]

St. John Baptist hails Him as the Lamb of God Who takes away the sins of the world. He was the Lamb of God, not as propitiatory sacrifice of sin, because that the typical male lamb of the Levitical

---

[1] St. Matt. i. 21, αὐτὸς γὰρ σώσει τὸν λαὸν αὐτοῦ ἀπὸ τῶν ἁμαρτιῶν αὐτῶν, not from the results of sin, but from sins themselves.

ceremonial never was.[1] Neither was He a piacular Lamb of God in any fulfilment of Isaiah's prophecy. If you read that prophecy attentively you will see that it alludes to nothing but the meekness and silence of the suffering Messiah, and not at all to any sacrificial character or act. Nor is Jesus the Lamb slain in expiation for sin from the foundation of the world, because that would imply eternally predestinated sin, and make God the Author of evil. No; but the Lamb of God beheld by the visionary of Patmos in the midst of the Throne is a symbol of the eternal and essential self-outyield of God through His Son; the leonine power of the Omnipotent, manifested to St. John, and to him visible only as a lamb, only as love.[2] Dispossess your mind for the nonce of traditional exegesis, and you will discern that in the New Testament the Lamb is everywhere a symbol of love and the beloved. The sign is congruous with the thing signified. Therefore the profounder sense of the Baptiser's misinterpreted phrase is, that Jesus as the Lamb of God is the manifestation of the essential character of the indwelling Life of the world, Who is Eternal Love, God our Saviour, the Forgiver of Sins.[3]

---

[1] Lev. xvi. 3-7; iv. 28-30; v. 6; xii. 6; xiv. 22, 12. In short, the sin offering could be almost anything but a male lamb.

[2] Rev. v. 5, 6. One of the elders said unto me, behold the lion . . . and I beheld, and lo, a lamb.

[3] This truth was perceived, if I understand his words, by the founder of the Society of Friends. — Fox, *Journal*, 28.

THE FORGIVENESS OF SINS. 167

This infinite and eternal outyield of self, this intimate nature of Life itself, which is essentially expansive, abundant, outflowing, this sacrifice which is named Love, does not necessarily involve pain and death.[1] In finite beings this sacrifice may be attended with pain, because the outgoing self dashes against limitations, but in the Infinite the outgo of self is unlimited, unrestrained, and returns within

---

[1] In the sacrifices of the Israelites the first idea was that of presenting food to God. Ex. x. 9, xviii. 12; Lev. iii. 11, xxi. 6, 8, 17 ff., xxii. 25; Judges vi. 19; Ezek. xliv. 3, 7, 15, 16, 29, 30; Jer. vi. 20; Amos v. 21, etc. Though fruit and drink were offered to God, animals were preferred, perhaps because they were means of a more patent transfer of life to God. From the peculiar construction of the Hebrew in Gen. iv. 7 it might be inferred that an earlier notion of sacrifice was primarily that it was propitiatory, and that originally animals alone were held to be acceptable for sacrifice. In animal sacrifice among the Jews the chief object was the offering of life, by means of the blood in which the life was supposed to reside. From the Levitical Code to the Talmud the slaughter of the sacrificial victim was regarded as merely incidental, and it was performed with the least possible torture to the animal; no stress whatever being laid upon pain and death in this sacrificial custom. The offering of the blood was the matter of highest importance. This offering was not for a substitution, but for a gift to God of representative life. This may be seen by an examination of the ceremonials of the Passover, the Day of Atonement, and the various bloody sacrifices. This idea of the self-yielding of life, though not unperceived by the Jewish doctors, was fulfilled by Jesus. All this view of the meaning of the sacrifice of Jesus might appear to contradict Acts xx. 28; Eph. i. 7; Heb. ix. 12; 1 Pet. i. 18, 19; Rev. v. 9, which have been assumed to signify unquestionably a commercial ransom. All these texts refer to the result of Christ's work rather than to the process. The

the bosom of God as His supreme jubilation. Our Lord in His double nature felt both the Divine and the human impulse to sacrifice; for once He exclaimed, "I have a baptism to be baptised with, and how am I pained until it be consummated."[1] It cannot be denied that such being the significance of the Lamb symbol, it was inevitable that the Lamb Himself should be put to death. Yet clear as was this issue at times in His consciousness, as in the words just quoted, in other hours His consciousness became dimmed. In the agony in the garden He prayed that if it were possible the cup might pass from Him, and on the cross when He uttered the cry of extreme dereliction. But because He was the supreme Revelation, the Parousia of shoreless Love, of infinite self-surrender of that Life which is self-subsistent, death was the inevitable goal towards which He in His true humanity developed. Because He is the utterance, the Logos of eternal Love, He is indeed the Lamb of God, but His blood is not a

---

result, as Theophylact points out, was release from slavery, removal of bondage. A complete discussion of the terms λύτρωσις, καταλλαγή, and ἱλασμός would involve a dissertation upon Hellenistic Greek. In Heb. ix. 16, 17, διαθήκη should be translated "covenant," and διαθέμενος "covenanter." Cf. Hatch, *Essays in Biblical Greek*, 47. A covenant is a mutual agreement, and not of necessity a bargain involving some "consideration."

[1] St. Luke xii. 50, πῶς συνέχομαι ἕως ὅτου τελεσθῇ. Συνέχομαι connotes that tension of soul in one who is holding himself prepared for extreme effort.

symbol of a formal forgiveness of sins any more than it is of a material fountain of cleansing. But it is, if the sign fits the thing signified, the effluence of the life powers of the Son of God, to vitalise human spirits, welling up within them as their consciousness of the reality of God grows more distinct; a fountain which, as the hymn hath it, is

> " of sin the double cure,
> Saves from wrath and makes me pure."

That Jesus perceived His own mediatorial saving work lay in the actual losing of life, is clear from the words with which the account of the last Passover begins: "Having loved His own which were in the world, He loved them *to the end*,[1] unto completion, unto consummation of love, which is utter self-surrender.[2]

The unvarying teaching of Jesus is that of the removal of sin;[3] and in His parables He makes it clear that our Father, God, never changes His attitude towards us, because God is changeless Love. Theology has termed this changeless Love, 'prevenient grace,' and 'pardon.' Because God is always love the pardon is awaiting acceptance, and implies change in man, not in God. The Immanent God is pardon awaiting reception in the consciousness of the soul of man.[4] The gospel discloses that God is

---

[1] εἰς τέλος. Cf. τετέλεσται, St. John xix. 30.
[2] St. John xiii. 1.   [3] ἄφεσις τῶν ἁμαρτιῶν.   [4] Is. lxv. 24.

seeking man, not that man is looking after God. It cannot be too often repeated and emphasised that this is clear from the parables of the Lost Coin, the Lost Sheep, and of the Prodigal Son, as elsewhere in our Lord's teachings. When Jesus by miracle, which is parable in action, teaches His redemptive and absolving work, He forgives sins not by a fiction of a forensic declaration or by the imputation of merits and the pardoning of the guilt alone, as folk-faith and Roman law have led men to think, but He absolves sins in fact; that is to say, He removes them. Then Divine Love, which is pardon, enters the consciousness of the Soul. To the paralytic He says in effect, "In order that men may know that I do remove sins, I remove your paralysis; arise and walk." Nowhere does He speak of Himself as a substitute for men. His life and ministry were the ransom[1] of many from sins. This Jesus distinctly teaches.[2] Into the apostolic development of the idea of Christ's work as

---

[1] λύτρον, literally means of loosing.

[2] St. Mark x. 45, ἀλλὰ διακονῆσαι καὶ δοῦναι τὴν ψυχὴν αὐτοῦ λύτρον ἀντὶ πολλῶν. Note here first that λύτρον, ransom, that is, means of release, stands in apposition to διακονῆσαι, which means to minister, as well as in apposition to δοῦναι; consequently both are elements of the ransom, and, second, observe δοῦναι τὴν ψυχήν, to give the living soul, need not be restricted to the significance of dying, as has been assumed, as though it were ἀποδοῦναι. For the term covers the whole lifelong out-yield of self which uttered itself in its consummation on Calvary. Weiss, *Bibl. Theol.*, I. 101, n. 5.

a Forgiver of sins, that is to say, a Remover, Redeemer, I cannot now enter; but I venture to beg you to teach, upon this foundation that I have endeavoured to uncover, a theology which is ethical, and above all a doctrine of the Atonement which is ethical. Jesus suffered, it is true, vicariously, but not substitutionally.[1] The author of the Epistle to the Hebrews distinctly puts aside all survivals of primitive folk-faith whether Semitic or Aryan, and every notion of Jesus as a propitiatory or substitutionary sacrifice for satisfaction or for compensation.[2] The old sacrifices were, he says, but shadows having indeed some small moral sanction, but now that the real ethical Sacrifice is manifested and established, these old and defective forms and notions are removed.[3] It is said that Jesus, because He is the Son of God, and thus is Infinite, must suffer in order that by infinite suffering He can atone or pay the price for our sins which, in their culpability, are infinite, Godward. But if our sins be infinite, Godward, then are also our good deeds and

---

[1] Weiss, *Bibl. Theol.*, I. 421, n. 2, 422, n. 4, 424, nn. 6, 7 ; Ritschl, *Critical History of the Christian Doctrine of Justification and Reconciliation*, 411. Hodge, *Systematic Divinity*, II. 470, in order to escape from the objectionable theory of the equivalent satisfaction, distinguishes between penal and pecuniary satisfaction. But further on (II. 540 and III. 175) he, for other exigencies, flatly contradicts himself; first he repudiates and afterwards asserts a grossly commercial theory of the Atonement.

[2] Pfleiderer, Hibbert Lectures on Influence of Apostle Paul.

[3] Heb. x. 9.

virtues infinite; and since two infinities are equal, they cancel one another. However, there is an objection deeper than the dialectic to this theory; it is that God does not suffer. Whatever suffers can die or become more perfect. Men cannot put on themselves the merits of another, even of the Son of God, as their remote ancestors masked themselves with the face of the merciful rain-god, supposing that thus for the nonce they became holy.[1] Our Lord Jesus is the Mediator of a better covenant. Avoid, therefore, artificial theories of forgiveness and absolution, and learn your doctrine of the atonement not from Justin Martyr, Anselm, Aquinas, Luther, Calvin, Bushnell, or Magee, but from the New Testament; for theologians have been propounding a doctrine of forgiveness which belongs to that stage of human development where the savage paints the corpse in order that in the other world the deceased may appear righteous, and where for a similar intention Clytemnestra covered the face of the murdered Agamemnon with a golden mask, — if we may believe the late Dr. Schliemann.

III. We ought not to feel surprised that the theologians of the early Church were powerfully influenced by both their notions of demonology, and by the tradition of the scapegoat, in their reception of the redeeming work of Christ. Following the anal-

---

[1] E. R. Emerson, *Masks, Heads, and Faces, passim.*

ogy of the scapegoat, many of them[1] taught that Jesus was in His death a sacrifice and satisfaction paid to Satan. Justin Martyr added,[2] as it is only right to say, that the teaching of Jesus was a power which removed sins of men, and Irenæus[3] also taught that the life of Jesus, meaning thereby the life of our Lord, according as it was lived by example, effected remission of sins. Irenæus goes on to say[4] that the purpose of the Incarnation was to reveal to man the character of God, in order that man might live according to God. This doctrine of forgiveness is repeated by Clement the Alexandrian. Origen in a like manner was conscious of the ethical manner of Christ's operation in the removal of sins of, says he,[5] "all those who not only believe, but enter upon the life which Jesus taught, and which elevates to friendship with God and to communion with Him every one who lives according to the precepts of Jesus." The epistle of Diognetus, if it belongs to the reign of Marcus Aurelius,[6] is a striking example of the early emancipation from the notion that Christ's death was to propitiate an angry God, and from the belief that the Divine Sacrifice of Calvary was a manifestation of eternal wrath. "He hated us not, nor bore us malice."[7] The idea of sat-

---

[1] Buel, *Dogmatic Theology*, c. xvi. [2] Apol. I. 23.
[3] *Against Heresies*, II. 22, 4. [4] V. 16, 2.
[5] *Against Celsus*, III. 28.
[6] See Bishop Lightfoot's *Introduction*. [7] Ch. ix.

isfaction or compensation for sin, in order to satisfy a principle of justice, dimly implied in Justin Martyr,[1] is liberated by Tertullian[2] into a moral and rational factor. Tertullian applies the term *satisfactio* "to such as make amends for their own sins by confession and by repentance which shows itself in works."[3] At this point is the beginning of the doctrine of Penance, as mutual public acknowledgment of wrong, exomologesis, was the starting-point of the custom. It was Anselm, in his *Cur Deus Homo*, who fixed upon the later Theology of the Western Church the dogma that, although there might be other methods of salvation within the resources of an omnipotent God, yet, nevertheless, the Eternal Father did choose the death of Christ to manifest His love toward man; and that since Christ was sinless, and death is God's reward for sin, Christ earned by a sinless death a reward, or merit, and as He was infinite, His merit was infinite. Human nature could not have been restored to the favour of God, unless compensation had been made for its sin, that is to say, its merit was complete destruction or else infinite torment; but by the love of Christ, in a bargain with the Father, His infinite merits were substituted in place of the infinite demerits of mankind, and so the price was paid to Justice, and the compensation

---

[1] *Dialogue with Trypho*, 103.
[2] Tertullian, *De Pœn.* v. et seq.
[3] Hagenbach, *Hist.*, I. 260.

accepted. This is the Anselmic scheme of salvation. This legal theory was the logical outcome of the idea of a remotely transcendent God, with Whom our relations are according to the provisions of the Roman law. "That the satisfaction made to God should be valid for men; it was not necessary that they should be aware of this meaning of the death of Christ; all that was necessary was their imitation of the self-surrender, which was perfectly realised in Him. The forgiveness of sins on the part of God, which follows upon the satisfaction made, does not come through the very person who made the satisfaction, but comes, so to speak, alongside of Him." [1] Anselm's notions of Divine ransom were undoubtedly shaped by the Teutonic custom of *Wergeld*, bloodmoney, whereby the criminal made pecuniary compensation for his crime. Abelard reasonably inquired why it was that our Heavenly Father must needs have taken this tortuous way of forgiving our sins. He also observes that if Christ ransomed us from the power of the devil, His redemption availed for the non-elect only, because over the elect the devil had never had any power. If this objection be good, then that Catechism which terms our Lord "The Redeemer of the Elect" might be improved in phraseology. Further into this savage forest, *selva selvaggia ed aspra e forte*, it is not necessary to proceed.

[1] Ritschl, *History of Christian Doctrine of Justification and Reconciliation*, 34.

Concerning the doctrines of the Atonement on their Godward side, I am not called in question; and if I were, I should be incompetent to give a certain solution. "How and in what particular way it [the sacrifice of Jesus Christ] has this efficacy [expiation of sin] there are not wanting persons who have endeavoured to explain; but I do not find that the Scripture has explained it. We seem to be very much in the dark concerning the manner in which the ancients understood atonement to be made, *i.e.* pardon to be obtained by sacrifices. And if the Scripture has, as it surely has, left this matter of the satisfaction of Christ mysterious, left somewhat in it unrevealed, all conjectures about it must be, if not evidently absurd, yet at least uncertain."[1] The history of the development of those doctrines, and likewise of theories of the Sacraments, show how the vast and world-wide institution of propitiatory and expiatory sacrifices inclines Christian thought to take some formal method of salving the conscience, and to substitute ritual acts for moral redemption. Has this coil come from beginning Theology at the wrong end? I suspect so. Although the first idea in Holy Scriptures is the idea of God, for centuries past the world has been taught to begin its religion with the idea of sin. Perhaps a survival of the mental disposition of primitive man was the origin of this error; perhaps also, if we may say it without failing in respect to one of the greatest

[1] Bishop Butler, *Analogy*, V. 6.

intellects in the whole history of the development of Christian Theology, St. Augustine's exceptional personal experience in unsaintliness had something to do with the choice of this special point of view. It has been accepted as an axiom that Augustine carried into practice the theory of Plato, "*Quidquid a Platone dicitur, vivit in Augustino*"; but in this special subject it is difficult to see Plato in Augustine's theory of sin and its remedy. At any rate, Christian instruction has been made to begin with —

> "Man's first disobedience, and the fruit
> Of that forbidden tree, whose mortal taste
> Brought death into the world, and all our woe."

A candid student finds it difficult to understand why emphasis was laid upon this narrative, rather than upon that of the fall of the angels where the pre-Christian Jews placed it, or upon the sin of Babel, or upon the deluge, each of which is equally a pre-Abrahamic, Chaldean antiquity. And so, for generations, even innocent babes and sucklings have been diligently taught as the first thing which they ought to know, in order that they might be good, and go to Heaven, —

> "In Adam's fall
> We sinned all."

One word to close this section. The distinction between Christianity and paganism lies in this, that in paganism man is seeking after God, and in Christianity it is revealed that God is seeking after man. To me, most of these atonement theories to which I have alluded look very like man seeking after God. It was not the Father God, but the Jews who cursed Jesus; it is not the Father God, but the " father of lies," who destroys both soul and body in hell.

IV. *a.* How shall we teach Christ's doctrine of the forgiveness of sins? Hitherto much mischief has arisen from too much method. The ground of sin, *reatus, peccatum, culpa, pœna,* original sin, actual sin, guilt, and penalty, have been harmfully sundered. It is dangerous to dissect a living man, and vivisection of the soul always makes mischief in Theology. Let us cease to seek for precision by this method of anatomy. Original sin is a fact. Original righteousness is equally a fact. Original sin is something which no one who has observed the result of habit in shaping the will and moulding the character that pass from parent to child, would ever think of denying; but to take up the words of the Ninth Article of Religion, and say, in the old traditional sense, that this of itself is guilt, that these inherited tendencies are subject to full moral responsibility, and that in this way they deserve God's wrath and damnation, is nothing less than to go straight against the Lord Jesus' rebuke of that very theory of primitive culture which had been revived by the Jews in the case of the man born blind. The words of our Lord were:

"Neither hath this man sinned nor his parents, but that the works of God should be made manifest in him."[1] In a sense profoundly true, sins, whether hereditary or actual, guilt and penalty, are all bound together in the bundle of life. Godward they are identical. Time, which belongs to the condition of human thought, may separate them through the human apprehension, yet in Eternity they are one.

b. Sin is its own terrible penalty, and the penalty of sin is sin, an awful impetus of degeneracy,[2] which, if unchecked, goes down to death. It has been said with approval that guilt is the fear of punishment.[3] Better would it be to lay aside this sentiment of primitive culture and say guilt is the anticipation of the consequence of sin; better still, that it is the sense of self-degradation, the strong desire to sin again, which the loss of God-consciousness entails. Liability to penalty is a common definition of sin, but this is the legal idea. In saying that sin is its own punishment, we find guilt to be liable to punishment translated into terms of personal experience, which teaches progressive propensity to sin.

c. There is a further lesson in our Lord's words concerning the man born blind which is timely for these days of pessimism. Pessimism doubts and despairs of life, because it cannot solve this problem of

---

[1] St. John ix. 3.
[2] Drummond, *Natural Law in the Spiritual World*, 97 ff.
[3] Archbishop Secker, Works, VI. 146.

pain in the world, and declares that our earth is the City of Dreadful Night, whose sole gospel is suicide. Even this consolation is denied us by Schopenhauer, on the ground that self-destruction is an assertion of the "will to live." For him the misery of life lies in the "will to live," and the world is the "will to live." How near was Schopenhauer to the mind of Christ only to completely miss it! The doctrine of Jesus is that pain is an element of personal redemption. The world is the "will to live," but to *live aright*. The evolution of life is a grand manifestation of the works of God as it mounts upward upon the steps of pain, the world's great altar stairs that slope through darkness up to God, where the Hidden Love manifests Himself in the cosmical process of Sacrifice. It is to Richard Wagner that modern thought owes a debt for having brought to its consciousness the almost forgotten truth of the gospel, that pain is not a curse, but a way of redemption. This is the answer which St. Paul made for pessimists of the first century. Creation is made subject to vanity, not wilfully or arbitrarily, but by reason of Him who hath subjected the same in hope, etc. The old theories, which in their doctrines of satisfaction confused sin and pain, had nevertheless in their heart this truth, that pain is an element in the remission of sins, in the redemption of the body. It is, however, more an exponent than a factor in redemption. As I have already said, wherever in the world is life and growth, there is pain. Pain, then, is the evidence of the stress of the upward movement of life, of the conversion of material to spiritual. Pain accompanies the forgiveness of sin, not as a compensation or vengeance, but as that birth-pang of which St. Paul speaks. The evolution of the world is an *ewige gebürt*. All progress in the history of humanity has come from men of sorrows. The secret of Jesus was to go to meet pain, to take up the cross; and the crucifixion is the highest expression of infinite love. The Cross is the revelation of the nature of the Eternal One. To the pessimism of our day and of all days the Cross reveals the true significance of suffering, "That the works of God might be made manifest." Through suffering, Jesus Christ, the leader of the drama[1] of history, the leader of our salvation therefore, is perfected. The Supreme Sufferer is the sinless sufferer, Immanent Eternal Love manifested in Time; therefore it could not be that He is cursed of God. Sin brings suffering, but not all suffering is brought by sin.

d. Evil in the world, I mean cosmical evil, is only privative. "Evil is null, is nought, is silence implying sound"; this is true Augustinian doctrine. Evil results from finiteness, and it is the inalienable complement of present limitations. But when the will takes up this negative, and, by what I may term a psychological magic, transmutes evil into sin, then

---

[1] ἀρχηγός, Heb. ii. 10; xii. 2. cf. Vaughan *in loc.*

the quality becomes positive.[1] Sin is not a substance or thing; it is not a poison or a dye. All Theology founded on such notions veers away from the realities of life. Sin is the quality, or the manner, of the exercise of the will, which results in disturbance of relations, and in an attitude of disfavour; that is to say, of dis-grace towards God the Righteous One. Sin is a discord which wounds the harmony of the Divine and human wills. The human will in Him, Christ, made one, atoned, if you wish it, with the Father's, " in which will we are made holy."[2]

e. Sin deadens the God-consciousness by sundering between God and the conscious soul. This severance results in loss of perception of the good. By sin we consequently lose faith in God and in man, faith in moral perfectibility, if not even in moral possibility, and in our divine sonship. Tennyson, in his *Vision of Sin*, and Browning, in his *Soul's Tragedy*, trace out this process of a soul's death. To attain to God-consciousness we must have faith in Jesus Christ, simply because that consciousness is of the sort which is effected by the actualisation in moral and spiritual existence of the individual man, of the historic life of Jesus Christ.[3] St. Paul teaches

[1] ἁμαρτία nowhere in the New Testament has a negative sense. — KEIM, *Jesus of Nazara*, V. 408.

[2] Heb. x. 10, ἐν ᾧ θελήματι ἡγιασμένοι ἐσμέν.

[3] Indeed, the doctrine of Justification by Faith, when unswathed from its theological mummy wrappings, is found to be precisely this rational truth. To this end was his κένωσις, humiliation. Every

that the *man* Christ Jesus is our Mediator, as Theodoret says, ἐπανθρωπήσας γὰρ ἐμεσίτευσεν. This truth has, from the survival of the pagan notion of divine mediators, been in danger of oblivion, and so the New-Testament doctrine of mediation has been obscured by later theologians.[1] If you are interested in the study of the doctrine of the Atonement, consider it from this point, — Jesus the Mediator in His humanity. In His whole life and death He is the self-revelation, the visible image of the invisible Saviour God; hence it is said that the destiny of man is to live according to the life of God.[2] Thus God and man are at one in will and in purpose; they are united in practical consciousness, for God-consciousness is no mere intellectual illumination or mystic trance, but a sense of righteousness which comes from living the Christly life. At its beginning it is written, "Ye shall be as gods knowing good from evil," and at its end, "Be ye perfect, even as your Father in Heaven is perfect."

f. Since sin is a quality of action caused by choice, its fundamental relations to life may be defined. Again, I say life is essentially appetite, desire, will, love, — all phases of the one thing. Therefore sin

---

life must pass through the Christ-process, which is a filling up of the Kenosis, albeit in a less perfect way; in this He is our only Mediator and Redeemer: a Mediator of a better covenant than that of substitutionary and piacular immolation.

[1] See Bishop Ellicott's Notes on 1 Tim. ii. 5, 6.
[2] 1 Pet. iv. 6, ζῆν κατὰ Θεόν.

may be described as life defective, or life distorted,[1] which, you perceive, is the same as saying that sin is love, or will, or desire, or appetite, defective or distorted; for example, hate is love defective; avarice, love distorted. In his *Inferno* and *Purgatorio*, Dante has fully and scientifically illustrated this theory of sin. Love he symbolises by warmth and fire, the want of love by torpor and cold. Those who had sinned by love distorted are tormented with flames, those by love defective are tortured with cold and ice. The arch-traitor is the farthest away from God, and at the point of indifference, the place of intensest cold. And the love of God which to the sinners is pain, to the penitents of purgatory becomes a cleansing flame; and in paradise thrills the elect saints with the warmth and ecstasy from the Divine Life which is love. Jesus came to supply the life defective, that we might have life, and have it more abundantly, to straighten the love distorted by justifying, or, as we would say, rectifying it; that is, making it right or just. This is what it is to take away sins. In both Greek and Hebrew the words for forgiveness signify removal, and nowhere do I find them used to denote a removal of guilt alone or of penalty alone.

g. God Himself cannot forgive sins which are unforgivable since they remain in the soul. Yet His love changes not, only we are not receptive of

---

[1] *A Theory of Sin*, by Orbey Shipley, would be interesting to read in connection with this.

that love which, relative to sins removed, we name pardon; the love which abiding in us we become conscious of only as sins are done away. We may with more ease forgive those who have wronged us than those whom we have wronged. In some true sense, it may be said that we find it hard to forgive God Whom we have wronged. Only as we yield to that Divine Life which presses against the soul,

"With scarce an intervention, presses close and palpitatingly;"

only then are our sins forgiven, and the Divine Life enters into the soul, and enters according to the measure that we lift up the gates of the soul by metanoia and lovingness. This assoilment is ethical, that is to say, it is actual; it means that the Life of God has entered into the consciousness of man; it means that man's will is made straight, justified, and that is the same as to say that he lives according to God. The greater the metanoia, the deeper the soul realises or understands the Divine Love; "for to whom little is forgiven, the same loveth little."[1] Aristides, in his Apology for the early Christians, says of them: "Those who grieve them, they comfort and make their friends."[2] What Heathen or Jewish

[1] St. Luke vii. 47. In this place the "for," δέ, indicates not the ground, but the effect of forgiveness.

[2] It is curious that in the Septuagint the Hebrew word for justice, which is usually translated by δικαιοσύνη, righteousness, is nine times translated by ἐλεημοσύνη, and three times by ἔλεος, loving kindness, charitableness, and mercy.

moralist had ever before dreamed of such a sublime charity! It is God's charity revealed in Jesus. It is the sinner who is to be pitied, not the righteous who is sinned against. It is the sinner who, in the quest of the Holy Grail, is lost in blindness, though the chalice of Divine Life floats ever near him; for the blessedness of the Divine Vision is revealed only to those who are pure in heart. The selfish cannot grieve because they are blind and dead. The harder hearted the sinner, the more jocund. Perhaps no two men ever lived harder, narrower, and more selfish during their career of success than Charles the Second of England and Napoleon the First of France. Millions adored them and would have gladly died for them. They loved no man. No grief or pain of sympathy clouded their intense self-satisfaction. What place in God's providence have such souls? Where in them is the place of one small seed of self-redemption? Shall they as bubbles on the infinite ocean of the Eternal Being burst, and their individual existence be gone forever? This is one of the deepest of the deep enigmas of life, and it leads us to turn with a sense of relief from Philosophy and History to the Lord Jesus Christ. God seeks for man. It is the sinner who draws from our Father God, the "Tear of Divine Compassion"; it is not jealousy for his own glory.[1]

[1] Hagenbach, I. 266. Origen, Comm. on St. Matt. vi. 14, teaches forgiveness of enemies as one of the means of obtaining forgiveness for one's own sins.

> "Alas! alas!
> Why, all the souls that were, were forfeit once;
> And He who might the vantage best have took
> Found out the remedy. How would you be,
> If He which is the top of judgment should
> But judge you as you are?"

h. Abstractly speaking, perfect forgiveness of sin would mean the restoration of things to their pristine condition. In fact, forgiveness is something more and something less. It is something more because Divine Life, "our daily bread," has entered into the soul's consciousness.

> "Impulses of deeper birth
> Have come to him in solitude."

The forgiven sinner, by the stress of his redemptive effort, has risen, as St. Augustine has somewhere said, upon stepping-stones of his dead self to higher things. The pardon itself is progressive because the forgiveness is a process; is, in short, the removal of sin. Like Donatello of Hawthorne's *Marble Faun*, the man who has passed through sin and its forgiveness, though he can never again be innocent, yet, at the same time, with a knowledge of evil, he has got the knowledge of good, and has tasted that gracious sense of pardon which accompanies removal of sin and the quickening of God-consciousness. He has learned, also, that he is not a law unto himself; that there is a Power outside him not himself that makes for righteousness; that forces for good do mysteriously prevail in this world, else long ago it would have passed away into nothing. An unnoticed sign of the existence of God pervading the world, is the gradual but evident extermination of evil from the world. We, individual men, repent and abandon our sin, and we are assured that in consequence our relation to God is right. But what becomes of the results of our sin, the ever-widening circle of the wave of a bad influence? If moral forces be indestructible, as physical force is said to be, then long ago the world must have become utterly corrupt and filled with violence. On the contrary, the history and the present conditions of human society demonstrate that the world is always growing better, that a mysterious process of moral and spiritual improvement is going on. How can we account for this removal of moral evil from the world, this extinction of sin, save by the presence of the Immanent Holy One, Who somehow neutralises the evils that men do which live after them, and which they are not able afterwards to remedy.

The immanence of God in His world is, therefore, like the presence of the holy waters of Ezekiel's vision, a presence at once vivifying and purifying. It is only this which gives us hope, and can save a tender and loving soul from utter despair. The beautiful idyl of the gospel brings to us light as from beyond the years, and hope profound as the fathomless love of God.

> "Is not God i' the world His power first made?
> Is not His love at issue still with sin
> Visibly, when a wrong is done on earth?"

Again and again by St. Paul is God named the Saviour, and yet we forget Jesus is a Saviour, just because He is the manifestation of the Saviour God. From this thought man learns also that somehow he has fallen back in the onward, upward movement of the universe of that Hidden Love by Whom are all things, through Whom are all things, and in Whom are all things. The prodigal returns to his father's house; but though thankful for the father's love, the reformed son can never be as if he had not once wasted his substance in riotous living. The story of Eden represents a psychical, if not an historical fact. Sin means loss, irretrievable loss; it means also inclination to further sin. In Jesus alone we trust. Against the impulse to sin, which, by the heredity of original sin is so strong within us, He fought and conquered, He alone; the brute inheritance He cast away. Therefore so can we. Thus He is our soul's Saviour, our only Redeemer, and in His will, as we make it ours, are we made holy. Let us then against a despondent pessimism, and an equally desperate positivism, preach Jesus, Who in His holiness demonstrated moral possibility and human perfectibility, in the removal of sins, and let us try to make clear what is that first function of the Church of God. Magnificent were the commission and power with which

Christ endowed His Church,[1] when He breathed upon it and said, "Receive ye the Holy Ghost: whose soever sins ye remit they are remitted unto them; and whose soever sins ye retain, they are retained." Not by any potent word of sacramental absolution are the sins of the world done away; that word, at its highest power, is but the assurance of a hope. But the actual removal of sins and evils is the serious and solemn work which has been given to the Church to perform in this world. The sorrows of human souls, their doubts, their fears, their desperation, their grief, their moral blindness, — these the Church is bidden to remove. The diseases, the pains, the social injustice and oppression, the inequalities and the harshness of commercial and social life, and all the manifold ills which in all days make human life sad, — these it is the duty of the Church to remove; these, first of all, gentlemen, in as far as you are endowed by the Church with a power of absolution, it is your duty to remove. Too long has the *parousia* of Christ been withheld from the world by the persistence in men's hearts of faith in survivals of magic and of mechanical religiosity. Too long the triumph of the Church has been delayed by the blindness of theologians and their indifference to social wrongs.

> "'Tis not by guilt the onward sweep
> Of truth and right, O Lord, we stay;

---

[1] St. John xx. 22, 23. Cf. St. Matt. xvi. 19; xviii. 18, 19.

> "Is not God i' the world His power first made?
> Is not His love at issue still with sin
> Visibly, when a wrong is done on earth?"

Again and again by St. Paul is God named the Saviour, and yet we forget Jesus is a Saviour, just because He is the manifestation of the Saviour God. From this thought man learns also that somehow he has fallen back in the onward, upward movement of the universe of that Hidden Love by Whom are all things, through Whom are all things, and in Whom are all things. The prodigal returns to his father's house; but though thankful for the father's love, the reformed son can never be as if he had not once wasted his substance in riotous living. The story of Eden represents a psychical, if not an historical fact. Sin means loss, irretrievable loss; it means also inclination to further sin. In Jesus alone we trust. Against the impulse to sin, which, by the heredity of original sin is so strong within us, He fought and conquered, He alone; the brute inheritance He cast away. Therefore so can we. Thus He is our soul's Saviour, our only Redeemer, and in His will, as we make it ours, are we made holy. Let us then against a despondent pessimism, and an equally desperate positivism, preach Jesus, Who in His holiness demonstrated moral possibility and human perfectibility, in the removal of sins, and let us try to make clear what is that first function of the Church of God. Magnificent were the commission and power with which

Christ endowed His Church,[1] when He breathed upon it and said, "Receive ye the Holy Ghost: whose soever sins ye remit they are remitted unto them; and whose soever sins ye retain, they are retained." Not by any potent word of sacramental absolution are the sins of the world done away; that word, at its highest power, is but the assurance of a hope. But the actual removal of sins and evils is the serious and solemn work which has been given to the Church to perform in this world. The sorrows of human souls, their doubts, their fears, their desperation, their grief, their moral blindness, — these the Church is bidden to remove. The diseases, the pains, the social injustice and oppression, the inequalities and the harshness of commercial and social life, and all the manifold ills which in all days make human life sad, — these it is the duty of the Church to remove; these, first of all, gentlemen, in as far as you are endowed by the Church with a power of absolution, it is your duty to remove. Too long has the *parousia* of Christ been withheld from the world by the persistence in men's hearts of faith in survivals of magic and of mechanical religiosity. Too long the triumph of the Church has been delayed by the blindness of theologians and their indifference to social wrongs.

"'Tis not by guilt the onward sweep
 Of truth and right, O Lord, we stay;

[1] St. John xx. 22, 23. Cf. St. Matt. xvi. 19; xviii. 18, 19.

> 'Tis by our follies that so long
> We hold the earth from Heaven away."

Let us then in our teaching reduce our Theology, if I may so say it, to sociology. Let us strive to make clear the moral, not magical, effect of the Divine Passion, thus freeing God from the inability to save His children, where the dogmas of scholastic theory have imprisoned Him in that marvellous, complex, and perplexing edifice of a Theology whose foundation is a substitutionary sacrifice, and whose windows are materialistic theories of the Sacraments.

THE RESURRECTION.

Εἶδος γάρ τι μεταβολῆς, καὶ πάντων ὕστατον, ἡ ἀνάστασις ἥ τε τῶν κατ' ἐκεῖνον τὸν χρόνον περιόντων ἔτι πρὸς τὸ κρεῖττον μεταβολή.
ATHENAGORAS, *On Resurrection*, XII.

The peculiar doctrine of Christianity is the Resurrection of the body, not the immortality of the soul.
EDGAR, *The Gospel of a Risen Saviour*.

    Sit if ye will, sit down upon the ground,
    Yet not to weep and wail, but calmly look around.
        Whate'er befell,
        Earth is not hell;
    Now, too, as when it first began,
    Life is yet life, and man is man.
    For all that breathe beneath the heaven's high cope,
    Joy with grief mixes, with despondence hope.
    Hope conquers cowardice; joy grief;
    Or at least, faith unbelief.
        Though dead, not dead;
        Not gone, though fled;
        Not lost, though vanished.
        In the great Gospel and true creed,
        He is yet risen indeed;
            Christ is yet risen.
A. H. CLOUGH, *Easter Day*.

'Αλλὰ φύσει οὖν τις ἡμῖν, θνητὸς φύσει ἐγένετο ὁ ἄνθρωπος; οὐδαμῶς. τί οὖν ἀθάνατος; οὐδὲ τοῦτο φαμέν. ἀλλὰ ἐρεῖ τίς οὐδὲν οὖν ἐγένετο, οὐδὲ τοῦτο. ἐγὼ μὲν, οὔτε οὖν φύσει θνητὸς ἐγένετο οὔτε ἀθάνατος. εἰ γὰρ ἀθάνατον αὐτὸν ἀπ' ἀρχῆς ἐπεποιήκει, Θεὸν αὐτὸν ἐπεποιήκει· πάλιν εἰ θνητὸν αὐτὸν πεποιήκει, ἐδόκει ἂν ὁ Θεὸς εἶναι τοῦ θανάτου αὐτοῦ· οὔτε οὖν ἀθάνατον αὐτὸν ἐποίησεν, οὔτε μὴν θνητὸν, ἀλλὰ καθὼς ἐπάνω προειρήκαμεν, δεκτικὸν ἀμφοτέρων· ἵνα ῥέψῃ ἐπὶ τὰ τῆς ἀθανασίας, τηρήσας τὴν ἐντολὴν τοῦ Θεοῦ, μισθὸν κομίσηται παρ' αὐτοῦ τὴν ἀθανασίαν, καὶ γένηται Θεός· εἰ δ' αὖ τραπῇ ἐπὶ τὰ τοῦ θανάτου πράγματα, παρακούσας τοῦ Θεοῦ, αὐτὸς ἑαυτῷ αἴτιος ᾖ τοῦ θανάτου.

THEOPHILUS OF ANTIOCH,
To Autolycus, Bk. II.

Sive ergo caro, secundum communem fidem, sive corpus, secundum Apostolum, dicitur quod resurget, ita credendum est, sicut Apostolus definivit, quia quod resurget, in virtute resurget, et in gloria; et incorruptibile resurget et spirituale corpus; quia corruptio incorruptionem non possidebit.

The Preface of Rufinus to St. Pamphilus' Apology for
Origen, ROUTH's <i>Reliquiæ Sacræ</i>, IV. 341.</div>

Particularly the Resurrection of our bodies, restoring our perfect manhood to us (a point wholly new to the world, which no Religion had embraced, no reason could descry), was hereby so exemplified, that considering it, we can hardly be tempted to doubt of what the gospel teacheth about it.

Dr. ISAAC BARROW, Works, II. 427.

SYNOPSIS.

INTRODUCTION:
    Relation of this subject to what has gone before.

I. — BIBLICAL THEOLOGY:
    a. The Resurrection of Jesus.
    b. The change in His body due to the victory of the spirit.
    c. Peculiarities of the risen body.
    d. Relation between the Resurrection of Christ and the Resurrection of the dead. The apostolic reception of the idea of the Resurrection.
    e. The Pauline development of the Resurrection.
    f. Moral Resurrection.
    g. Spiritual Resurrection.
    h. Cosmical Passion and Resurrection.
    The Resurrection an answer to Pessimism.

II. — TRADITIONAL THEOLOGY:
    The development of this Revelation in Historic Christianity was from the first not fully received. The opinion of Clement, of Ignatius, of Justin Martyr, of Epiphanius, Arius and Eusebius, of St. Irenæus, of Clement of Alexandria, of Theophilus of Antioch, and of Hippolytus touching the Resurrection.

III. — COMPARATIVE RELIGION:
    a. Theories of folk-faith which became factors in the development of the Christian Theology of the Resurrection. Jewish literalism and materialistic speculation.
    b. Early theories about the life of the ghost, in Semitic folk-faith, in Norse legend, and in mediæval and modern superstition.
    c. The Egyptian theory of the Resurrection of the body.

    d. Its influence upon the popular Religion and the Theology of the early Christians, and its survival to the present day. Its influence in the development of the cultus of relics and of some burial customs. Irreconcilable with the Pauline doctrine.

    e. Gross literalism in the early development of the Theology of the Resurrection and the influence of this literalism upon the religion of the Middle Ages. Aquinas's attempt to develop the doctrine of the Resurrection. The Resurrection in modern folk-faith.

    f. Some revivals of ancient and primitive theories offered as substitutes for the Christian doctrine of the Resurrection.

IV. — PRACTICAL CONCLUSION:

    The ethical force of the true teaching of the Resurrection, and its answer to the scientific and moral scepticism of the day. The Resurrection the necessary result of the Immanence of God in human consciousness and in the world.

THE RESURRECTION.

Gentlemen: —

Because in God we live, and move, and are, because the kingdom of God is as Leaven hidden in the meal of humanity, because by forgiveness of sin that vitalising Power permeates the deeds and the consciousness of men, transforming them as leaven transforms, it results that there is a Resurrection of the dead,[1] as the symbol of Constantinople correctly words it. It is congruous that we should come, after determinating what we mean by asserting the belief of a Triune God in the Church, and in remission of sins, to the Christian doctrine of the Resurrection. For such is the logical development of human receptiveness, and such is the eternal order in Divine operation. To believers only, Jesus after His Resurrection appeared. The sceptics of Emmaus did not discern their Lord until after their understanding had been opened.

I. *a.* Just what was the nature of the Resurrection of Christ? Of this we ought to have some definite opinion before we go on to discuss the Resurrection of the dead in general, because our Lord was " the first-

[1] ἀνάστασις νεκρῶν.

fruits of them that slept." His first proclamation of His own Resurrection was under the figure of the sign of the prophet Jonah,[1] who was sacrificed in order to propitiate a hostile power and yet appeared alive again. After the first important peculiarity, — namely, that He is the first to rise from the dead, — the second point to be noticed is that this rise shall be[2] "after three days," or, on the "third day." This is the next distinctive characteristic; but there is a much larger meaning which demands our attention.

b. In distinction from prevailing notions of the Resurrection, as I shall point out later, our Lord signifies that His uprise will be to a higher plane of existence,[3] where there is neither birth nor death. This characteristic of the Resurrection has not received the attention which its importance demands. This transition through death and Resurrection to loftier or larger conditions of life Jesus calls[4] a baptism, and the Resurrection life the new birth,[5] because it is a transition from a lower to a higher environment as physical birth is conceived to be individualisation of impersonal life. The Resurrection appears from this teaching of the New Testament to be a transition, that is, an ascent into superior conditions of existence. Yet from our Lord's words, "Destroy this temple, and

---

[1] St. Matt. xii. 40.   [4] St. Luke xii. 50.
[2] St. Mark. viii. 31; ix. 31; x. 34.
[3] St. Mark xii. 25.   [5] St. Matt. xix. 28, παλινγενεσία.

in three days I will raise it up," [1] and, "I have power [2] to lay down my life and power to take it again," it is evident that Christ's body is, before the Resurrection, and afterwards, essentially the same, however different the potencies and attributes. This body of our Lord underwent a change which we cannot describe, but of which the effects are definitely recorded. It was a process beginning with the dawn of His consciousness, and of this change the Transfiguration was a revelation. With the quickening of His God-consciousness those divine powers and operations which, in assuming the limited and progressive soul of a man as His organon He had relinquished, He gradually reassumed as these same powers assimilated and transmuted the deathfulness of His humanity. He increased in wisdom and in stature and in grace Godwards and manwards,[3] and learned obedience by the things He suffered in the days of His flesh.[4] This growth in righteousness and in the consequent keen discernment of what is righteousness with the expanding realisation of Infinite and Eternal realities, is spiritually the state of divine Sonship, a sonship born not of blood nor of the will of the flesh nor of the will of man, but of God,[5] and as He is, so

---

[1] St. John ii. 19.   [2] St. John x. 18, 19, ἐξουσία.

[3] χάριτι παρὰ Θεῷ καὶ ἀνθρώποις, St. Luke ii. 52. Winer, *Greek Grammar of N. T.* § 48, d.

[4] Heb. v. 7, 8.   σάρξ distinguishes the ante- from the post-resurrection body.   [5] St. John i. 12.

are we in the world;[1] that is to say, each man must pass through the human experience of Jesus Christ in His inner life. Now with the Incarnate Lord this growth or process was the gradual victory of the Spirit over the flesh, so that in some way the centre of vital energy, of desire and will, was removed from the exterior court of the body and of the soul, into the inner sanctuary of the Spirit and the Sanctum Sanctorum, where is the Shekina of God. This removal in one aspect is called metanoia. For this reason it was said that it was not possible that Jesus, Whose life's centre was removed into the sphere of the Eternal within Him, should be holden of death; because death is the victory of body over spirit. This vanquishment of body by spirit was utterly consummated in Gethsemane, and then and there Jesus became distinctly and abidingly conscious that His hour was come to pass up into that higher and interior sphere of existence where alone He could perfect His work of salvation. The death of Jesus was necessary not only as a supreme manifestation of whom He is, and whom He reveals, but also as the means of transition of His Divine-human Person to the next higher sphere of His humanity, — foreglimpse of that far-off divine event to which the whole creation moves. For His risen Body, which is identical in substance with the body of His Bethlehem birth, is nevertheless dominant over limitations of time, space, weight, impenetrability, and inertia.

[1] 1 John iv. 17.

c. It appears that at times His risen Body was luminous,[1] that He moved with the celerity of thought,[2] that He passed through closed doors, through the rock at the mouth of His tomb, and the swathings of His dead body, stiffened as they were with unguents, even retained somewhat the shape [3] of His body, as they lay in the tomb. Yet Jesus did not appear unclad.[4] He did take food,[5] and He points out to the disciples that a spirit, or ghost, has not flesh and bones [6] as He has.[7]

[1] St. John xxi. 4, πρωτας δὲ ἤδη γινομένης; Aquinas, *Summa*, III*a*. 54, 3, *et Supplem.* LXXXII. 1.

[2] *Summa*, III*a*. 84.

[3] St. John xx. 1–9.

[4] St. John xx. 15.

[5] St. Luke xxiv. 30, 43; St. John xxi. 13.

[6] St. Luke xxiv. 39; St. John xx. 27.

[7] So much has been made of this expression "flesh and bones," that a portentous structure of theology, the doctrine of the "Precious Blood," has been reared upon it. The curious may read on the subject De Ponte, V. 24; Suarez, III*a*. tom. ii.; Disp. XLVII. 3; St. Tom. Aquinas, III*a*. liv. 2. Aquinas acutely observes, "Sanguis autem ille qui in quibusdem ecclesiis pro reliquio conservatur, non fluxit de latere Christi, sed miraculo dicitur effluxisse de quadem imagine Christi percussa." See also De Maistre, *Soirées de St. Petersbourg*, II. Appendix; Delitzsch, *Bibl. Psychol.*, *passim;* Bengel, *Gnomen*, *Heb. xii. 24;* à Lapide, *1 Pet. 1–19.* The theory is that the blood of Christ arose apart from His body and is still separate, and beheld in heaven as the glassy flaming sea before the Throne. The idea has arisen probably from a too literal interpretation of the sacrificial offering of the blood wherein was the life, and from too great stress laid upon the death of Jesus as a propitiatory sacrifice. It is easy to see why Protestants hold-

d. The actual relation between the resurrection of Christ and that for which we say in the creed that we have an anticipation,[1] is expressed in His own words: "I am the Resurrection, and the life: He that believeth in me, though he were dead, yet shall he live: and whosoever liveth and believeth in me shall never die."[2] By the raising of Lazarus He uttered the same gospel; and yet a theology of transcendence has been virtually murmuring, "This is a hard saying; who can bear it?" and has gone about to invent a mechanical upraising for a spiritual uprising,—a power acting from without, instead of a vitalising energy from within. The way the earlier writers of the New Testament discuss the Resurrection of Jesus is striking, and of deep significance. They do not go about to prove the fact itself: for them there can be no more question of its reality than of the sun. They are filled with its light and splendour. Their attention is engaged in what the

ing such a theory of the Atonement as I describe in the last lecture (see p. 175) lean towards this speculation and allow it to affect their eucharistic doctrine. Scholastics, after Aquinas, insist that for the integrity of Christ's risen body the blood must have been entirely collected and placed in his veins. This doctrine is symbolised where you see in old paintings of the crucifixion angels holding a chalice to catch the flowing blood. On the other hand, the legend of the Holy Grail, imported into the West from Oriental folk-faith, shows how ancient and deep-seated and persistently surviving in the Teutonic mind was the anti-Thomist opinion of the permanent separation of the body and blood of Christ.

[1] προσδόκωμεν.   [2] St. John xi. 25, 26.

Resurrection reveals. In the light of Christ's Resurrection they see light, and the world appears to them as never before. The character and meaning of the Resurrection, rather than the bare fact of a miracle, occupy them. They do not search for evidences of the Resurrection, because the Resurrection is in itself to them an evidence of the largest significance. The Jews had required of Jesus a sign in the natural world, of His power and authority in the spiritual realm.[1] The apostles confidently gave the signs of His authority and power in the spiritual world as proof of His power in the natural world. What caused this reversal of logic? The mental attitude of the disciples had been uplifted to a plane where they endured as seeing Him who is invisible; they had mounted to those high, shining tablelands of spiritual consciousness and comprehension to which our God Himself is sun and moon. The New Testament-writers exult in the larger thought which had come to them when Christ said, "Touch me not"; for while they flagged not in affection for the Christ with Whom they had walked in the ways of Galilee, Samaria, and Judea, they nevertheless beheld, as it were, the Christ Who is now in the whole world, the essential Christ Whose law of life became manifest to them wherever they looked, Whose face, grown large

---

[1] In one instance, at any rate, Jesus afforded this sign, the healing of the paralytic (St. Matt. ix. 6), to which I have already made reference. The sign had a peculiar significance.

as the boundless stretch of the heavens, looked down upon them, — a countenance blessed and beautiful, — "*Aspettata in ciel beata e bella Anima.*" Also for us, again, in these latest days, the ethical and cosmical resurrection process is become proof[1] which is sufficient, clear, and unshakable of the historic uprise of Jesus Christ from the dead. Unless, indeed, there be a Resurrection, the world is a vulgar, paltry, squalid town of banishment, "where," says one, "with the shifting dust we play and eat the bread of discontent." Straightway after the Resurrection, or rather after Pentecost, the apostles proceeded to develop the grand and inspiring doctrine of the resurrection of the dead.

e. St. Paul began with asserting that Jesus is the power of God unto salvation,[2] a salvation from death[3] through the rectification[4] of life, due to our Lord as a revealer[5] of what righteousness is, and what is its operation unto deathlessness.[6] The apostle goes on to declare that the inner force which Jesus has liberated in the world is not a theory or a doctrine, but a positive power,[7] which makes men saved, safe, sound, healthy, holy,[8] and causes the

---

[1] Renan, *Les Apôtres,* 44.   [2] Rom. i. 16.
[3] Rom. v. 18–21.   [4] δικαίωσις.   [5] Rom. i. 17.
[6] St. John vi. 39.   [7] 1 Cor. iv. 20, δύναμις.
[8] Rom. i. 16; 1 Thes. v. 9; 2 Thes. ii. 13; 2 Tim. ii. 10; Rom. iv. 25. Weiss, *Bible Theol.* I. 434, appears to have forgotten this when he remarked concerning Jesus, "His Resurrection has not, like His death, a significance as being the means of procuring salva-

Resurrection of the dead. Hence St. Paul evidently doubts [1] a uniform Resurrection of the dead; he himself strains every power to attain unto the better Resurrection by living into the life of Jesus Christ. Consequently, while St. Paul cannot be said to deny [2] the Resurrection of the wicked, he certainly does contemplate a distinction between the Resurrection of the just and that of the unjust; for, to go no further, he said that every seed would have its own body, and that one star would differ from another star in glory, in the Resurrection of the dead. He also distinguishes former resuscitations; *e.g.* of the widow's sons in the Old Testament from the better Resurrection [3] coming from Jesus, the First-fruits [4] of them that slept. The evangelist in recounting the miracles of Christ's raising from death Jairus' daughter, the widow's son of Nain and his friend

---

tion." Without the Resurrection, the death of Jesus could not atone. The death of Jesus upon which Paul laid stress was a death unto sin; this was the atoning death, of which the physical death was the last number of the series. 2 Cor. v. 19 ; Gal. iii. 13, iv. 4 ; Rom. viii. 3.

[1] Phil. iii. 10.

[2] It is not true for Weiss to say, II. 89, I. 57, that a Resurrection of the godless may not be assumed from the New Testament, for see St. John v. 25, or that St. Paul does not know of such a Resurrection, for see Acts xxiv. 15. The wicked, it is true, are already judged, Weiss, II. 4, 18, n. *b*, but, for that matter, so have the righteous passed from death unto life.

[3] Heb. xi. 35.

[4] 1 Cor. xv. 20.

Lazarus, uses not the word meaning to resurrect, but that which signifies to awake or to arouse.[1]

f. This better Resurrection is a transformation of the corruptible and psychical into the incorruptible and pneumatical body.[2] Lotze's observation,[3] is therefore strictly in the Pauline spirit, when he says that a Resurrection of the same material body would mean only a continuance of this life during the existence of the body which it animates. St. Paul teaches a change and a transformation of the body, but no loss of substantial identity and continuity. The natural body is evolved in this life from the Psyche (or soul), the heavenly body is evolved from the Pneuma (or spirit). Thus much concerning the Pauline psychology: more would be beyond our purpose. St. Peter [4] likewise calls attention to the spiritual body of the Resurrection of our Lord, intimating that it belongs, like baptism, to the process of the justification, which we have seen to be the rectification of life. He also shows that the energy, or dynamic impulse, to Resurrection is essentially within man, and that it resides in his pneuma, or spirit.[5] It is clear that this spiritual Resurrection of Jesus is only the starting-point

---

[1] Not ἀνάστασις, but ἔγερσις, St. Mark v. 41; St. Luke viii. 54, vii. 14; St. John xii. 1. See St. Matt. xxvii. 53, for the ἔγερσις, not ἀνάστασις, of the saints at the crucifixion.

[2] 1 Cor. xv. 43–52.   [3] *Microcosmos*, 480.   [4] 1 Pet. iii. 21.

[5] 1 Pet. iii. 18. Cf. Weiss, *Bibl. Theol.* I. 229, n.

and the impulse of the general Resurrection of the body. It is, in fact, the first Resurrection, and mention is made of it in Rev. xx. 5. I understand that it was concerning this spiritual Resurrection, which is the ground and condition of the bodily Resurrection, that our Lord spoke when he said of some that [now] "they have eternal life; . . . they have [already] passed from death unto life," and that they will not taste death because, at the last day, He essentially having permeated them, will raise them up.[1] It was a misunderstanding of these words concerning the spiritual process of the Resurrection which anciently caused Hymenæus and Philetus "to err concerning the truth, saying that the Resurrection is passed already,"[2] so that no other is to come; and this obsolete heresy has in our own day been revived by rationalism, theosophy, and Christian science.

g. St. Paul after thus evolving the Christian idea of the Resurrection of the dead, until it is presented as a rise to a higher plane, by the out-working and unveiling in Jesus of the hidden Love Who is deathless Life, finds that this wonderful reality has also a subjective application which is quite true; a death unto sin and a Resurrection unto righteousness.

"Yea, the Resurrection and Uprise
To the right hand of the Throne — what is it beside,

---

[1] Weidener, *Bibl. Theol. of the New Testament*, I. 109; Milligan, *Revelation of St. John*, 226, note *b*, and Appendix II.
[2] 2 Tim. ii. 18.

> When such truth, breaking bounds, o'erfloods my soul,
> And as I saw sin and death, even so
> See I the need and transiency of both,
> The good and glory consummated thence."

h. There is in that golden letter attributed to James, the brother of the Lord, a striking expression, of which we could easily make too much, as probably Jacob Böhmen did. St. James alludes to the " wheel of nature,"[1] which, if we might be allowed to use Hegelian phrase, should be translated the *Wheel of Becoming*, *i.e.* of continually coming into existence. From a certain attitude, nature has seemed to man nothing other than such a vast, terrific whirl. To the man of sensibility there is something even more than saddening in this aspect; the conflict in nature is a bitter tragedy. The world of animal life is filled with cruelty, ferocity, and crime. Violence could almost be termed the condition of lower animal existence. Everywhere the strong preys upon the weak, everywhere there are terror and flight, rapacity and pursuit. From the tiniest insect to the strongest kings of the carnivora, each animal destiny is a lifelong, incessant warfare. Everywhere nature, like the Hindu goddess Kali, is smeared with blood and cruelty. How much better is the aspect when we mount from wild beasts to the higher stage of civilised man, nay, even to the region and history of religion? Taking a generality familiar to all: At

---

[1] iii. 6, τροχὸς τῆς γενέσεως

the beginning it seemed for the first six centuries that Christianity was destined to cover the whole earth, as the waters cover the sea. The Church waxed rich and splendid and powerful, kings sat in her councils and her word went forth into all lands; but in the seventh century arose a hostile power, Islam, that rode forth in the name of the Prophet, with the scimitar and with fire. Like a tornado or the forest conflagration, it spread rapidly and irresistibly until itself became convinced that its inheritance was nothing less than the whole earth. But Islam, too, was checked in its onward spread, and for centuries its boundaries have not been enlarged. Then rose the Papacy of the Middle Ages, the power and the recognised authority. It ruled the kings of the earth with a rod of iron, and broke them in pieces like a potter's vessel. In the days of Gregory and Innocent and Boniface, men could imagine no power likely to arise upon earth which could ever check the sway of God's vice-gerent. But Protestantism arose and swept across Europe, sudden, swift as a whirlwind, and the splendid fabric of the popes melted away like cloud cities. Scarcely a century had past when Protestantism, too, had reached its limits, and to a standstill it came and at a standstill it has since remained. With the fall of the ideal of the rule of the Church arose the ideal of the rule of kings; but that, too, has gone the way of human theories, and, in our own time, the conflict which has arisen is not over the throne of pope or of king, but it is the tense, hand to hand, silent, terrific struggle of class with class. And as Nature in her blindness is filled with fierce and deadly conflict, so history demonstrates that human life, in all its various manifestations, is but a succession of strifes, of bitterness, and of pain: as one who would seem to have ascended to the Olympian heights of calm intellectual mood, and there in philosophic satisfaction had donned his singing robes, chants to us, —

> "Like a vast wheel that spins through humming air,
> And time, life, death, are sucked within its breath,
> And thrones and kingdoms like sere leaves are hurled
> Down to its maelstrom; for its wind of death
> Sweeps the wide skies, and shakes the flaring suns,
> So fast the wheel spins, and the glory runs."

The facts of history and of life, such as these, have brought us in our own days face to face with a practical problem of thought, with the riddle of things which has been called "the mystery of pain." This question which presses upon the teachers of religion cannot be ignored as one of mere theory. It is a fundamental question of living thought, "Why is the world so filled with agony of mind and of flesh?" It is a question which seems unanswerable, which, in melancholy minds of pessimists, has suggested the poetical idea of *Weltschmerz*. The philosopher has suggested that it is inconceivable that God should have created a world in which these very conditions of conflict should not press upon us, in which gloom and perhaps despair should not prevail. Pain must predominate in the world; it is the potency of life and progress, and must equal, if it do not outweigh, pleasure; because of the pain and lassitude which inevitably follow when the nervous excitement which we call pleasure ceases. The exhaustion of the nerve force in pleasure weakens the pleasure and becomes pain, so that it is difficult to distinguish between the highest degrees of pleasure and of pain. We weep for joy as well as for sorrow; an extremely high musical tone causes a sensation difficult to discriminate — is it pleasurable or is it painful? "Our sweetest songs are those that tell of saddest thought." The reason of this is that pleasure may be characterised as indirect; it is relief from pain, and arises simply from the sense of relativity. Hope, which is the mainspring of all life, which is the spur to all endeavour, gives but a momentary satisfaction in the attainment of its end; it is the pleasing anxiety of hope, which of itself is a pain, that makes existence possible. Gratification, satiation, would result in repose, stagnation, and consequently in death. Finally, pain, by its very nature, more easily than pleasure, enters into human consciousness; hence pain, it would seem, must always outweigh pleasure.

Now, even if we do not agree with Von Hartmann, the statement of Mr. Hinton is hardly controvertible:[1] "A life from which everything which has in it the element of pain is banished becomes a life not worth having; or worse, of intolerable tedium and disgust. There is ample proof in the experience of the foolish among the rich that no course is more fatal to pleasure than to succeed in putting aside everything that can call for endurance. The stronger and more generous faculties of our nature, debarred from their true exercise, avenge themselves by poisoning and embittering all that remains." From this it is clear, that when we carefully examine the contributions of philosophers towards a solution of the problem of pain, we discover that they do scarcely more than restate the question in terms which are rigidly positive and pitiless. The ancients, gazing at the great whirl of life, the relentless turning of the "Wheel of Becoming," conceived it to be the manifestation of the wrath of the gods, a vortex of blind necessity, or the twirl of the distaff of Clotho, who spins the fate of souls and spheres. But in the vivid light of the riven tomb, St. Paul discerns that this universe, which is the progressive utterance of Infinite Love, is going through a vast passion, which is the tragic drama of its time history, until, through the awakening of the divine sonship in each man, and the consequent spiritualisation of his body, there will be a passage and a return of the universe unto the spiritual sphere. If, therefore, we are puz-

[1] *Mystery of Pain*, 47.

zled by the enigma of life, and by that passion as manifest in humanity as in nature, by the martyrdom of man which saddened Æschylus and Buddha and many a man since, we shall find the only solution in the principle that St. Paul dwells upon as the manifestation of the Resurrection.

The passion which is in the heart of Divine Love reveals itself alike in the heart of man, in the process of nature, and on the Cross of Calvary.

> "God draws a cloud over each gleaming morn, —
>   Would you ask why?
> It is because all noblest things are born
>   In agony.
> Only upon some cross of pain and woe
>   God's Son may lie:
> Each soul redeemed from self and sin must know
>   Its Calvary."

The epistle to the Romans contains Paul's rationale of the struggle for existence, which, based upon the principle of the Resurrection, is his solution of the problem of the existence of evil, sin, and death. He says, "I reckon that the Passion of the present is of no account in comparison with the glory that shall be revealed to-usward. For the earnest expectation of creation awaiteth the revealing of the Sons of God. For creation was subjected to vanity not of its own choice, but by reason of Him who hath subjected it in the hope that even creation shall be liberated from the bondage of the corruption into the glorious freedom of the children of God. For we know that the whole creation groaneth together, and suffereth birth-pangs until now. And not only that, but ourselves also, though we have the first-fruits of the spirit, groan together within ourselves awaiting an adoption which is the emancipation of our body. For we by hope were saved."[1]

I take these words of St. Paul to mean that the Resurrection through Jesus is that liberation or emancipation which he terms the redemption of our body. I never think on these words of St. Paul without recollecting the admirable exposition of them made by Mr. Fiske in his *Destiny of Man*, and afterwards summed up in the *Idea of God:* "We see man still the crown of the universe and the chief object of divine care, yet still the lame and halting creature, loaded with a semi-brute inheritance of original sin, whose ultimate salvation is slowly to be achieved through ages of moral discipline. We see the chief agency which produced him,—natural selection which always works through strife,

[1] λογίζομαι γὰρ ὅτι οὐκ ἄξια τὰ παθήματα τοῦ νῦν καιροῦ πρὸς τὴν μέλλουσαν δόξαν ἀποκαλυφθῆναι εἰς ἡμᾶς. ἡ γὰρ ἀποκαραδοκία τῆς κτίσεως τὴν ἀποκάλυψιν τῶν υἱῶν τοῦ Θεοῦ ἀπεκδέχεται. τῇ γὰρ ματαιότητι ἡ κτίσις ὑπετάγη, οὐκ ἑκοῦσα, ἀλλὰ διὰ τὸν ὑποτάξαντα, ἐφ' ἐλπίδι διότι καὶ αὐτὴ ἡ κτίσις ἐλευθερωθήσεται ἀπὸ τῆς δουλίας τῆς φθορᾶς εἰς τὴν ἐλευθερίαν τῆς δόξης τῶν τέκνων τοῦ Θεοῦ. οἴδαμεν γὰρ ὅτι πᾶσα ἡ κτίσις συστενάζει καὶ συνωδίνει ἄχρι τοῦ νῦν· οὐ μόνον δέ, ἀλλὰ καὶ αὐτοὶ τὴν ἀπαρχὴν τοῦ πνεύματος ἔχοντες, ἡμεῖς καὶ αὐτοὶ ἐν ἑαυτοῖς στενάζομεν υἱοθεσίαν ἀπεκδεχόμενοι, τὴν ἀπολύτρωσιν τοῦ σώματος ἡμῶν. τῇ γὰρ ἐλπίδι ἐσώθημεν. Rom. viii. 18–25.

— ceasing to operate upon him, so that until human strife shall be brought to an end there goes on a struggle between his lower and higher impulses, in which the higher must finally conquer. And in all this we find the strongest possible incentive to right living, yet one that is the same in principle with that set forth by the great Teacher who first brought men to the knowledge of the true God."[1]

Clearlier in the run of the ages is the Divine developed in human consciousness, and the broken spectrum of the One Light[2] loses its dark lines. Modern science, which some men have distrusted as utterly godless, is making thought receptive of the most spiritual teaching of Jesus. The hidden Leaven of Divine Life is leavening the world, and the Church, and the souls of men, is solving the dark problem of evil, and is atoning pain and love. The strife of the world is a redemptive process, an upward stress of the Life that permeates and pervades star mists and saints. Of this interpretation of God in human destiny an apt symbol was set forth by the magic hall which Merlin reared for Arthur's court: —

> "Four great zones of sculpture, set betwixt
> With many a mystic symbol, gird the hall:
> And in the lowest beasts are slaying men,
> And in the second men are slaying beasts,
> And on the third are warriors, perfect men,
> And on the fourth are men with growing wings,

[1] John Fiske, *Idea of God*, 165.   [2] 1 John i. 5.

> And over all, one statue ... with a crown,
> And peak'd wings pointed to the Northern Star."

Finally, though we do hereupon, with the sanction of Biblical Theology, affirm the Resurrection of the dead as a result, or a moment, in that process which is both individual and universal,[1] because of the nature of the Immanent God, Who is Love, Who is Life, we no more deny that God raises the dead than we deny that God creates us; albeit by the process of natural generation.

II. Although the apostles, and Paul in particular, spread out such a grand exposition of the Christian idea of the Resurrection, yet the sub-apostolic ages made little further progress; to that "fugitive and gracious light shy to illumine" their receptiveness was blinded. Indeed, owing to the survival of cruder notions, and also to the influence of philosophy, there was among the Patristic writers a distinct retrogression of consciousness of the idea of the Resurrection. The first epistle of Clement draws its argument for the Resurrection from the worn example of the Phœnix, of pagan fable, and cites the Old Testament, and not the New, in support of the doctrine. It shows a complete misapprehension of the Resurrection of those who are made alive in Christ. In that homily, commonly called the Second Epistle of Clem-

---

[1] It is from ignoring this truth of St. Paul's that Weiss finds Rom. iv. 25 and vi. to be unintelligible, and denies by innuendo a Resurrection of the wicked. Cf. *Bibl. Theol.* I. 437, 5.

THE RESURRECTION.

ent to the Corinthians, a materialistic theory of Resurrection is boldly expressed as "in this very flesh."[1] St. Ignatius, however, in his opinion of the Resurrection, perceives no distinction between the flesh[2] and the body.[3] Tatian[4] points out that the Christian idea of the Resurrection differs from that of the Platonists, Stoics, and Epicureans. With the Stoics, Tatian conceives of a cyclic consummation,[5] when the dispersed particles of the body shall be recongregated, and there will be a Resurrection of bodies.[6] In this theory of Tatian we perceive a survival of the theory of the Egyptians. According to this view the world will last only so long as enough shall have lived on it to require, at the consummation of the cycle, all the particles of matter to recompose their bodies. What standing-ground will then be left for the bodies thus resuscitated? Justin Martyr had ideas which were altogether as crude. In one place[7] he teaches a double Resurrection, and in another[8] a single Resurrection. His formula is the "resurrection of the dead,"[9] and it is evident that in one place by his reference to St. Matt. xxii. 29, 31, he may not necessarily mean by "the dead,"[10] corpses. Epiphanius, the Orthodox, is contented to say "resurrection of dead,"[11] while

---

[1] ἐν τῇ σαρκὶ ταύτῃ.   [2] σάρξ.
[3] σῶμα. See Bp. Lightfoot's *Apostolic Fathers*.
[4] c. vi.   [5] συντέλεια.   [6] ἀνάστασις σωμάτων.
[7] *Apol.* 81.   [8] *Apol.* 52.   [9] ἀνάστασις τῶν νεκρῶν.
[10] νεκροί.   [11] ἀνάστασις νεκρῶν.

Arius, the arch-heretic, and Eusebius, the semi-Arian, stickle for "resurrection of flesh."[1] The theory that the Resurrection of the wicked ought to be in the flesh,[2] in order that in the flesh they might suffer appropriate torments, was certainly the popular Jewish opinion of that day, and gained authority from our Lord's use of the phraseology then in vogue. Though subtly it implies a dualism, nevertheless it was adopted by many of the Fathers, and ran its course through the Middle Ages, as may be seen in many a painted window, carving, and mural painting in the Gothic churches. These grotesque fancies of retribution were abundantly ridiculed by Rabelais and Quevedo y Villegas. One has only to read over the entertaining tales of the *Legenda Aurea*, and the quaint dramas of the Middle Ages, to be impressed with the certainty that these notions of the Resurrection were nothing better than survivals of ancient fancies, of Tartarus, of the Egyptian land of Amenti, of the Hindu abode of the dewas, of the dusty subterranean kingdom of the Akkadian god Mul-lil, lord of the ghost world, and, further back, of the ghost land of primitive folk-faith.

St. Irenæus[3] denies that man is essentially immortal. Immortality he takes to be the gift of God, Who by some interior operation of the consecrated elements of the Eucharist,[4] will cause the particles of

---

[1] ἀνάστασις σαρκός.   [3] *Against Heresies*, V.
[2] σάρξ.   [4] *Against Heresies*, V. 3.

the body to reintegrate and be revivified. Perhaps it was a belief like this which caused the Christians of the Catacombs to place the Eucharistic food in the mouth of the corpse before it was walled up in its narrow bed. St. Irenæus, speaking of the Resurrection, uses the term "raising from dead."[1] In one place,[2] the thought of Irenæus is that the indwelling Holy Spirit does by His gifts transmute the animal or psychical (commonly called carnal) into the spiritual body; and again by his expression, "laver that leads to incorruption,"[3] he has been understood to imply that Holy Baptism is the beginning of that process which culminates in the Resurrection of the dead. This we may accept as true, if the inward and spiritual grace of man corresponds to the outward and visible sign. St. Clement of Alexandria[4] does distinctly join immortality with baptismal regeneration. Theophilus of Antioch of all the anti-Nicene Fathers appears to have afforded to the teachings of apostolic tradition the most considerable receptivity. By analogy of the processes of the natural body, Theophilus indicates what may be conjectured of the Resurrection of the spiritual body. Tertullian, who wrote a treatise *On the Resurrection of the Flesh*, believed not in a Resurrection, but in a resuscitation of the flesh, into which the soul is recalled; as you might see pictured in the sepulchral

---

[1] ἔγερσις ἐκ νεκρῶν.
[2] *Heresies*, I. 10.
[3] *Against Heresies*, III. 17, 2.
[4] *Pæd.* I. 6.

pictures and in the Book of the Dead of ancient Egypt, where with a magic touch of the crux ansata, the jackal-headed god Anubis calls back to the mummy its soul, which is represented in the form of a winged creature; or as the Greek Hermes Psychopompos was fancied by the Neoplatonists and like mystics to resuscitate the dead. The pictures on the walls of the Catacombs show that these pagan beliefs had passed over into Christianity. It is by a poor evasion that Tertullian expounds [1] Paul's words, "Flesh and blood shall not inherit the kingdom of God," to signify only fleshly works. In this he had, however, the bad example of what Irenæus had written [2] a few years before. St. Hippolytus says that the unrighteous will receive their bodies unransomed from the bondage of disease and pain,[3] but the risen bodies of the godly will be not able to suffer.[4] The gross judaising of the Western theologians in the second century appears distinctly at the close of Irenæus' great work [5] where he says that this earth will be renewed in order that the risen flesh may dwell in it. Since Irenæus omits to inform us what earth sinners are to inhabit, we might infer from this and from other passages [6] that he did not believe in a Resurrection

[1] *On Res.* 50.   [2] *Heresies*, V. 3, 9.   [3] φθορά.
[4] *Against Plato.*   [5] *Against Heresies*, V. 36.
[6] *Against Heresies*, II. 34; V. Cf. St. Theophilus to Autolicus, II. 37; Tatian, *Ag. the Greeks*, XIII.; St. Justin Martyr, *Tryph.* V.; St. Athan., *Against the Gentiles*, II. 14–16; *On Incarnation*, III., also IV.

of the unjust. From all this it is sufficiently evident that anti-Nicene theology was hindered by survivals of folk-faith from receiving the gospel of the Resurrection. From the second century to our own day the Idols[1] of the Den and of the Theatre, *i.e.* folk-faith and philosophy, have dominated the thought of the Christian theology of Resurrection.

III. *a.* Let us now turn and examine this folk-faith. For the aspiration of the Jew at our Lord's time, the land of Canaan sufficed for an everlasting Heaven. The Jew was nothing if not literal. He read the rolls of the ancient prophets, and from them he understood that upon his own Mount Zion should be set up the literal throne of the Messiah, and there should be his Court and Hall of Audience; thence should emanate decrees levying taxes upon all the nations of the earth for the benefit of the remnant of Israel. The Messiah's Kingdom which the Jew of that day expected was a veritable empire of the world, an autocracy more sublime and opulent than dreamed of by the Julian Cæsars. It was said that in the Messiah's day it would come to pass that each Jew would have twenty-eight hundred slaves, and that his other wealth would be simply beyond calculation. To this Paradise on earth the good Jew was to be revivified, said the Pharisee, and that by means of some indestructible germ of life, some part of the body which could not decay. The story goes that a Roman emperor once demanded of a

---

[1] See above, page 3.

Jewish Rabbi how it was possible that there could be a Resurrection of the dead after their bodies had long been completely dissipated through corruption and decay. The answer given was that there is in the body a bone called luz, the *os sacrum*,[1] which is indestructible, and which contains the germ of life, retaining it to the Resurrection. Then the emperor made a test; a luz bone was procured, it was boiled, was put into fire; with pestle and mortar, with sledge and anvil, they tried to pulverise and destroy this bone. No success. Even acids would not eat it. The emperor was convinced. Some supposed that the indestructible germ of human life resided in some bone, in the shape of a small hair-like worm. Descartes put the seat of the soul in the pineal gland. Paley and Bishop Courtenay believed that the mind utterly perished with the body, but at the Resurrection God called it anew into existence.

[1] It is possible that this legend about the os sacrum had an Egyptian origin, because in Egypt the os sacrum was a symbol of eternal goodness, as the permanent and imperishable foundation of all things. This bone, together with a heart surmounted by a cross, was often pictured upon Egyptian coffins, and in Egypt it denoted a son devoted to his father. In Christianity the symbol has in part survived in the cult of the Sacred Heart. The late Dr. Lundy told me that he was one of a party in Egypt who had procured a mysterious bundle of some mummified object. After unrolling many a wind of cloth they found carefully preserved in the centre an os sacrum. See *Horapollinis Hieroglyphica*, II. 10,—διότι δυσπαθές ἐστι τὸ τοῦ ζῴου ὀστέον; and Sharp, *Vocabulary of Egyptian Hieroglyphics*, 624, 625, 1012.

To return to Jewish theology: the Rabbi Eleazar asked, "And will not the righteous that die outside the land of Israel live again?" Rabbi Illaa replied, "They will, by rolling" (underground to the land of Israel). Rabbi Abba Salla Rabbah put forward a very forceful question in regard to this, viz.: "Will not the rolling occasion distress to the righteous?" Abaii replied, "Tunnels will be made for them through the ground." Carna said, "There is reason in the words, 'And thou shalt carry me out of Egypt, and bury me in their burying-place,' Gen. xlvii. 30; for our father Jacob knew that he was a perfectly righteous man, and if the dead outside the land of Israel will live again, why should he trouble his son to carry him out of Egypt? The reason is he feared lest, if buried in Egypt, he might not be worthy enough to escape the distress of rolling through the subterranean tunnels from his grave to the land of Israel."[1] Such is the Jewish theology of the Talmud, and I am told that to this very day Polish Jews will bury wooden forks with their dead in order that at the last day the dead resuscitated may burrow their way underground from where they lie to the land of Canaan, when they will emerge to the surface of the soil.[2] So the Christians of the Middle Ages would bury in a campo santo, in soil brought from the Holy Land (as now we use conse-

---

[1] *Kethuboth*, fol. IIIa.
[2] Hershon, *Treasures of the Talmud*, 285.

crated ground), and they would inter the corpse with its face to the East, in order that at the Resurrection the man might face the literal geographical region whence Christ should come to judge. The sun-myth has, I grant you, been worn to rags, but this concept of the coming of Christ from the literal East is nothing other than a survival of an element of the solar myth. The early Christians, says Aristides in his *Apology*, forbade the burning of bodies as sacrilegious, for it militated against the idea of the Resurrection of the body. There is upon the earth more than one race of mankind which will not eat of "the sinew which shrank," *nervus ischiadicus*, because they believe it to be the germ of the Resurrection body.[1] Shall we therefore wonder that in such an environment, even the sweet reasonableness of the Alexandrians was confused, and that Origen, as it appears, thought that the Resurrection would be due to the permanence of some organ or atom of the body, and that the Resurrection body itself would assume the convenient shape of a globe.

b. Back of this notion of the Resurrection, or rather resuscitation, through the endurance of the life principle in some incorruptible material portion of the body, lies a more ancient concept. The patriarch Joseph requested that his body should be embalmed and carried to Canaan in order that he might sleep with his fathers. This desire, so frequently

[1] *Religion of the Semites*, 360, n. 2 ; *Golden Bough*, II. 126.

found expressed in the Hebrew Scriptures, answers to the actual Semitic folk-faith. It is not a figure of speech. According to this faith the dead in their tombs slept, and dreamed, and sometimes became distinctly awake to the affairs of the world outside the walls of their vaults. To this folk-faith at least one reference occurs in the gospels.[1] For the Jews said that when the tribes were carried away to captivity, sounds of weeping and lamentation were heard, as they passed along by it, from within the tomb of their great ancestress Rachel. The Northern nations had a similar belief,[2] that the dead dwelt inside the barrows, the great family burial mounds, and there in the darkest depth of night they awoke from their slumber and held unholy revels. Later on, the people of mediæval Europe believed that Charlemagne, crowned and throned in the burial crypt beneath the dome at Aachen, was only sleeping and waiting to start up into life, and at the last extremity to defend his realm against the Norsemen, who already in his lifetime had caused the great emperor a foreboding unto tears. Barbarossa, too, as we all know well, sits in solemn death slumber, beneath the Kyffhausberg, while the watchful eagles circle round the mountain peak, and whisper in the ear of the dead emperor the course of events as Christendom passes through the years of

---

[1] St. Matt. ii. 18; Jer. xxxi. 15.
[2] *Corp. Poet. Boreale*, II. 4, 14, and elsewhere.

its history. Thus in the ancient Norse myth the ravens of Odin, flying in circles about his head, spied out the doings of the world and reported them to the All-Father. Our own Western Indians will talk to the skull of a relative, or they will whisper in the ear of a corpse the message which they desire to send to their dead ancestors. We ourselves speak of our dead as "turning in their graves," when anything occurs which we feel sure would have distressed them if still in life. Pins, we know, should never be put in a shroud, for they are disagreeable to the dead. In the city of Birmingham, England, in the year 1886, a dead body was exhumed in order that the pins that had been put in the shroud might be removed, and the dead lie in comfort in the grave.[1] In Ireland, to this day, it is believed that the touch of the hand of a corpse will cause milk to flow. Among English peasants we are told that it is not uncommon to seek the cure of disease from the touch of a dead man's hand; and it is notorious in ecclesiastical annals that in Corfu the consecration of the bishop is effected by the imposition of the dead hand of St. Spiridion, the only extant Nicene Father. From all this it is clear that the primitive belief that the soul of the dead remains attached to the body has never entirely perished out of modern civilisation. Mediæval Europe, driven nigh to madness by wars of Investiture, Crusades,

[1] *Folklore Journal*, V. 162.

Papal Interdicts, the Black Death, and the Dancing Mania, saw skeletons rise from their graves, and with bitter satire dance the dance of death. This same survival of the pagan theory of the persistent continuance of the soul with the body is most admirably set forth in Robert Browning's poem, *The Bishop orders His Tomb at St. Praxed's Church*, where the dying man says to his sons: —

> "I shall fill my slab of basalt there,
> And 'neath my tabernacle take my rest. . . .
> And then how I shall lie through centuries,
> And hear the blessed mutter of the mass,
> And see God made and eaten all day long,
> And feel the steady candle-flame, and taste
> Good, strong, thick, stupefying incense-smoke!
> . . . Leave me in my church, the church for peace,
> That I may watch at leisure if he leers . . .
> Old Gandolf, at me, from his onion-stone."

c. It was the ancient Egyptian opinion that if the corpse of a man could be kept from decay for three thousand years, a cycle during which one of its several souls, the *ba*, completed a period of existence in the land of Amenti, the ghost world, then the *ba* soul, and also the *ka* soul, which had during this period remained in the tomb, and must be furnished with food and drink, would return to their former body and revivify it,[1] or in lieu of the body, the *ba* would

---

[1] J. A. S. Grant Bey, *Ancient Egyptian Religion;* Renouf, Hibbert Lectures.

take up with a clever portrait image and reanimate it. It is to this belief that we owe the remarkable realistic statues of earliest Egyptian art, the portrait statue of the Lady Nefert, who died some six thousand years ago, and of Khaf-ra, who departed this life three thousand six hundred and sixty-six years before our era,[1] leaving a large number of images of himself in order that when, at the end of the cycle of three thousand years, the *ba* soul returned from the land of Amenti, it might not fail to find at least one form to inhabit. This doctrine of resuscitation was the core of the Egyptian theory. Their speculative theology was embodied in the myth of Osiris, and, with their moral theology, in the Book of the Dead. Both of these were concerned with the revivification of the body. The lifelong purpose of the Egyptian was by any means to attain unto the Resurrection of the dead. The likeness of the story of the passion, death, and resuscitation of Osiris to the Christian gospel was recognised by Tertullian, — and why? Because Tertullian held not the Christian idea of Resurrection taught by Jesus, and rehearsed by Paul, but rather a superstition, not yet in these days of ours abandoned, that the soul or spirit is material. Hence Tertullian sees no impropriety in styling Osiris the Egyptian Christ. It is

---

[1] Brugsch, *Egypt under the Pharaohs*, 37. It is probable that to this belief the Greeks owed their first Art impulse, for they derived their earliest Art from Egypt at this period.

clear from his treatises[1] that Tertullian held the Egyptian doctrine of resuscitation and not the Christian doctrine of Resurrection. Tertullian's phrase[2] is "with the restitution of flesh."[3]

d. The Catacombs prove that folk-faith rather than philosophy closed the consciousness, of the Roman Church at any rate, against the Christian doctrine. For lamps were shut in with the corpse in the grave, to light the dead as they lay in the tomb, —

"To chase the spirits that love the night."

The Eucharist was placed in the mouth of the corpse. From some epitaphs it is evident that opinions not much differing from the Egyptian obtained also among the early Christians. Here is one: "I adjure all holy Christians, and thee, keeper of happy Julian, by God and by the fearful day of judgment, that his tomb may never at any time be violated, but may be guarded even to the end of the world, in order that I without hindrance may return to this life, when He shall come to judge the living and the dead."[4] The feeling that the Resurrection depends upon the preservation of the material remains survives in many a form to this very day. The kings of Spain are dead and turned to stone that they may not perish utterly.

[1] *De Virg. Vel.*, c. i., and *Adv. Prax.*, c. ii.
[2] *De Prescr.*, c. xiii.
[3] *Cum Carnis Restitutione.*
[4] Bennett, *Christian Archæology*, 256, 529.

Witness the fear recently expressed that somehow cremation might interfere with the Resurrection. Strongly was the idea of the epitaph from the Catacombs repeated in that famous epitaph whose malediction Miss Bacon dared: —

> "Good frend for Iesus sake forbeare
> To digg the dust encloased heare:
> Blest be ye man y^t spares thes stones,
> And curst be he y^t moves my bones."

From the half-realised conviction that somehow life lingers for a long while, if not forever, in or about the remains of the dead, has arisen the belief in the sacredness of the tombs of the saints, the use of these tombs for Christian altars, or, according to the Roman Church, the making of every altar into the tomb of a saint by placing relics therein. Harnack[1] traces the development of the cultus of relics, and points out the survival of fetish and magic elements therein. To this survival is due also the belief in the efficacy of the bones or relics of the saints for miracle working; among the native Australians the charm to produce sickness is the yountoo.[2] The yountoo is a small bone from the leg of one man, wrapped in a piece of flesh cut from another man, tied with hair from the third man. The Talmud[3] says that for "twelve months, as long as the body is

---

[1] *Dogmenges.* II. 7, n. 2, 41, n. 2, 416.

[2] King, *Supernatural*, 144.

[3] *Sabbath*, xv. 26.

still uncorrupted, the soul hovers up and down"; but Maimonides said that for three days the soul hovered over the body, and then if it found the countenance unchanged flew away. In my part of the country it is customary to bury on the third day, not sooner. Then there remains for us to notice a contrary theory which arises from this same notion. This theory is that the body is a clog to the soul, and should be burned away in order that the soul may soon be freed. This thought inquires, —

"Why, if the Soul can fling the Dust aside,
And naked on the Air of Heaven ride,
Wer't not a Shame — wer't not a Shame for him
In this clay carcase crippled to abide?"

According to this theory every effort to quickly and completely destroy the body ought to be made. It is, indeed, a common opinion among Greek Christians, that in punishment for the sins of the soul the body of one who has died excommunicate simply becomes hard and black as iron, and will never decay until its excommunication is removed with the full rites of the Church.[1] The modern Greek's curse is, "May the earth not eat you"; and if he finds a corpse undecayed, it is to him a sure proof that the same is a vampire who at night comes forth from his grave to drink the life-blood of cattle and of men.[2] Vampirism came, we are told, from

[1] Picart, III. 125.
[2] Garnett, *Christian Women of Turkey*. The Greek called the coffin sarcophagus, "flesh-eater."

the ancient Babylonians who had inherited it from the prehistoric Summero-Akkadian religion, where Mul-lil restrained the spirits of the dead from returning to the earth and devouring living flesh and blood and so getting bodies again.[1] It is plain that from this came the popular superstition about ghouls. The lasting bond between soul and body implied a notion of a fleshly Resurrection, which you may see emphasised in the Jewish Apocalyptic books of the two centuries before our era. Now against this theory of Resurrection St. Paul determinedly girds.[2] The Pauline teaching is, at all events, clearly this, the victory of the spirit, we might almost without hesitation say the doctrine of the transformation of matter, an abolition of dualism by the uplift of matter to a higher plane. Philosophy in the West, with its obstinate adherence to an obsolete theory of atoms, and to the belief in the self-subsistence and eternity of matter, coupled with folk-faith in vampirism and the like, has survived in the dogma of fleshly revivification, as the Latin creeds show.

e. The Gnostic Christians, because of their orientalism and tendency to dualism, revived the notion of no Resurrection of the dead, and they asserted that Christ's Resurrection was seeming only, docetic, and

---

[1] Sayce, Hibbert Lectures. Consequently rites of necromancy usually involved the shedding of blood. Cf. *Od.* XI. 36, 97.

[2] Pfleiderer, Hibbert Lectures.

that human souls in general would be revived without a Resurrection. Both the Gregories, of Nazianzus and of Nyssa, adopted spiritual ideas of the Resurrection similar to those of Origen. St. John Chrysostom improved still further upon the idea of the theologians who had preceded him. Indeed, he approached the Pauline position; but the disrepute into which Origen had fallen caused a reaction from his reasonable way of developing theological ideas. The old Roman Creed, instead of saying Resurrection of the body or Resurrection of the dead, both of which are the doctrine of Christ, according to Scriptural and primitive testimony, said "Resurrection of the flesh." Rufinus went further and said, "Resurrection of this flesh"; and St. Jerome, not satisfied with this degree of literalism, went on to reassert with grossest sensual detail his faith in the resuscitation of the flesh.[1] Even Prudentius, in a hymn, exults that, without the loss of tooth or nail, the grave should cast him forth.[2] Both Theophilus of Alexandria and Epiphanius echo this notion of the early stage of culture. St. Augustine, however, at first opposed such crude literalism, and denied the resuscitation of the flesh, stating a Resurrection of the body;[3]

---

[1] Hagenbach, *Hist. Doct.* II. 91; Harnack, *Dogmenges.* I. 74 ff., 151 ff., 223, 232, etc.

[2] *Nec me vel dente vel ungue Fraudatum revomet patefacti fossa sepulchri.*

[3] *De Fide et Symb.*, c. x.

but in later life in his *Enchiridion*[1] he gives us a grotesque picture of the Resurrection, suitable as a text for the Etruscan gloom and terror of that Last Judgment in the Campo Santo of Pisa, long supposed to be the work of Orcagna. "From the beginning no one in Christian theology," says Harnack, "taught the naked immortality of the soul. The Christian doctrine of immortality was bound up in the thought of the Resurrection." In the Middle Ages the great rationalist Aquinas made some effort to develop from the point, where the Fathers had left it, the Christian doctrine of the Resurrection, but he was hampered by the Arabian philosophy of the materiality of the soul, and by Aristotle's doctrine of form and matter, as it had been accepted by the Church. The *Summa*, as is well known, teaches four principal qualities of the risen body:[2] clarity, agility, impassibility, and subtlety. The doctrine of the soul's consciousness in the intermediate state was in the Middle Ages strongly emphasised and set forth by the effigies of that time, which were carved with eyes open and hands joined in prayer. The *Divina Commedia*, after the year 1300, must have made the life of the unseen world very vivid to Christian imagination, distinct like those glowing domes of incandescent iron, when Dante first beheld the city of Dis against the

---

[1] c. lxxxviii.
[2] *Summa Theol.* I^a. 97, III^a. 54 ff.; *Supplem.* 83 ff.

dense blackness of the subterranean world. Modern Protestantism represents the dead as though they were unconscious, "Asleep in Jesus." Look at the Byzantine or at the pre-Raphaelite paintings of the dead Christ on His Cross. There you find no *pietas*, with limp and powerless body, but Christ upright, strong, with eyes wide open, that look past you into the secrets of Eternity, and a countenance vivid with a mystic and solemn joy. It is the boast of modern Spiritism that it revives faith in the dual nature of man and in the conscious state of the dead, even though of disembodied spirits. Nevertheless, epitaphs and hymns still go on asserting the ancient heresy of the soul's sleep in death, — a notion thoroughly pagan, even if Athenagoras did broach it, a notion without foundation in the teaching and example of the Lord Christ. Nowhere does the New Testament literally teach that death is a sleep.[1] How slowly Christian receptiveness corresponds to revelation! How grotesque our survivals of primitive folk-faith, in that astonishing structure of Christian theology where, —

> "Fiends and dragons on the gargoyled eaves
> Watch the dead Christ between the living thieves."

f. As substitutes for the Christian doctrine of the Resurrection, there have been offered to modern civilisation some theories of re-incarnation, trans-

---

[1] Delitzsch, *Bibl. Psych.* 490.

migration of souls, and of Karma. These are, all of them, revivals of a faith belonging to lower stages of religious culture, and finding response in receptiveness of the same grade. Likewise we are earnestly bidden to content ourselves with joining, " The choir invisible of those immortal dead who live again in lives made better by their presence." Quite noble, but quite as superfluously impersonal! sounds like an invitation to a Barmecide feast. Transmigration is definite. The Jewish Talmud teaches it. Cain is said to have had three souls: one passed into Jethro, one into Korah, and the third into the Egyptian whom Moses slew. The doctrine of Pythagoras is well known. Plato fancied that souls of very superior people passed into separate stars, and his own epigrams upon the soul of his dead son Aster are among the most touching and beautifully humane bits of verse in Greek anthology.[1] That there could not always have been among Greeks of the highest culture and spiritualistic temper of mind a complete absence of the idea of the revivification of the body, appears from the use which the Greek dramatists made of the pathetic stories of Persephone and Eurydice, of Alcestis and Medea. Indeed, the Lesser Mysteries of Eleusis, to which the Greek plays, which were the dramas of the Dionysia, belonged, must in setting forth their peculiar mythos, have laid stress upon some idea of the Resurrection;

---

[1] Bergk, *Anthologia Lyrica*, 109.

and we can guess therefrom that the Greater Mysteries enlarged and intensified the hope. Modern theosophy endeavours to revive in Western Christendom the doctrine of Karma. It was the teaching of Sakya Muni that to attain blessedness one must gain extinction of consciousness of existence, at any rate of individual existence. This attainment is to be acquired by abandonment of the will to live, that is, the will to assert self-existence.

> "This is the doctrine of the Karma. Learn!
> Only when all the dross of sin is quit,
> Only when life dies like a white flame spent,
> Death dies along with it.
>
> "Say not, 'I am,' 'I was,' or 'I shall be.'
> Think not ye pass from house to house of flesh
> Like travellers who remember and forget,
> Ill-lodged or well-lodged. Fresh
>
> "Issues upon the Universe that sum
> Which is the lattermost of lives. It makes
> Its habitation as the worm spins silk
> And dwells therein."

"Kill out ambition, kill out desire of life, kill out desire of comfort," says *Light on the Path*, our modern theosophic treasury of devotion.

> "Then Sorrow ends, for life and death have ceased;
> How should lamps flicker when their oil is spent?
> The old, sad count is clear, the new is clean;
> Thus hath a man content."

According to this theory, it is by annihilation of the will that blessedness is attained, for the flame of life is blown out — Nirvana, such was the doctrine of Gautama Buddha. Now this is the very opposite of the teaching of Jesus. He says, in effect, "Acquire the intensest personality, and will of such sort as shall re-incarnate itself, not by being born down into the world in many successive earthly bodies, but up out of the world in one spiritual, heavenly body, and upon some loftier level of life." Strictly considered, Karma is not at all a religious idea, but is merely a statement of the theory of the permanence of physical force.

IV. We owe thanks to Hegel for putting modern thought in the way of receiving the Pauline teaching of the Resurrection of the body. Hegel it was who pointed out [1] the evidence of a process of Resurrection in the history of humanity. The theory of the evolution of physical life absolutely demands our acceptance of the fact of a Resurrection, as Robert Browning shows at large in his poem, *Easter Day*. And thus the Resurrection becomes for us, as I have tried to show, the only true solution of the mystery of pain. In the Light of the Cross of Calvary and of the tomb in the garden, pain and death are beheld as steps in the stairway to a higher life. In pain and grief we recognise a sure token of the glorious fulness of the life to which humanity must eventually attain. The

[1] *Phil. Hist.*, 56.

Resurrection gives us a meaning of life; not that life is, as Bunyan so beautifully puts it, but a pilgrimage, nor that life is a probation, in the sense that God from His far-off Heaven has reached down an arm and put us into the world to try us, if perchance we may fail; but in the light of the Christian Resurrection life is seen to be growth; my own dim life should teach me this; life also is an education, God's word teaches me that and God's world also. Nature, like some august Sybil of gigantic stature, as Michael Angelo painted her high on the shadowy vaultings of the Sistine Chapel, is chanting the oracles of Eternal Wisdom, who, reaching from one end to the other mightily, doth sweetly order all things. Growth, says the cosmic hymn, without Resurrection is impossible. Somewhere there must be an open gate to the world, or the procession of progress is stopped. Somewhere the stream of life has an outlet into that immortal sea that brought us hither, else, dammed up, the river of Life would set back and form dead waters. In the light of evolution, progress, and growth we lack no certitude of the Resurrection of the dead. Individual character, or soul, demands that there be a Resurrection. Unless there be a spiritual uprise, unless a mastery of spirit and its potencies for righteousness, over flesh and sense, we could not increase in wisdom and stature, and favour with God and men.

> "Poor vaunt of life, indeed,
> Were man but formed to feed
> On joy — to solely seek, and find, and feast."

This is what I alluded to in explaining the process of the rise in the spirit of the sense of divine sonship, that manifestation of the sons of God for which the creation is groaning in birth-pangs, the eternal birth, a process which Pessimism perceives only as irremediable woe: —

> "The weariness, the fever, and the fret
> Here where men sit and hear each other groan."

In the light of the first Easter morn the meaning of agony in flesh and spirit is revealed to be the condition of the ever-continuing birth into the knowledge of God, which is eternal life, because it is the identity of truth and life. Knowledge, not existence, is the description of eternal life which Jesus gave. Thus it is that God speaks in the soul and through the soul of man, and the word becomes flesh. Let us so teach the Resurrection that its ethical import will so vitalise the dogma, that men may comprehend that it is something more than an historic fact about which the Church labours to show that the testimony was sufficient, something more than an historic fact which was given as evidence that what Jesus said was true; but rather in the apostolic spirit, let us endeavour to make men comprehend how the Resurrection is a factor of human life and character, and how the Resurrection of our Lord Jesus in the measure that it is actualised in our personal lives becomes the power unto a Resurrection of the dead. Thus life may be clear in its purpose and plain in its continuity, thus that life of the world of nature, that inner force that works in wondrous ways of unfolding, of expansion, of dominance over matter and the transmutation of it, may be seen to operate in the world of souls. The soul that grows strong in righteousness, the righteousness of the Lord Jesus Christ, because it gains the victory of the Spirit, shall rise from the dead, because it is not possible it shall be holden of death. Finally, in the unity of the divine process, we see how pain and death are always and everywhere the inevitable transition, the resultant Resurrection unto life. The revelation of God in the world and in Christ shows us that

> "As a god self-slain on his own strange altar,
> Death lies dead."

Nature therefore in the old sense of the word, *Natura*, meant just this process of birth, and natural science reveals to us that there is going on always in the world a process of the victory of spiritual over material elements, and of transferrence of the centre of the output of energy from matter to spirit. From that centre it energises forth, changing and controlling all from its spiritual force centre, generating that spiritual body which it is not possible should be holden of death. Therefore we look for a Resurrection of the dead.

ETERNAL LIFE.

The mere article of a future life is not in itself the test of superiority of one creed over another, for besides that it may be grossly misconceived, the bare image of a futurity is nothing, and merely shows a different condition of the popular fancy.

J. B. MOZLEY, D.D., *Lectures*.

Now wherever a man hath been made a partaker of the divine nature, in him is fulfilled the best and noblest life and the worthiest in God's eyes that hath been or can be. And of that eternal Love which loveth Goodness as Goodness for the sake of Goodness, a true, noble, Christ-like life is so greatly beloved, that it will never be forsaken or cast off. This life is not chosen in order to serve any end, or to get anything by it, but for the love of its nobleness and because God loveth and esteemeth it greatly.

Theologia Germanica, c. 28.

> Wem Zeit ist wie Ewigkeit
> Und Ewigkeit wie Zeit,
> Der ist befreit
> Von allem Streit.
>
> JACOB BÖHME.

We think that the way of blessings and prosperous accidents is the finer way of securing our duty, and that when our heads are anointed, our cups crowned, and our tables full, the very caresses of our spirits will best of all dance before Ark, and sing perpetual Anthems to the honor of our Benefactor and Patron God: and we are apt to dream that God will make His Saints reign here as kings in a millenary kingdom, and give them riches and fortunes of this world, that they may rule over men, and sing psalms to God forever.

Bp. JEREMY TAYLOR, Sermon, *Of God's Method of Curing Sinners*.

Faustus.
>When I behold the heavens, then I repent,
>And curse thee, wicked Mephistophilis,
>Because thou hast depriv'd me of these joys.

Mephistophilis.
>>Why, Faustus,
>Thinkest thou heaven is such a glorious thing?
>I tell thee, Faustus, it is not half so fair
>As thou, or any man that breathes on earth.

Faustus.
>How prov'st thou that?

Mephistophilis.
>'Twas made for man, therefore is man more excellent.

>>>Marlowe, *Tragical Historie of
>>>Doctor Faustus.*

SYNOPSIS.

INTRODUCTION:
> The Christian idea of Eternal Life unique.

I. — COMPARATIVE RELIGION:
> Three classes of theories of future life.
> > *a.* Transmigration or Re-incarnation.
> > *b.* Continuation, on this earth, beyond it.
> > *c.* Retribution, — vindictive, compensative, reformatory.

II. — BIBLICAL THEOLOGY:
> Contrast the teaching of Jesus, which is that Eternal Life is of the present. This is particularly set forth in St. John's Gospel, which is especially the gospel of life; and it follows necessarily that such is the nature of Eternal Life if God be immanent in this time-world. A further examination into the nature and characteristics of Eternal Life.

III. — Obstacles to the Reception of the Gospel of Eternal Life; the part played by clericalism and the notion of a commercial atonement in nursing survivals of folk-faith in the eschatology of the Church; and the tendency to substitute dogma for life as an easier way of making Christians. The force of the moral sanction of rewards and punishments — now passing away — still measurably valid where it remains efficient. Eternal Life manifested on Calvary as the Revealment of the Immanent Love. God Eternal, because infinitely holy. Jesus gave His life, rather than His death, for the world. Eternal Life is to live according to God. This gospel teaching of life eternal finds modern Science accommodating herself to it, — and also Philosophy.

IV. — This doctrine of Eternal Life is real, and therefore a saving doctrine, for which reason we find it helpful to preach and consoling to teach.

ETERNAL LIFE.

GENTLEMEN : —

The apostle Paul in a profound and richly significant passage declares that the changeless purpose and favour of God were given unto men from the beginning of time, but were clearly manifested by an Epiphany, which was Christ Jesus, Who rendered death ineffectual and brought to light life and incorruption.[1]

This signifies the revelation of a new truth, not the republication of an old idea upon a new and Divine authority. In order that we may detect the absolute novelty of this Christian doctrine we must first examine what ideas of immortality already were extant in the world, and in the examination we shall observe their effects upon Christian Theology.

I. The primitive culture of mankind held in its religious consciousness three typical theories of the future life.

a. The earliest was the conjecture of the transmigration of souls or their re-incarnation, to which I

---

[1] 2 Tim. i. 8, 12, ζωή, ἀφθαρσία.

have already alluded.[1] This theory fancied that the human soul, after leaving its body at death, must find some other sort of body, and therefore will enter a tree, a stone, or some beast or man. The Karens are in constant fear lest they shall become possessed by the wicked spirit, *la*, of some one who has died.[2] Some of the negro tribes upon the gold coast believe in three parts of man, — his body, his soul or ghost, and his indwelling spirit or *kra*. They suppose that this *kra* existed before the birth of the individual man, and at his death will at its first opportunity enter into some other body or thing.[3] If unable to find a tenement, it wanders around about the earth as a malignant demon; the soul or ghost, however, at death, proceeds to the land of the dead, and there remains. The Navajo Indians, likewise, believe man is body, soul, and spirit, and that the spirit was pre-existent and is indestructible. Other North American Indians, when their little children die, will bury the bodies along the wayside, in the hope that the soul of the dead child may re-enter the body of its mother as she passes by, and so be born again. Negroes in harsh slavery have been known to commit suicide in order that they might be born again, and by good

---

[1] Tylor, *Prim. Cult.* II. c. 12.

[2] *The Karens of the Golden Chersonese*, 128 ff.

[3] This suggests the probable source of the early Egyptian theory of the return of the soul after death to reanimate the mummy or a portrait image.

hap into liberty in their own land. The continuation of family names from generation to generation had, no doubt, its origin in this belief. The story of the Pied Piper of Hamlin is a legend which arose from just this sort of animistic speculation about the soul's life and transmigration. Many savage peoples believe that everything has its ghost, and that when a tree dies, its ghost travels to the spirit land. Hindu philosophy developed this notion of the travelling of spirits, and their pre-existence, in an ethical way, making the transmigration of an individual soul up from the stone to the Buddha, through many thousand births, a vast and complicated solution to the problem of life and the mystery of evil. The low-caste Sudra hopes, by a righteous life, to be born again as a Brahmin, who by knowledge of the Vedas, and meditation upon the same, will ultimately be absorbed in the Deity as a drop of water in the ocean.[1]

"Om! Mani padmi, Om! the Sunrise comes,
The dewdrop slips into the shining Sea"—

is Sir Edwin Arnold's favourite formula of a Buddha passing into Nirvana.[1] Greek Philosophy heard of this notion of metempschychosis when on a visit in Egypt and the East, was charmed with its poetry and picturesqueness, but never seriously adopted it.

[1] At this point Brahminism and Buddhism agree. See Sir Monier Monier-Williams, *Buddhism, passim; Brahminism and Hinduism, passim.*

Individualism was too strong in the bracing air of Hellas and on those Ionian

> "Sprinkled isles,
> Lily on lily, that o'erlace the sea."

With Plato and Pythagoras a theory of metempsychosis remained an eclectic speculation, held in solution, it is true, but not definitively colouring their philosophical systems. Ritualistic Brahminism taught that in order to avoid the retribution of the re-incarnation of the soul in many successive births, men must offer sacrifice. A singular parallel of the development of religious thought is observed by comparing the relation of the Brahminic sacrifices to the hymns of the Rig Veda, with that of the Levitical code to the later psalms. It is just possible that these two lines of development were contemporary. From the Satapatha-Brahmana, translated by Sir Monier Monier-Williams, I quote what tells its own story.

> "The gods lived constantly in fear of Death —
> The mighty Ender — so with toilsome rites
> They worshipped, and repeated sacrifices
> Till they became immortal. Then the Ender
> Said to the gods, 'As ye have made yourselves
> Imperishable, so will men endeavour
> To free themselves from me: what portion then
> Shall I possess in man?' The gods replied,
> 'Henceforth no being shall become immortal
> In his own body; this his mortal frame
> Shalt thou still seize; this shall remain thy own,

This shall become perpetually thy food.
And even he who through religious acts
Henceforth attains to immortality,
Shall first present his body, Death, to thee.'"[1]

The later Jewish philosophy of the Middle Ages adopted the theory of migration, or gilgul, the rolling on of souls through successive incarnations; but this was evidently an alien importation into Judaism. In vain will sincere scholarship seek to find the doctrine of metempsychosis authorised in the New Testament writings. Attempts have been made to see signs of the Jewish belief in the transmigration of souls in the words[2] of St. Matthew's gospel, "Some say that thou art John the Baptist, some Elias, and others Jeremias, or one of the prophets." Nothing more was indicated in these words than the popular opinion that these men had not really died, but fallen asleep, and ready to start up to deliver Israel; an opinion which perhaps survived in many a legend of early Jewish Christianity, as, for example, those of Prester John, and of the Seven Sleepers of Ephesus. Appeal has been made to St. John's gospel,[3] "Master, who did sin, this man or his parents, that he was born blind?" to show that Jesus taught re-incarnation. The obvious import of the passage is the rabbinic doctrine of the inherited guilt and its penalty. This last doctrine has survived in our

---

[1] Sir Monier Monier-Williams, *Brahminism and Hinduism*, 24.
[2] xvi. 14.   [3] ix. 2.

grosser forms of the theology of original sin, in traducianism, and likewise in the notion of a revivified body, into which, as into a house, the soul shall enter at the last day, instead of the Resurrection body concerning which our Lord Jesus Christ taught. Again, that saying of Christ's, "If ye will receive it this *is* Elias which was for to come,"[1] has been explained by a rigid literalism in a way to support the theory of transmigration of souls. Further it is not worth our while to pursue this form of an evolution from animism, this dream of the Pantheist and poet, this brave attempt to solve the enigma of sin and pain. After the days of the Gnostics and the Manichees the teaching of transmigration of souls fell out of sight in Christendom. It really belongs to emanation theories. Here and there in the history of Christian thought there have been sporadic survivals of the notion; for instance, the Druses in the East, some mediæval popular sects, Scotus Erigena, the Knights of the Order of the Temple, probably, and the peasants of the Slavic churches at the present time. There have been also revivals of the opinion by some Platonists, such as Henry More and Thomas Taylor, and by students of Oriental Theosophy. I have said thus much only because in this bric-a-brac age there have been attempts to revive this theory and to commend it to Christian teachers. The late Professor Francis Bowen, whose memory I revere, was

---

[1] St. Matt. xi. 14, αὐτός ἐστιν Ἠλείας ὁ μέλλων ἔρχεσθαι.

of the opinion that a "firm and well-grounded faith in the doctrine of Christian Metempsychosis might help to regenerate the world." Professor Bowen has passed behind the veil, and perhaps now he knows. For my part I cannot conceive of a doctrine of metempsychosis which is Christian, which does not destroy moral responsibility in man, and which is not totally irreconcilable with that revelation which our Lord Jesus Christ gave both in Himself and in His words and works, of the nature of eternal life. The weakness of all forms of the doctrine of metempsychosis is that they make the article of death sacramental; they either present the future as an anti-climax or as a contradiction to the law of the permanence of forces; they presume that the human will raised to the nth power can neutralise itself; and, finally, they find for this theory no evidence in the ground of personal experience or in the analogy of nature. The Fathers of the Church, Tertullian, Irenæus, Augustine, and Origen, carefully weighed the theory of metempsychosis, and agreed in rejecting it.[1] The whole system of speculation has, however, been adopted by individual religious writers as an escape from the cruder horrors of an arbitrary, *ab extra*, Tartarus, which had come down to us from primitive culture.

b. We now consider the common theory of continuation. According to this theory of primitive folk-

---

[1] Tertull. *De Anima*, c. xxxi.; Iren. *Hær.* II. 33; Aug. *Faust.* xx. 21; Orig. *Cels.* VIII. 30, etc.

faith, the soul goes forth from the body and continues its existence in the spirit land as a naked, pale, soft, vague, shadowy thing. This thought has been precisely expressed in the Latin epigram called Hadrian's Address to his Soul, —

> "Little, courteous, wand'ring thing,
> Whither wilt thou turn thy wing,
> The body's friend and guest?
> Pale and naked, cold as clay,
> Forgot, alas! thy wonted play,
> Where wilt thou take thy rest?"[1]

In some parts of Christendom they will not sweep the house for days after a death, and they will not leave sharp-pointed objects lying about, nor will they shut a door abruptly, for fear of hurting the poor ghost. In his journey through the threefold world of the dead, Dante was detected by the resident ghosts because he cast a shadow and moved what he touched.[2]

The souls of the heroes whom Odysseus saw were but pale presentments of their former selves until

---

[1] *Animula, blandula, vagula,*
Hospes, comesque corporis,
Quae nunc abibis in loca?
Pallidula, rigida, nudula,
Nec, ut solas, dabis joca?

[2] *Siete voi accorti,*
Che quel di retro move ciò ch' ei tocca?
Così non soglion fare i piè de' morti.
  Inferno, XII. 80.

they had lapped the blood of the sacrifice. Their occupations in the shadowless land were the same as they had been under the light of the sun. In that dream region of the ghosts, says Mr. Tylor,[1] the soul of the dead Karen with the souls of his axe and cleaver, builds his ghost house and harvests his ghost rice; the shade of the Algonquin hunter pursues the souls of beaver and elk, walking upon the ghosts of his snow-shoes, which had been buried in his grave; the fur-wrapped Kamtchatkan in the spirit land drives a spirit dog-sled; the Zulu ghost milks his ghost cows and drives the spirit cattle into their ghostly kraal. The South American lives on the spirit lands, sometimes sick and sometimes well, in pain and in comfort. All these primitive folk expect to live forever in the spirit land a shadowy continuation of their existence in this. In the hills of the dead, the barrow-tombs of the Scandinavians,[2] the Norse warrior, it was believed, fought and feasted, feasted and fought on forever. The Ainu believed that the souls of the dead lingered long near the grave, and that by contact with them the living became ceremonially unclean, and, worse than this, that by character ghosts are universally mischievous. They endeavour to persuade the goddess of fire to lead the souls of the dead as soon as possible to the ghost

[1] *Prim. Cult.* II.
[2] *Long Lay of Brunhild*, and Excursus I., Sec. 3, *Corp. Bor. Poet.* II.

land, where, it is believed, the soul of the dead will continue forever to work and play and eat and sleep as in this life.[1] The Jewish souls of the dead, *rephaim*, in their tombs slumbered a half-conscious trance, or, according to a later notion, remained semi-somnolent in the hollow caverns of the underworld, and resented all interference from a necromancer such as the witch of Endor. So it became a crime in Israel to rouse the souls of the dead from their empty slumber — empty; for, says Koheleth,[2] "there is no work, no device, no knowledge, no wisdom in Sheol." In Egypt, however, by help of the pictured walls of the serdab of his tomb, the soul ploughed and reaped in the spirit land of Amenti; with aid of the same pictures he drove his oxen and played chess with his wife.

In earlier ages of Egypt both food itself and actual articles of furniture and implements of life were placed in the tomb with the dead; but later on, it was hoped that the representation of the articles might be sufficient for the ghostly representation of the man. In a like manner, the Chinese who anciently offered to their dead ancestors all sorts of sacrifices, of things in themselves, have now concluded that paper representations are sufficient to burn to the souls of the departed. The ghost of the ancient Egyptian was

---

[1] J. Batchelor, *Ainu of Japan*, Chaps. XV., XVI.
[2] Eccl. ix. 10, Ps. lxxxviii. 11; Robertson Smith, *Relig. of the Semites*, 217.

supposed to eat the offerings of the dead, food and drink, placed before the door of his tomb, a door which had been perforated in order that the *ba* soul might come forth and relieve its hunger. Likewise the Mahometans to this day feed the ghosts of their dead, and they also place within the tomb a seat convenient for the angel who comes to judge the dead shortly after his burial.[1] So the soul of the savage needs his weapons and armour; even his wives must be despatched with a bludgeon or their legs broken, and they thrown into the grave, that they may accompany him to the land of spirits.[2] The Karens will impoverish themselves in order that the deceased shall be thoroughly equipped for the next world.[3] When the coffin is lowered into the grave, everything that a man could need or desire is thrown in with it, according to the ability of the mourners.

A common consent assigned the country of dead souls to the regions of the evening land, beyond the setting of the sun and baths of all the western stars, or to that realm of fancy, the land east of the sun and west of the moon. For good ghosts there were

[1] See Picart, Tome V., and D'Herbelot, under *Akhrat*.

[2] *The London Standard*, 1890, gave a long account of the Iu-Iu rites which occurred at the death of a Calabar king. By accident English traders entered the village, and discovered the body of the dead king lying in a great pit, and seven of his wives with broken limbs placed beside him.

[3] A. R. McMahon, *Karens of the Golden Chersonese*, 419. Cf. Batchelor, *Ainu*, 204.

also the islands of the Hesperides, full of the stately repose and the lordly delight of the dead, where also is the tree of the apples of life, wondrous, beautiful, and serpent-guarded, and where a fountain of eternal youth is always casting up its sparkling jet. This creation of fancy we see enter in some form as an element in the Jewish idea of the Messianic age, and then pass over into the millennarian visions of Papias and the early Christian Church. Of this early form of the idea of eternal life we have still left in the Creed the phrase, "Life of the world to come," literally of the "coming age,"[1] which phrase is a Hebraism for the Messianic age, and also the earthly Paradise of the Millennium for the souls of the righteous. That dream passed away long centuries ago, so long that the phrase of the Creed no longer connotes for us what it did for the early Christians, but we have a more sure hope. A further development of this idea reached out beyond the earth. One of the seers[2] of the Enoch writings thought of the world as a flat disk covered over by a hollow hemisphere. Just outside the rim of this inverted cup he found the abode of the spirits, who, if any man went to the edge of the world and called, would come to him, whether from the "vasty deep" or elsewhere. Perhaps it was from this pre-Christian Apocalyptic book that the Manichee developed his picturesque and

---

[1] τοῦ μέλλοντος αἰῶνος.
[2] Book of Enoch, iv. 1, v. 1, xi. 2, etc.

peculiar theory of the redemption and purgation of souls after death.[1] Our Teutonic ancestors imagined that the dead dwelt beneath the earth in Niflheim, Nidgard, or in Helheim, a cavernous region where perpetual gusts of sleet and snow were driven through the dun air.

In these earlier theories, as thus far you may have perceived, the ethical characteristic has hardly emerged clearly into consciousness. The thought which underlay them was generally that of an impartially unmoral necessity of existence. The question had hardly become evolved beyond the concepts of pleasure and pain. Consequently these primitive notions, save by their imagery, have feebly affected the development of Christian Theology. I suspect that this shadowy continuation theory, emptied as it is of moral quality, has somehow subtly survived in Christian Theology, in the theory of essential or native immortality, which, notwithstanding the protests[2] of Justin Martyr, Tatian, Irenæus, Theophilus of Antioch, Clement the Alexandrine, Arnobius, and Lactantius, ultimately has dominated Christian Eschatology. Possibly also it suggested those nebu-

---

[1] See Archelaus, *Disp. with Manes*, c. xi.

[2] Barnabas, xx. ; Clement of Rome ; 1 Cor. iii., ix., xxxv., xvi., xlvii., vii.; Ignatius, *To Polycarp*, ii., *To Romans*, vii. ; Hermas, *Sim.*, iii. ; *Didaché;* Justin Martyr, *Tryph.*, v. ; *Apology*, xxxix., xlii., lii. ; Tatian, *Graec.*, xiii., vii., xv. ; Theophilus, *To Autol.* I. 11, 37 ; Irenæus, *Her.* II. 34, etc.; Clement of Alex., *Paid.* I. 3 ; Arnobius, *Against Gentiles*, II. 14-16, etc.

lous creations, the *limbus infantum* and the *limbus patrum*, states of neither weal nor woe. For the theologians have not, I think, determined which of these lies nearest hell. Universal restoration also, in so far as it obliterates moral distinction, is a survival of the same primitive theory. Jesus teaches [1] that few will be saved, — Universalism begs to differ, and says "all will be saved."

c. Succeeding the notion of a bare continuance came the higher thought of compensation and retribution in the future life. Man got ideas of law and justice in this world, and projected them into the other. He figured to himself that God is vindictive, or is retributive, or is compensative, or is reformatory. So in the religions of the reflective races of the earth, the ethical element — I mean sin and its consequence in a future life — ever arises into a great moral motive power. In later days the Norse warrior came to think that he would be forever debarred from Valhalla, should he die peacefully, and therefore he required that, at least, a spear scratch should be made on his body, if he found himself dying of disease. A similar temper led Christians to seek to die in monastic habit, or with the cord of St. Francis about them. The newspapers gave account of a curious custom of the Russian Church which was recently performed at the funeral of the Grand Duchess Paul. Before the coffin was

[1] St. Matt. vii. 14 ; Luke xiii. 23.

finally closed upon the corpse, the Metropolitan placed in the hand of the dead this writing: "We, by the grace of God, prelate of the holy Russian Church, write this to our master and friend, St. Peter, the gate-keeper of the Lord Almighty. We announce to you that the servant of the Lord, Her Imperial Highness, the Grand Duchess Paul, has finished her life on earth, and we order you to admit her into the Kingdom of Heaven without delay, for we have absolved all her sins and granted her salvation. You will obey our order on sight of this document which we put into her hand."

To all Semitic races[1] belongs the myth of a sea of outer darkness which surrounds this world, into which all that is evil will be cast, when the earth shall be purified for the abode of the saints. But the Aryan races, as indeed some of the Semites, conceived of a place on the earth, or at the end of it, where for an æon, fires should torment the ungodly. According to the institutes of Vishnu,[2] the inhabitants of heaven are able freely to inspect the sinners in hell, who hang head downwards. This arrangement serves the double advantage of enhancing the bliss of the gods and saints, and of increasing the agonies of the damned.

The Jew, likewise, bade you mark that there was

[1] Cf. Izdubar Epic of Chaldea, Book of Enoch, Koran, and Samaritan Book of Joshua.

[2] *Hindu Literature, or the Ancient Books of India*, 151.

but a hand-breadth between the flames of Gehenna and Abraham's bosom. The essence of these doctrines of a future state is this, which already I have hinted at as being a survival from a primitive stage of culture, that physical pain purges away moral evil. This has always been taken for granted in the development of religious thought; and Schopenhauer makes grimly merry that our world offers so much more material for constructing a graphic image of hell than for a definite picture of heaven. Because physical pain has been assumed to compensate for spiritual sin, asceticism appeared, whereby, in Hindustan, a man, or even a demon, may become greater than the gods; and in the Roman Church it is believed that a man is able to accumulate in this way such a store of merits that Almighty God can refuse him nothing. This fundamental theory has been accepted without question, and it lies at the base of some of the popular doctrines of the forgiveness of sins, and of the atonement, as it is termed, of our Lord Jesus Christ. If you believe that the merits acquired by our Lord by His suffering and death on the Cross are substituted for our sins, that is, reckoned as our merits, then logically you ought to believe in the mediation of saints, in the appropriation of their merits, and in indulgences, and all the rest of the system. But if you do accept this system, be quite clear in your mind about this one thing, that its fundamental idea arose at that stage of the development of mankind where man does not distinguish between moral and physical evil.

Turn to the sacred books of the East, or to the Egyptian Book of the Dead, or to the pictures and sculpture on temple and tomb and church, and you will perceive to what this theory of a retribution *ab extra* has led. The thought of the relation between God and men was thereby everywhere degraded into the notion of the exaction of a price, or a barter or a bargain of some sort. Thus while on the walls of the Egyptian temple[1] were painted the scales of Mat, goddess of Justice, wherein the human conscience was outweighed by the feather of truth, so on the walls of mediæval churches were painted the great balances of God, wherein He weighed the good of a soul against its sin.

"It is by no breath,
Turn of eye, wave of hand, that Salvation joins issue with death."

In one sense Dante's theory of rewards and punishments was just and rational, and Dante, we know, voiced the scholastics. In the *Divine Comedy*, God is seen as Love unaltering and all-pervasive, which to the holy is warmth and light of profound bliss, but to the ungodly the same all-embracing Love is either tormenting flame or cold and darkness. Everything depends upon the attitude of the individual soul towards God. Implicitly, therefore, the "wrath prin-

[1] See plates in Lepsius' *Egypt*.

ciple" is human and subjective. In the earlier days of Christianity the idea of future compensation so warped the minds of Christian theologians that many of them could see in the divine death nothing higher than the payment of a price. This thought survives in the doctrine of Indulgences. In fact, all theories of sin which sunder sin and its penalty fall into this snare of reviving the old idea of compounding for guilt, and of placating a vindictive God by satisfying the demand of his iron *lex talionis*.

Not without some excuse has this theory been stated as "the immolation of an innocent God, by an all-loving God, to satisfy a perfectly just God." We have not so learned the gospel of Jesus. Later speculations of primitive men went so far as to evolve [1] the idea of sensuous torments which have no end, thus setting up an eternal contest between good and evil. This doctrine, it is said, was brought by the early Christian theosophists from Persia, and has been preserved for us in Augustinian theology, which only transfers the *mise en scène* to a future world of heaven and hell. Is not this virtually making an omnipotent God impotent to overcome evil? Is it not, in effect, bringing into the theological world *Die Götterdämmerung*, which Wagner's acute intellect has seized upon to point out this suicidal element in Christian Theology. Read, I pray you, Mr. Browning's poem, *Ixion.* If evil be able to resist God, then

---

[1] Distinguishing between the *pœna damni* and the *pœna sensus*.

it is stronger than God, and by it God is blotted out. In Wagner's famous opera, the sin of Odin brings on the conflagration of Valhalla.

To take up the words of Ixion to which I have already alluded: —

"High in the dome, suspended, of Hell, sad triumph, behold us!
  Here the revenge of a God, there the amends of a Man.
Whirling forever in Torment, flesh once mortal, immortal
  Made — for a purpose of hate — able to die and revive,
Pays to the uttermost pang, then, newly for payment replenished,
  Doles out — old yet young — agonies ever afresh.

"— When Man pays the price of endeavour,
Thunderstruck, downthrust, Tartaros-doomed to the wheel, —
Then, ay, then, from the tears and sweat and blood of his torment,
  E'en from the triumph of Hell, up let him look and rejoice!
What is the influence, high o'er Hell, that turns to a rapture
  Pain — and despair's murk mists blends in a rainbow of hope?
"What is beyond the obstruction, stage by stage though it baffle?
  Back must I fall, confess, 'Ever the weakness I fled'?
No, for beyond, far, far is a Purity all-unobstructed!
  Zeus was Zeus — not Man; wrecked by his weakness I whirl!"

In this way Mr. Browning illustrates forcibly the *reductio ad absurdum* of that subtle dualism which underlies the theological doctrine of punishment of sin by means of sensuous pain. Nobler and gracefuller was the temper of those old heathen of the Nile Valley who called none dead but the wicked: the good man they reverently named "That yesterday who sees endless days." The ghost world of rewards and punishments has filled an immense space in Christian Theology from the days of the Apocryphal Gospel of Nicodemus, the visions of the Nitrian monks, the dreams of Furseus, Alberigo, and of the ecstatic nuns of the Middle Ages. In all religions, as I have already said, the torments of the other world have formed the *pièce de résistance*. The journey of Odin in the *Voluspa*, Orpheus, Odysseus and Æneas, Yama and Gwynnidion, the visions of Enoch and St. Brandan, Dante and Swedenborg, Bunyan and John Miller, are exponents of this universal mythos. The survival of the primitive idea of innate and essential immortality, that is of "an immortal soul," a phrase found nowhere in the Bible, was with the aid of Platonic philosophy transplanted into Christian Theology, and gave rise to all this curious mythology to which I have referred.

II. In distinct contrast to all this system are the teachings of Jesus. Not the future life, but the present, He set forth as the motive of righteousness. He taught the conditions of Eternal Life. Everlastingness is a human corollary of eternity. Nothing is more striking than our Lord's silence concerning the scenery of the world unseen. It is true that He freely makes use of phrases, terms, and popular fancies then in vogue, to convey His doctrine; but in order to indicate that such terms do not literally answer to the realities, He uses all of them impartially, though they are formally contradictory. Of the place and environment of the spirits of the dead He makes no picturesque revelation. By means of the parable of Dives and Lazarus He distinctly declines to allow the fear of future punishment to be furnished as a motive for godliness. Nowhere in His teaching does He substitute other worldliness for unworldliness; nowhere holds up a scheme of future rewards and punishments, as a reason for godly and righteous living in the present time. In the Old Testament the right life is long. "That thy days may be long," is the incentive which is given in the Commandments, repeated in Deut. v. 33 as the motive for the whole Decalogue; "that ye may prolong your days in the land which ye shall possess." But our Lord starts with a new proclamation, one which is deeper and more intimate with the very essence of life. He came that we might have life and have it more abundantly.[1] His kingdom is a kingdom of Life, and into this kingdom of the new life each one of us must be born: "Except a man be born from above[2] he is not able to enter into the kingdom of God." "Except a man be born of water and the spirit he is not able to enter into the kingdom of God." Jesus added, "He that believeth on Me hath eternal life";[3] "*hath* eternal

---

[1] St. John x. 10, καὶ περισσὸν ἔχωσιν.

[2] St. Jer. iii. 3, ἐὰν μή τις γεννηθῇ ἄνωθεν.

[3] ἔχει ζωὴν αἰώνιον. Not only is the present tense emphatic, St. John vi. 47, but αἰώνιον does not denote duration, whatever it may connote.

life," it is a present possession of which Christ is speaking. He goes on to say further, "He that heareth My word and believeth on Him that sent Me *hath* eternal life,[1] and shall not come into condemnation, but *is passed* from death unto life." The statement is here more emphatic. The true believer *now* has eternal life, and already *has passed* out of the deathful condition into consciousness of life eternal, the living, eternal, immanent God. So it is a matter not of the future, but of the present, because we are in God now. The Beatitudes were, every one, given in the present tense. It is an error to suppose that life eternal is nothing more than a continuation of this life, brought about either by a fiat of God, or by a bargain with Him, or because the soul is essentially indestructible as if it were a piece of God. God is eternal because He is perfectly holy. Eternal life is something different from any continuation of life beyond death; it is a transformation of a human life (which has consciously sinned), so that it cannot cease or die. Therein is fulfilled the old theological dictum: "Man is made able not to die, in order that he might become not able to die." Eternal life therefore is the quality rather than the quantity of life, the quantity being a result of the quality. Again, when He proclaimed[2] Himself the Bread of Life, He said with intensity, "Verily, verily, I say unto you, he that believeth on Me *hath*

---

[1] ἔχει ζωὴν αἰώνιον, St. John v. 24.   [2] St. John vi. 47 ff.

everlasting life," etc.; and, "Whoso *eateth* My flesh and drinketh My blood *hath* eternal life": therefore, unless we now have eternal life before the grave, we cannot with certainty expect to have it afterward.

> "No, no! the energy of life may be
> Kept on after the grave, but not begun;
> And he who flagged not in the earthly strife,
> From strength to strength advancing — only he,
> His soul well-knit, and all his battles won,
> Mounts, and that hardly, to eternal life."

The sinless infant who has never by voluntary sin and the knowledge of evil been separated from the consciousness of the indwelling God, may grow in wisdom and holiness throughout the eternal years, though his little span of life in this world gave him no room for effort; but he who has once barred out God-consciousness must of himself remove that bar. In the prologue to his gospel, St. John alludes to these sayings of our Lord, gathering them up in one great vision of the meaning of the world and of its life in relation to God. For he writes,[1] "That which was made was life in Him, and the life was the light of men, and to as many as receive Him He gave power to become the sons of God, which were born of God." This eternal life physical death cannot interrupt, as

---

[1] St. John i. 3, 4, 12, 13, ὃ γέγονεν ἐν αὐτῷ ζωή ἐστιν, καὶ ἡ ζωὴ ἦν τὸ φῶς, κ.τ.λ. Cf. the critical note of Tischendorf which establishes this reading.

Jesus says,[1] "Whosoever liveth and believeth in Me shall never die," and of Himself, in a sense which may be explained at another time, He said,[2] "This is the bread which came down from Heaven that a man may eat thereof and not die"; "He that eateth of this bread shall live forever," or, as He puts the same idea in other words, "If a man keep My saying he shall never see death."[3] To this bright positive of life there is a dark negative,[4] "Verily, verily, I say unto you except ye eat the flesh of the Son of man and drink His blood ye have no life in you." Therefore we learn that in the present, without waiting for a future world beyond death, the want of eternal life signifies that the soul is dead.[5]

> "They pass me by like shadows, crowds on crowds,
> Dim ghosts of men, that hover to and fro,
> Hugging their bodies round them, like thin shrouds
> Wherein their souls were buried long ago:
> They trampled on their youth, and faith, and love,
> They cast their hope of human-kind away,
> With Heaven's clear messages they madly strove,
> And conquered, — and their spirits turned to clay:
> Lo! how they wander round the world their grave,
> Whose ever-gaping maw by such is fed;
> Gibbering at living men, and idly rave,
> 'We only, truly live, but ye are dead.'
> Alas! poor fools; the anointed eye may trace
> A dead soul's epitaph in every face!"

[1] St. John xi. 26.
[2] St. John vi. 50.
[3] St. John viii. 51.
[4] St. John vi. 53.
[5] Cf. *Divina Commedia, Inferno,* xxxiii. 121-124.

Thus Biblical Theology repeats the one and unvarying lesson touching eternal life; it is life actually and ethically in the "everlasting now," whether here or hereafter. This must be true, if indeed in God we live and move and have our being. Out of the moral action comes the intellectual conviction, and at length out of this arises the spiritual consciousness of divine sonship and life in God, which is life eternal. Only by living the kind of life God lives does man know God. Only by this knowledge of God does he know his divine sonship; this is life eternal to know Him, the only true God and Jesus Christ whom He hath sent. It was in the perfectness of this consciousness that Jesus said, "I am the life," "I am the Resurrection and the life," "he that eateth Me the same shall live by Me."[1] Can we determine more clearly the nature of this eternal life? Observe, first, that in the New Testament between the Greek words *soos*, safe, and *zoos*, alive, there is no vast difference in meaning, and in form but the difference of a not very different letter. Radically these two words are the same. In the gospel of Christ salvation and life are terms so nearly related as to be almost interchangeable. The life that is saved is called real or actual life.[2] Only he that hath life is saved, and the life that he has is eternal. The connection between salvation and life

---

[1] St. John xi. 25. Cf. 1 John iii. 15.
[2] 1 Tim. vi. 19, ἡ ὄντως ζωή. Cf. Olshausen, *Opuscula*, 187.

is that Jesus saving the world from sins (not their guilt or punishment only) rightens (rectifies or justifies) it, and life becomes eternal in the measure it is rightened or rectified; it cannot die, and of its own inherent nature comes to a Resurrection. But what, more definitely in the terms of Biblical Theology, are the characteristics of life eternal? First, it is God-consciousness,[1] an abiding recollection of the Immanent Love. Are we to understand that this knowledge of God is an intellectual apprehension, or a speculative idea, a "sensed conversion," or a *unio mystica* of rapture and trance? Is it an Hegelian out-working of the Immanent Divine Mind into consciousness in the heterogeneous world and in the brains of men? Is it this the gospel teaches? Not at all! The gospel knowledge or gnosis is the identity of creed and deed:[2] "Hereby we do know that we know Him if we keep His commandments." We may approach the understanding of this subject of eternal life from another side. In St. Matthew's gospel [3] Jesus makes entry into the kingdom identical with the beginning of eternal life: "If thou wilt enter into life, keep the commandments." This He said to the rich young man who had asked, "What good thing shall I do that I may have life eternal?" At the end our Lord's comment is, that a rich man shall hardly enter into the kingdom of God. In St.

---

[1] St. John xvii. 3.
[2] St. John vii. 17 ; 1 John ii. 3.   Cf. 1 John iii. 7.   [3] xix. 16–24.

Luke x. 25 the old misconception of eternal life as a future reward, instead of a present condition, is corrected by the parable of the good Samaritan, wherein eternal life is displayed in the concrete present. In short, as we have already seen, the kingdom of God is the obverse, of which eternal life is the reverse, upon the coin of human life. Again, eternal life is like a grain of mustard seed because it grows. Such is the very nature of life, to grow. Eternal life grows forever. Again, God is the living God, not lifeless matter, mechanical force, a stream of tendency, or an abstract first cause. He is living because He is infinitely holy. This is the key to the meaning of "eternal life." They who are unholy are alienated from the life of God,[1] and are therefore dead; they have no life in them. Eternal life, says St. Peter,[2] is to live according to God, or in St. Paul's phrase,[3] to be alive unto God. This life begins with an altered mind towards God.[4]

The second Petrine Epistle[5] contains this further development of the idea of eternal life, that those who live according to God, conscious of their divine sonship, are partakers of the divine nature, that Christ was God in flesh, and therefore to live accord-

---

[1] Eph. iv. 18. [2] 1 Pet. iv. 6.
[3] Rom. vi. 11. [4] μετάνοια εἰς Θεόν.
[5] θείας κοινωνοὶ φύσεως, 2 Pet. i. 4. Delitzsch, *Bibl. Psychol.* 172, 404; S. Tom. Aq., *Summa*, I^a. 1, 13, 9; I^a. 2, 110, 3, et 112, 1, et 113, 9, et 114, 3, etc.

ing to Christ is to live according to God. Eternal life, then, is godly life, infinite in its power of growth and expansion: it is the life of love which God is, even the life of unself which is love, the boundless joy of giving self, as it is written, "He that findeth his life shall lose it; he that loseth his life for My sake shall find it." Eternal life is, therefore, not the addition of anything to the soul, any more than it is a reward laid up in a future world, but it is a quality in the character. Eternal life is a manner of life unto the formation of character. Each man's character is his book of final doom. In this manner of life, justification and righteousness are met together.[1] This is the teaching of the Holy Scripture[2] concerning Eternal Life.

III. Simple and clear as are the sayings of our Lord, when without any bias or prepossession they are received, how soon the theologians of the Church, in many instances and bearings, lost the comprehension of their profound and saving sense! Receptiveness was limited and misshapen by precedent influences and contemporaneous environment. The

---

[1] If we translate δικαίωσις "justification," we ought to translate δικαιοσύνη "justness"; but if we translate δικαιοσύνη "righteousness," then we should translate δικαίωσις "rectification," for righteousness is the result of a life that has been rectified or rightened, and such a life is eternal.

[2] Cf. *Le Problème de L'Immortalité*, par E. Petavel-Oliff; *Life in Christ*, by Edward White; Harnack, *Dogmengeschichte;* Martensen, *Dogmatics*, Secs. 125–147.

old folk-faith persisted in the mental convictions of the converts to the Christian Church, and it was impossible that that faith should be at once completely expelled. Moreover, that clerical theory of the Church which early arose favoured external and legal methods of apprehending the teachings of Jesus. A desire for the rapid spread of the Church found, "rod and candy for child-minded men," an easier way of making church-members than the apparently hopeless task of changing the character of the candidates. So we encounter early in the history of Theology a survival of primitive culture in the notion that life after death has its value and significance in being a retribution or compensation for the life before death. The thought of human life, as growth and progression and as self-retributive, does not seem to have emerged clearly into Christian consciousness. The common notion of the law of life was that of sordid compensation, "an eye for an eye, a tooth for a tooth." "All the ancient Fathers," says Haag,[1] "agree in teaching that the souls immediately after death repair, not to Heaven, for this opinion was held to be a gnostic heresy, but to Sheol or Hades, the subterranean world, where they awaited the last judgment." Men forgot the gospel that

---

[1] Haag, *Hist. des Dogmes Chrétiens*, II. 316. Cf. Hermas, *Pastor*, Sim. IX. 16; Irenæus, *Her.* V. 32; Justin Martyr, *Tryph.* 80; Tertullian, *De An.* lv.; *De Resurrect.* xliii.; Lactantius, *Institut. Div.* VII. 21.

future life, or immortality, is the corollary or result of life being in the present of an eternal character. It was forgotten also that Jesus taught that the future is the outcome of the present, not a gift which shall meet us beyond the door of death. Godliness *is* great gain. Men forgot that to be born again was simply to begin to live spiritually, after the institution and the example of the godly life of Jesus, historically manifested. They forgot that to eat His flesh and drink His blood was, as He explained, to keep His commandments; they forgot that this Christ-life was simply the life of pure and unselfish love, like divine love, not passional; and consequently they erected a formal and external theory of the Sacraments, analogous to the Hebrew system of sacrifice, and such sacraments had but a feeble and notional hold upon the moral life of man. But this theory exactly suited the imperialistic idea of the Church, and without such a theory the hierarchical system would have had no *raison d'être*. Logical as was that theory, it had, in any age from Peter Lombard down, one fatal defect, — it did not save people from their sins proportionately to its tremendous assumptions. Its fundamental defect was a lurking scepticism concerning the value of human life; in fact, we might say that it was subtly atheistical. Hence for the many Eternal Life — that is to say, righteousness — appeared to be impossible in this world; at any rate, it was hardly begun before the grave. The effect of the many evils of the system was that, with all its intellectual acuteness and forcefulness, it made only a few unnatural saints, leaving the rest of humanity almost untouched by influences which make for a righteous life. This is only too evident to any one who studies into the details of the European history up to the sixteenth century sufficiently to discover what was the social condition of the masses.[1]

Many of the ante-Nicene apologists and controversialists were so accustomed to the transcendental philosophies of their day, that the theosophy rather than the ethics of Christianity attracted their attention. The tendency, therefore, was to offer to the cultivated or intellectual, the theoretical gnosis, and to the more emotional, ignorant classes, the mechanical or sensational gnosis. At any rate, of this they were sure, that knowledge, and not existence, is eternal life. In this way orthodoxy or speculative knowledge was offered as a means of salvation in this world, and a mysterious knowledge of God, called a beatific vision, was fancied as a reward in the other world, and substituted for eternal life in this world or elsewhere. This survival we owe to the shaman's hysteric trance on the one hand, and to the Neopla-

---

[1] Cf. Lecky, *History of European Morals;* *La Comédie et les Mœurs en France au Moyen Age,* L. Petit de Julleville; Lea, *Superstition and Force;* Owen, *History of Crime in England;* Pearson, *History of England during the Early and Middle Ages;* the works of Rabelais, and the poems of François Villon.

tonic refinements of speculation and transcendental theosophy on the other. Between folk-faith and philosophy the word of Jesus could hardly get a hearing. Conduct was put in place of character; that is to say in conventional language, good works were exalted above faith. God judges character, yea, it is self-judged; by faith are we justified or made just. Let us never in our teaching sunder justification and righteousness, because essentially they are one. The fault of the theologians of the early Church, if we may presume to point it out, is that they started the evolution of a dogma about salvation, which has always required an elaborate explanation to establish for it any bearing upon human life and character. Therefore the dogma has not been saving. It has held within it too little of the power of the personal Christ. The subject of Jesus' teaching was implicitly and explicitly *life*, its value, significance, and purpose. A precise point of His teaching was consequently this, that unless we have eternal life now, unless we are born again now, into a higher plane of existence, unless now we enter into Christ's life, will, character, existence, as it was on earth, there can be no ground to hope for an eternal life hereafter. "For life does not arise from us, nor from our own nature; but it is bestowed according to the grace of God. And therefore he who shall preserve the life bestowed upon him, and give thanks to Him Who imparted it, shall receive also length of days forever and ever. But he who shall reject it and prove himself ungrateful to his Maker, inasmuch as he has been created, and has not recognised Him Who bestowed, deprives himself of continuance forever and ever."[1] There is no longer in Christendom baptism for the dead, nor forensic imputation of the qualities of some other soul. Impossible! Such notions belong to the religious masked dances and dramatic representations of a poltroon savagery. No requiem mass, no sanctification in the article of death, no solifidian confidence, no probation in the underworld, is able to be given in exchange for eternal life. It is a question of the now, as predestination is a matter of the now, not of ages past; for our God is eternal, and eternity is the ever-present now. It is quite true that the conditions of salvation are in some sense not the least altered by the restatement of doctrine which I have made. God forbid that any one should think to alter and to amend the teachings of Jesus! But a variant and uncertain theology, defectively receptive of those teachings, we may well examine. True, eternal life is still everlasting life, the moment we import into it the thought of duration, but according to the readjustment or statement in this lecture, is not the whole idea, the entire meaning, changed? From the standing-point of this idea of eternal life, formal devices of theology and religion melt each as a cloud. Life gains vastly

---

[1] Irenæus, *Against Heresies*, II. 34, 3.

in ethical and spiritual import. Indeed, our own lives, by this truth, become so exalted that their preciousness and worth make all other considerations paltry, and most of all the supposition of anything like a commercial transaction with Him Who is the Infinite Immanent One, abiding in Eternity, Who containeth all within Him. From this concept of life eternal, as a present quality and fact, what peace and tranquillity come unto us! The petty cares of our environment are nothing to the eternity of life. "Our noisy years seem moments in the being of an eternal silence." As Böhmen uttered from intuition, "When [for any soul] time is as eternity, and eternity as time, then ceases all strife."

The old theory of rewards and punishments *ab extra* has served a use in the world. A theological police system, it was suited for a stage of imperfect development of the religious consciousness. This theory fed the poetry, art, and drama of the Middle Ages, elevated the papal chair, and sent forth the crusaders. In one of the chronicles of that time I once read a story which shows how evident to the paynim was the motive of the crusades. An old Moslem crone was seen going through the Christian camp bearing in one hand a flask of water, and in the other a pot of fire. When asked her purpose, she answered, "I am going to burn up the heaven of the Christian and to drown out his hell, so that these knights will return home from molesting us." Powerful as has been this doctrine in the past, useful as the turn it has served, it has nevertheless been an untrue statement of the religion of Jesus. Besides, its day is fast passing away, the temper of the world is changed. This doctrine has no logical place in scientific or rational theology. It is not an article of the Creed. It is not a part of the reasonable, religious and holy hope of the Christian. No longer do men clutch the pew in front of them to keep from falling down into a burning hell, which yawns just before their terrified imaginations, as some Jonathan Edwards thunders out the wrath of God. The wrath principle certainly does exist, but it exists in us, as the distorted medium through which we view eternal and changeless love. For wrath and fear and hope of gain are not the motives of that life eternal which Jesus brought to light. Yet for centuries they have been stinging thongs in the whip which a mistaken theology wielded to keep the child-men good. Even the heathen Marcus Aurelius had a nobler and worthier idea of life's meaning. "For what more dost thou want," said the imperial moralist, "when thou hast done man a service; art thou not content that thou hast done something conformable to thy nature, and dost thou seek to be paid for it? Just as if the eye demanded a recompense for seeing or the feet for walking. For as these members are formed for a particular purpose, and by working according to their several constitutions obtain what is their own, so also as man is formed by nature to acts of benevolence, when he has done anything benevolent or in any other way conducive to common interest, he has acted conformably to his constitution, and he gets what is his own."[1] Reward in the sense of *possession*, future or present, is not a part of the gospel of Christ. His teaching of reward is that it is in *being* something. Although the inexorable logic of the expanding consciousness of God as Love and Life, pulsing throughout the worlds and the spirits of men, has cast off, or is casting off, rude and mechanical notions of the vindictiveness or retribution from God, and of the future life as something pieced on to this, not developed out of it; nevertheless the moral sanction remains clear and unweakened. The soul that sinneth shall die. The imagery of Christ's teaching has this true meaning, truer than a conventional theology nursed in folk-faith has been wont to give; a significance, which no imputation theory, no invented vicariousness of guilt and penalty, and no materialised grace can nullify. God destroys the soul by creating conditions of existence, which, if not fulfilled, result in destruction, as surely as if He did it by a sudden and visible thunderbolt of annihilation.[2] Only, in God's sovereignty there is nothing

[1] *Meditations*, IX. 42.

[2] In the *Apocalypse* ζωή is regularly contrasted with the second death; also, read Drummond, *Natural Law in the Spiritual World*.

arbitrary, there are no legal fictions and equivocations, no theological evasions, whereby that which is unholy shall be counted as though it were holy, and enter into joy hereafter. Because life is growth eternal, life is growth and progress in this world and after it.

> "Come up hither. From this wave-washed mound
> Unto the furthest flood-brim look with me;
> Then reach on with thy thought till it be drowned,
> Miles and miles distant though the last line be,
> And though thy soul sail leagues and leagues beyond,
> Still, leagues beyond these leagues there is more sea."

The scope for progress is infinite for that life which is become eternal. Consequently, the development of individual spirits will be various; there are differences of progress. Heaven is no dead level of pious vacuities, nor is it a picturesque arrangement, as we see in Dante Rossetti's pictures of —

> "All the saints above,
> In solemn troops and sweet societies,
> That sing, and singing in their glory move."

To the children of the twentieth century this fancy, I expect, will not be attractive, or, what is of far more serious import, it will not be the object of a reasonable, religious, and holy hope. Even a child of our own day, a *fin de siècle* spirit, voices the protest of thousands against the unrealities of popular religious teaching.

"Behold," says Reynaud, "on the steps of this strange heaven the elect, seated side by side, all in rank assigned to them according to their short pilgrimage on earth, absorbed without distraction in the rigidity of their contemplation, and clothed forever in their terrestrial bodies, in which they were seized by death, as by the fatal seal of their eternal mutability. What are these phantoms doing? Are they living or dead? Ah! Christ, how this Paradise scares me. I prefer my life with its lights and shadows, its tribulations and pains, to that blank immortality, with its sanctimonious peace." Now, allowing for a little of that overcolouring which is characteristic of the French school, does not his picture represent correctly enough the ordinary and popular pulpit teaching? Does he not utter the protest of intelligent people? However, if any man does in these days what is right, solely in order to gain reward of such a heaven, or escape a burning hell, let that man well know that he has not Christ's life in him. Let him rest assured that he seeks his life only to lose it, for he simply and certainly exalts his own self-seeking to the throne of the Eternal. Therefore that man, if he be consistent, will go on and ascribe to the eternally living God, Who is ineffable love or unself, the motive of creating the world and men for His own glory, and good pleasure, "and for the praise of His glorious justice to ordain them to dishonour and wrath." No, a thousand times no, to such phraseology, though it be sanctified by generations of teaching, and by the blood of the covenanters. The "place of the skull" is not the altar of wrath; the death on Calvary was the supreme exhibition of eternal love; for, I repeat it, and with emphasis, the sacrifice of the Cross is essential to the purpose of Jesus, essential to His divine human character, essential, not accidental; for it was, is, and ever shall be, the outflowering, the culmination, in its utterance from eternity into the time-sphere, of the operation of Divine Love, Who is the heart of all, and beareth all in His heart. Thus is infinity focussed out of eternity into time. Having loved His own which were in the world, He loved them unto the consummation of love.[1] Hence the Cross is the essence of Christianity, as a manifestation of God to man. This is the purpose of the Incarnation. This is the manifestation of the very nature of life eternal; this life is in His Son, the actualisation in conduct and character of the principle of unself. Again, it has been pointed out that life means correspondence and conformation to the environment. If this be true, then only that life which is conformed to such desires, thoughts, volitions, and deeds, as are from their nature indestructible, will, when destructible things come to an end, have any environment. Therefore, from this point of view, the standing-point of modern science,[2]

[1] See p. 24, above.

[2] Recent studies in Biology and in Embryology furnish strong analogies to the Biblical Theology, of the nature and conditions of

we apprehend again the profound truth and reality of Jesus Christ's doctrine of life eternal.

By Philosophy, also, has this teaching been tested. Spinoza thought that a man would become immortal only as the elements of deathlessness entered into his character; so, when the destructible things pass out of existence, the man would be left with only indestructible elements of character, "saved so as by fire." If nothing eternal or imperishable have entered into the man, he will simply cease to exist, because in him there is nothing which will endure. Thus, in the meaning of the philosopher, as in that of the gospel, true life, and everlasting life, is eternal life, because it is that life which cannot be extinguished, to which death is only a phase, a transition, and which, being deathless and spiritual, re-arises from the dead, immortal, and a spiritual body.

IV. Let us, therefore, teach our people the real eternal life; for in this way only shall we help to build up strong and Christ-like characters. In this way only can we show life to be wholly solemn and full of dignity. Let us bid men cultivate a constantly abiding sense that life must be eternal now, if ever. In this way, also, the worth and nobility of human destiny come to us as a mighty inspiration. It is a consolation in those hours of depression when

eternal life; Drummond, *Natural Law in the Spiritual World;* Cæsar Malan, *La Génération Spirituelle; Revue de la Théologie et de la Philosophie,* Mai, 1879.

the sense of failure weighs heavily upon the soul, and the doubt whispers that life for us holds no further possibilities. Then comes borne in upon the soul the consciousness of that Love Hidden, yet manifest, in all the ways and works of our past. And the soul responds to the message which comes out from eternity, when the Spirit and the Bride say "Come, whosoever will let him drink of the water of life freely."

"Therefore to whom turn I but to Thee, ineffable Name?
Builder and Maker, Thou, of houses not made with hands!
What, have fear of change from Thee Who art ever the same?
Doubt that Thy power can fill the heart that Thy power expands?
There shall never be one lost good! What was, shall live as before;
The evil is null, is nought, is silence implying sound:
What was good shall be good, with, for evil, so much good more;
On earth the broken arcs, in Heaven a perfect round."

Life eternal inheres not in accomplishment, but in effort; not in material success, but in unselfish work; not in conduct, but in character. It is godly life, the life of God, and consequently immortal.

"Now unto the King eternal, immortal, invisible, the only wise God, be honour and glory forever and ever. Amen."

We began at the head of the stream of divine Providence, and have followed and traced it through its various windings and turnings, till we are come to the end of it and see where it issues. As it began in God, so it ends in God. God is the infinite Ocean into which it empties itself.

Pres. JONATHAN EDWARDS, *History of the Work of Redemption*, Works, edition of 1843, Vol. I. p. 510.

Donec me Dominus Deum Incarnationis potentia faciat.

ST. NILUS.

My faith in God rests on my faith in Christ as God manifest in the flesh — not as God and man, but as God in man. It is true that the argument for a Creator from the creation is by modern sciences modified only to be strengthened. The doctrine of a great first cause gives place to the doctrine of an eternal and perpetual cause; the carpenter conception of creation to the doctrine of a divine immanence; the Latin notion of an anthropomorphic Jupiter, renamed Jehovah, made to dwell in some bright, particular star and holding telephonic communication with the spheres by means of invisible wires which sometimes fail to work, dies, and the old Hebrew conception of a Divinity which inhabiteth Eternity, and yet dwells in the heart of the contrite and the humble, takes its place. But the theological argument is strengthened, not weakened, by the doctrine of evolution; creation is more, not less, creation because it is the thought, not the mere handiwork, of God. It is not possible even to state the doctrine of an atheist creation without using the language of theism in the statement, but the heart finds no refuge in an infinite or an eternal energy from which all things proceed. That refuge is found only in the faith that God has entered a human life, taken the helm, ruled heart and hand and tongue, written in terms of human experience the biography of God in History, revealed in the teaching of Christ the truth of God, in the life of Christ the righteousness of God, in the Passion of Christ the suffering of God. That God is in nature, filling it with Himself as the spirit fills the body with its omnipresence, so that all natural forces are but the expressions of the divine will, and all natural laws but the habits of divine action, — this is the doctrine of the Fatherhood. That God was in Christ; so that Jesus Christ was seen, in the three short years of His public life, to be what God is in His eternal administration of the Universe, — this is the doctrine of the Divine Sonship. That God is in human experience, guiding, illuminating, inspiring, making all willing souls Sons of God and joint heirs of Jesus Christ, — this is the doctrine of the Holy Spirit.

Rev. Dr. LYMAN ABBOTT, *Installation Address.*

BIBLIOGRAPHY.

BIBLIOGRAPHY.

Works to which reference is made in the preceding Lectures: —

De Origine, Progressu, Ceremoniis, et Ritibus Festorum Dierum Iudæorum, Græcorum, Romanorum, etc. Rodolpho Hospiniano Auctore; idem, Festa Christianorum, etc. 2 volumes in one, folio. 'Tiguri, ap. Wolphium, MDXCIII.

Cérémonies et Coutumes Religieuses de Tous les Peuples du Monde. Picart. 12 tomes in six volumes, folio. Paris, L. Prudhomme, 1807.

Primitive Culture, by E. B. Tylor, LL.D., F.R.S. 2 vols. 8vo. New York, Henry Holt & Co., 1889.

Researches into the Early History of Mankind, by E. B. Tylor, D.C., LL.D., F.R.S. 1 vol. 8vo. New York, Henry Holt & Co., 1878.

The Hibbert Lectures, 1878–1891. 12 vols. 8vo. London, Williams & Norgate.

The Golden Bough, A Study in Comparative Religion, by J. G. Frazer, M.A. 2 vols. 8vo. London, Macmillan & Co., 1890.

The Women of Turkey and their Folk-Lore, by Lucy M. J. Garnett. Vol. 1. The Christian Women. 8vo. New York, Charles Scribner's Sons, 1890.

Annual Reports of the Bureau of Ethnology. 5 vols. 8vo. Washington, 1882–1889.

Ethnology in Folk-Lore, by George Laurence Gomme, F.S.A. New York, D. Appleton & Co., 1892.

Die Deutsche Volkssage, von Dr. Otto Henne-am Rhyn. 8vo. Leipzig, Kruger, 1874.

Fetichism, by Fritz Schultze. Humboldt Library, New York.

Die Deutsche Götterlehre, Dr. Paul Herrmanowski. Berlin, Nicolai, 1891.

The Supernatural, Its Origin, Nature, and Evolution, by John H. King. 2 vols. 8vo. London and New York, Williams & Norgate, 1892.

Vedische Mythologie, von Alfred Hillebrandt. Ier Band. Breslau, Kœbner, 1891.

Records of the Past, edited by A. H. Sayce. 2 Series. Bagster, London.

Kaffir Folk-Lore, by G. M. Theal. London, Swan Sonnenschein, 1886.

Corpus Poeticum Boreale, The Poetry of the Old Northern Tongue from the Earliest Times to the Thirteenth Century, by Vigfusson & Powell. 2 vols. Oxford and New York, Macmillan & Co., 1883.

Prologomena to the History of Israel, by Julius Wellhausen. Translated. Edinburgh, Adam & Charles Black, n.d.

Religion of the Semites. First Series. The Fundamental Institutions, by W. Robertson Smith. New York, D. Appleton & Co., 1889.

Buddhism in its connection with Brahminism and Hinduism and its contrast with Christianity, by Sir Monier Monier-Williams. New York, Macmillan & Co., 1889.

Brahminism and Hinduism, or Religious Thought and Life in India, by Sir Monier Monier-Williams. New York, Macmillan & Co., 1891.

Studies of the Gods in Greece at Certain Sanctuaries Recently Excavated, by Louis Dyer. New York, Macmillan & Co., 1891.

The Apocryphal Gospels, translated by B. Harris Cowper, London, F. Norgate, 1881.

BIBLIOGRAPHY.

The Book of Enoch, translated from the Ethiopic by Rev. G. H. Schodde. Andover, W. F. Draper, 1882.

Die Gottesbegriffe des Talmud und Zohar, by Dr. Aron Hahn. Leipzig, Kaufmann, n.d.

The Talmud, Selections, by H. Polano. Philadelphia, E. L. Stuart, n.d.

Treasures of the Talmud, by P. J. Hershon. 8vo. London, Nisbet & Co., 1882.

The Kabbalah Unveiled, translated from the *Kabbala Denudata* of Knorr Von Rosenroth by S. L. MacGregor Mathers. 8vo. London, George Redway, 1887.

Bibliothèque Orientale. D'Herbelot. Folio. Mæstricht, MDCCLXXVI.

Le Juif Talmudiste, par M. L'Abbé Rohling. Bruxelles, Vromant et Cie. n.d.

La Kabbale ou la Philosophie Religeuse des Hébreux, par Adolphe Franck. 8vo. Paris, Hachette, 1889.

Études Orientales, par Adolphe Franck. 8vo. Paris, Lévy, 1861.

Jesus of Nazara, by Dr. Theodor Keim. Translated. 6 vols. Williams & Norgate, 1876.

Vie De Jésus, par Ernest Renan. Paris, Lévy, 1863.

Novum Testamentum Græce, Editio Octava Critica Major. 2 vols. Const. Tischendorf, Lipsiæ.

The Creeds of Christendom, by Philip Schaff, D.D. 3 vols. New York, 1874.

A Comparative View of the Doctrines and Confessions of Christendom, by G. B. Winer. Translated by W. B. Pope. Edinburgh, T. T. Clark, 1881.

Authoritative Christianity, The Decisions of the Six Ecumenical Councils, by James Chrystal, Translator, Editor, and Publisher. 1st vol. 8vo. Jersey City, 1891.

The Apostolic Fathers, Revised Texts, by the late J. B. Lightfoot, D.D., D.C.L., LL.D., Lord Bishop of Durham. 8vo. London, Macmillan & Co., 1891.

The Ante-Nicene Fathers. Translations of the Writings of the Fathers down to A.D. 325, by Rev. Alex. Roberts, D.D., and James Donaldson, LL.D. Revised by Bishop A. C. Coxe, D.D. 8 vols. 8vo. Buffalo, Christian Literature Publishing Company, 1886–1888.

History of Christian Doctrines, by Dr. K. R. Hagenbach. Translated. 3 vols. 8vo. Edinburgh, Clark, 1883.

Manuel de l'Histoire des Dogmes Chrétiens, par Henri Klee. Traduit de l'Allemand, par l'Abbé Mafire. 2 tomes. Paris, Lecoffre et Cie, 1848.

Lehrbuch der Dogmengeschichte, von Adolf Harnack. 3 Band. Freiburg, Mohr, 1888–1890.

Histoire des Dogmes Chrétiens, par E. Haag. Paris, 1892.

A Critical History of the Christian Doctrine of Justification and Reconciliation, by Albrecht Ritschl. Translated by J. S. Black. 8vo. Edinburgh, 1872.

The Philosophy of History, by G. W. F. Hegel. Translated by Bohn. New York, Macmillan & Co., 1884.

Masks, Heads, and Faces, by Ellen R. Emerson. Boston, 1891.

Die Christliche Mystik nach ihrem geschichtlichen Entwickelungsgange im Mittel und in der Neuern Zeit dargestellt, von Dr. Ludwig Noack. Konigsberg, Gebrüder Bornträger, 1853.

A Treatise of Dogmatic Theology, by Rev. Samuel Buel, S.T.D. 2 vol. 8vo. New York, Thomas Whittaker, 1890.

Christian Dogmatics: A Compendium of the Doctrines of Christianity, by Dr. H. Martensen. Edinburgh, Clark, 1860.

Systematic Divinity, by Charles Hodge, D.D. 3 vol. 8vo. New York, Harpers.

S. Thomas Aquinas' Summa Theologica. 8 vols. 8vo. New York, Benziger Bros., 1875.

Le Christ de la Tradition, par Mgr. Landriot, Evêque de La Rochelle et Saintes. 2 tomes. Paris, Victor Palmé, 1867.

Works of Mr. Richard Hooker in Eight Books of the Laws of the Ecclesiastical Polity. 1 vol. fol. London, MDCCV.

A Course of Sermons for All the Sundays of the Year, by Jeremy Taylor, D.D. 2 vols. fol. London, 1655.

Works of William Beveridge, D.D., Lord Bishop of St. Asaph. 6 vols. Oxford, 1817.

The Works of Joseph Butler, D.C.L., Lord Bishop of Durham. 2 vols. Oxford, MDCCCXXVI.

The Works of Thomas Secker, LL.D., Archbishop of Canterbury. 6 vols. 1811.

Bishop Overall's Convocation Book, MDCVI. London, 1690.

The Polity of the Christian Church, by A. A. Pelliccia. Translated. London, Masters, 1883.

A History of Philosophy, by Johann Eduard Erdmann. 3 vols. London and New York, Macmillan & Co., 1890.

Handbook of the History of Philosophy, by Dr. Albert Schwegler. Edinburgh, 1874.

Ancient Law, its Connection with the Early History of Society and its Relation to Modern Ideas, by Henry Sumner Maine. New York, Henry Holt, 1875.

Christian Archæology, by C. W. Bennett, D.D. New York and Cincinnati, 1888.

History of Mediæval Art, by Dr. Franz von Reber. Translated. New York, Harpers, 1887.

Didron, Christian Iconography. 2 vols. London, Bohn, 1851, 1886.

History of the Christian Church, by W. Moeller. Translated. London and New York, Macmillan & Co., 1892.

Ecclesiastical Polity of the New Testament, by Rev. G. A. Jacobs, D.D. New York, Thomas Whittaker, 1878.

The Destiny of Man Viewed in the Light of His Origin, by John Fiske. Boston, Houghton, Mifflin & Co., 1889.

A System of Biblical Psychology, by Franz Delitzch, D.D. Translated by Rev. R. E. Wallis. Edinburgh, Clark, 1867.

Biblical Theology of the New Testament, by Dr. Bernard Weiss. Translated. 2 vols. 8vo. Edinburgh, Clark, 1888.

The Constitution of the Presbyterian Church containing the Confession of Faith, the Catechisms, and the Directory for the Worship of God.

Justini, Philosophi et Martyris, Opera. Item Athenagoræ Atheniensis, Theophili Antiocheni, Tatiani Assyrii, et Hermiæ, etc. Coloniæ, MDLCLXXXVI.

S. Hippolyti, Refutationis Omnium Hæresium Libri X. Duncker et Scheneidewin. 8vo. Gottingæ, 1859.

Firmiani Lactantii Opera, Fritzsche. 12mo. Leipzig, Tauchnitz, 1842.

Arnobii adversus Nationes Libri, VII, Oehler. Leipzig, Tauchnitz, 1846.

M. Minucii Felicis Octavius. Firmicus Maternus, Paulinus, Commodianus. Leipzig, Tauchnitz, 1847.

Reliquiæ Sacræ, by M. J. Routh, S.T.P. 5 vols. Oxoni, 1846.

Le Problème de l'Immortalité, par E. Patavel-Olliff. 2 tomes. Paris, Fischbacher, 1892.

Essays in Biblical Greek, by Edwin Hatch, M.A., D.D. Oxford and New York, Macmillan & Co., 1889.

La Divina Commedia, di Dante Allighieri. Witte. Berlin, 1862.

INDEX.

INDEX.

A.

Abbott's, Lyman, Statement of the Theology of Divine Immanence, 290.

Abelard, his criticism of the Anselmic theory, 175.

Absolution. See Forgiveness.

After death, in primitive culture, 227, 277.

    in modern common opinion, 237.

Agnosticism, evolution of, 43.

Ainu theory of ghost-world, 257.

Albigensians, 69, 72, 110.

Altars, early, 15.

    why of stone, 17.

    why relics deposited in, 232.

Amiel, H. F., on the distinctive element of Christianity, 3.

    adjustment of religious teaching, 50, 73.

Ancestor worship, 38, 258.

Ancient temple, how different from a Christian church, 83.

Andrews, Bp., on Episcopal government of Church, 124.

Animism, 35, 71.

    survival of, in Pantheism, 43.

Anselm, St., on Atonement, 174.

Antiquity, value of appeal to, 2.

Apocalypses, pre-Christian, 8, n. 1.

Apocalypses, influence of, on Christian theology, 234.

Apocalyptic writings, their influence on common notion of heaven, 260.

Apostolic Church, 117.

Apostolic development of doctrine of the Resurrection, 204-208.

Apostolic Succession, 118. See Continuity, Tactual, and Episcopacy.

    its sign, 126.

    relation to the Church, 125.

Aquinas, St. Thomas, on Divine Immanence, 26, 67.

Arabian philosophy, 13.

Arbitrary God, in primitive folk-faith, 147.

    survival of the notion of, 148.

Arianism, 68.

Arius on Resurrection, 220.

Arnold, Sir E., quoted on Peace of the Church, 135.

Arnold, M., on decay of Faith, 75.

    on Eternal Life, 271.

    on Infallibility of the Church, 115.

Art, Byzantine, and the dead Christ, 237.

    of Greece, influence of theory of Resurrection upon, 230, n. 1.

Art, its influence on early survivals in Christianity, 71.
— of Early Egypt, influenced by folk-faith, 230.
Aryan Monotheism, more stable than Semitic, 41.
Athanasius, on deification of humanity, 51.
— on Divine Immanence, 66.
— on Eternal Logos, 60.
Athenagoras on Resurrection, 194.
Atonement, Anselmic doctrine of, 69.
— Bp. Butler on, 176.
Atonement, and magic, 84.
Augustine, St., 13.
— his influence on the development of the doctrine of forgiveness of sins, 177.
— on the Resurrection, 235.
— on the privilege of Peter, 106.
— his dualism, 266.
Authority, basis of, 23, 134.
Azazel, predecessor of Satan, 158. See Scapegoat, Substitution, Sinbearer.

B.

Bacon on human error, 3.
Baptism and resurrection, 221. See Irenæus, Justin, etc.
Baptism for forgiveness, 144.
Baptists, distinctive truth of the, 132.
Barbarossa, mediæval popular belief about, 227.
Barrow, Isaac, on Resurrection, 195.
Bible (the), a record of progressive reception of truth, 7.
Bohmen, Jacob, on Eternal Life, 246, 282.

Bowen, Professor Francis, on transmigration of souls, 253.
Brahm, 38, 116.
Browning, Robert, on Renaissance belief in consciousness of dead, 229.
— on extinction of evil, 267.
— on service of man, 138.
— on the perfection of the Universe, 289.
— on human progress, quoted, 33.
— doctrine of cosmic resurrection process, 240, 241.
— on remission of sin from the world, 189.
— on Christ in the world, 88.
Buddhism, 43, 83.
— its self-renunciation contrasted with the Christian self-renunciation, 113.
— and Brahminism at one in the doctrine of Absorption of the soul in God, 251, n. 1.
Burnt Column, the, 6.
Butler, Bp., on Atonement theories, 176.

C.

Calvinism and Neoplatonism, 12.
— and polytheism, 42.
— its idea of God, 148.
— and devil worship, 147, 152.
Catacombs, their influence on Christian doctrine, 9.
— their testimony to early Christian belief in resurrection, 231.
— their testimony to survivals of paganism, 222.
— See Art.

INDEX. 305

Catholic Church, Antenicene definitions of, 98, 99.
  Anglican definitions of, 78, 79, 93.
  Matthew Arnold's definition of, 115.
  true members of, 78.
  See Apostolic Church.
Catholicity, Jeremy Taylor on, 2, 131.
Ceremonies [see Ritual, Symbol, Sacrifice] relative to religion, 10.
  dramatic, 104.
Charlemagne, mediæval popular belief about, 227.
Christianises the Saxons, 10.
Christian religion, spread of, 8.
Christian Science, 19, 56.
Christmas, 11.
Chrysostom, St. John, on Resurrection, 235.
Church, definition of, in XIXth Article of Religion, 93.
  how constituted and instituted, 92.
  theory of, in early Latin theology, 96.
  undergoing a supernatural evolution, 118.
  relation of individual to, 94.
  and State united, idea of Hindu and Greek thought, 88.
  and World, 133.
  unity of, 103.
  "Notes" of, 97, 101.
  See Unity, Holiness, Catholicity, Apostolicity.
  article of, not in early creeds of East, 95.
  of West, 96.
  of Rome, effect of politics on, 17.
Clement, St., of Alexandria, on defective receptiveness, 3.
  on forgiveness, 173.
  on salvation in the Church only, 99.
  his gnosis, 100.
  of Rome, on Episcopacy and Succession, 119.
Clericalism, inevitable, 12.
  survival of Shamanism, 84, 127, 252.
Clough, A. H., on resurrection of society, 195.
Cobbe, F. P., on Mystery of Pain, 215.
Collegia of Rome, survivals in the Church, 88, 91.
Comparative religion, 17.
Communion with God, 275 and n. 5.
  with the god in Mexican religion, 154.
  with God in Hebrew ceremonial, 167, n. 1.
Congregational form of polity, a survival, 88.
Congregationals, their special truth, 132.
Constantine the Great, 6, 10.
Continuity of the Church, 127.
Conversion, sensible, survival of adeptism, 86, and of Shamanism, 149, 279.
Coronation stone, 16.
Cross, symbol of life not of death only, 165, 240.
Crucifixion in early Art, 49.
Culture, ancient, rejected by the Church, 12.
Cusa, Nicolas, on Divine Immanence, 67.
Cyprian, St., Theory of the Church, 99.

D.

Dance of death, 229.
Dante, on coequality of the Persons of the Trinity, 62.
  on dead souls, 272, n. 5.
  influence of his Divine Comedy on popular conceptions of state of dead, 236.
  on "donation of Constantine," 87.
  on punishment of sin, 184.
  on Immanence of God, 26.
  on Rewards and punishments, 265.
Death, eternal, 284, 288.
  of Jesus, its significance, 202.
Deism, 43.
Development of doctrine, 2, 20, 51.
Devil worship of primitive man, 147.
  worshippers, 152.
Dioceses, small, evils of, 122.
Diognetus, Epistle of, 173.
Dionysiac mysteries and mythos of the Resurrection, 238.
Dionysius the Areopagite and pantheistic mysticism, 44.
Divine vicegerents and the papal theory, 37.
Doctrine of Church Fathers, never any concensus of, 79.
  of the Holy Trinity, the, the true idea of God, 60-62.
  of Christian religion, some primary postulates, 21.
  Christian, Evolution of, 7, 18, 22, etc.
  Christian, pagan elements of, 7, 15, 67, etc. (see Survivals).
  how to separate paganism from, 73.

Doctrine, Christianity influenced by philosophy and law, 18.
  of sin over-analysed, 178.
Doctrines of the Christian religion, what are essential, 3, 26.
Dogma. See Doctrine.
Dualism, its basis, 61; its survivals, 72.
  in materialistic theories of Resurrection, 220.

E.

Eckehart's debt to Neoplatonism, 13.
  on Immanence of God, 26.
  on St. Paul's doctrine of evolution, 58.
Edda, on Odin's self-immolation, 161.
Edwards, Jonathan, on God the beginning and end of theology, 290.
Egyptian Art, originally realistic, 230.
  religion, 44.
  theory of resuscitation of the dead, 229.
"Elements" surviving in Christian belief, 71.
Eleusis and the Church, 83.
  and doctrine of Resurrection, 238.
Enoch, Book of, on the Millennium 260.
  on Azazel, 158.
Emanations, theory, 63.
Episcopacy a basis of unity, 129.
  its importance, 124-129.
  of the integrity of the Church, 127, n. 1.
  historic, 127.
  See Apostolicity.

Episcopate, historic, asserted in Book of Common Prayer, 78.
Erigena on Divine Immanence, 66.
Error, religious. See Survivals.
Eternal birth-process, a statement of Evolution, 181.
See Regeneration.
Eternal death, 284.
from failure to conform to the Environment, 265, 283, 287.
Eternal life, its *raison d'être*, 270, 275.
begins in the present, 271.
progressive, 285, 288.
according to the *Theologica Germanica*, 246.
Jeremy Taylor on, 246.
in teaching of Jesus, 269.
in Egyptian folk-faith, 258.
in the Edda, 257.
ethical doctrine of, 183, n. 2, 280.
and natural law, 287.
a present condition, 270.
Eternity of evil, not possible, 266.
Ethical form of the doctrine of the Resurrection, 242.
Euripides, his idea of divine sacrifice, 48.
Everlasting. See Eternal.
Evil is privative, 181.
Eternal, and Wagner's criticism, 266.
Evolution, and Resurrection in Pauline theology, 208.
St. Paul's statement of, 57.
of the Church, 211.
the cosmic passion, 58.
and theism, 291.
Expiatory sacrifice, its rational basis, 69.
Extinction of Sin, due to Divine Immanence, 188.

F.

Fathers of the Church, no consensus of doctrines of, 79.
Faith, Catholic, 2.
Fall of Man, a truth of psychology, 189.
Fear, the secret god of Rome, 148.
influence on development of theology, 153, 277.
in primitive religion, 148.
Feminine principle, 63, 64.
Fetishism, 37, 120.
Fichte, 26.
Fictions, theological, 140, 170.
Fire-worship, 14.
Fiske, John, on Romans viii. 18–26, 216.
quoted, on Pardon, 138.
Forcordination, 68.
Forgiveness of sins, in the Creed, 143.
not an evasion of penalty alone, 146.
not magical, 133, 185.
of sins, chief office of the Church, 144.
See Pardon.
Free-thought, hostility of Church to, 13.
François Xavier, St., on love of God, quoted, 40.

G.

Genius of Roman Emperor, 38.
Gibbon, Edw., on absolute revelation and conditioned receptivity, 9.
error about the eating of the slain god, 153.
Gilgul, a Rabbinic doctrine, 225, 253.

308   INDEX.

God, primary idea of, 32 seq., 35, 36, 39, 42, 45, 61.
   proofs of existence of, 31.
   knowledge of, 51, 74.
   in His World, Goethe on, 27.
   idea of, comprehends all theology, 33.
God-consciousness, 51.
   Fichte on, 26.
Götterdämmerung, its ethos, 266.
Goethe, 27, 31.
Ghost-world in patristic theology, 277 and n. 1.
   of primitive man, 250.
   of Egypt, 229.
Ghosts, feeding the, 15, 221, 259.
Gorham Case, 145, n. 1.
Gnosticism, 234.
   its problem, 63.
Gnosis of the Gospel, 274.
Grace, a theory of, 111, 182.
   double aspect, 201, n. 3.
Gregory the Great, St., on Divine Immanence, 66.
Ground of Authority, 134.
Guilt, inherited, 178.
   inherited, a survival of Ancient Semitic Materialism, 253.

H.

Haag on lack of agreement of the Fathers, 79.
Hall, Bp., on Episcopacy, 118.
Harnack on cultus of relics, 232.
Hartmann's explanation of the predominance of pain over pleasure, 213.
Harwood, G., on actual forgiveness, 139.
Hawthorne, Nathaniel, his psychology of sin and its forgiveness, 187.

Heaven, 270.
   in early folk-faith, 260.
   See Eternal Life.
Hell, a dualistic survival, 267.
Hegel on doctrine of the Trinity, 70.
   on Resurrection, 240.
Hesperides, 260.
Hierarchial theory of the Church, a survival of Shamanism, 127.
Higher Criticism and Theology, 5.
Hinton on Mystery of Pain, 214.
Hippolytus, St., theory of two resurrections, 221.
Historic Episcopate, 127.
   See Continuity of the Church, Apostolic Succession, Tactual, St. Spiridion, Ordination.
Holiness of God, the ground of His Eternal Existence, 275.
   the condition of life eternal, 276.
   of Church, 105.
   distinguished from Nirvana, 240.
Holy Ghost, a person, 64.
Holy Grail in relation to Christian doctrine, 203, n. 7.
Hooker, quoted on absolute necessity of Episcopal form of government, 117.
   on non-Episcopal Ordination, 126.
Hooker's Ecclesiastical Polity, 125, n. 1.
Hugo, Victor, on Cultus of Saints, 38.
Human Sacrifice, origin of. See Scapegoat.
Humiliation. See Kenosis.
Huntington, Bp., on functions of a bishop, 120 ff.

Hymnology, relative to ritual in development, 252.

I.

Idea of God, innate, 32.
   in Monotheism, 42.
Ignatius, St., theory of the Church, 98.
   theory of Resurrection, 219.
Illusion, theory of the world, 55.
Immanence of God, 26.
   in doctrine of the Fathers, 66–67.
   a Pauline doctrine, 65.
   a Johannine doctrine, 54.
   according to Ezekiel, 65.
   Tennyson quoted, 44.
   Shelley quoted, 45.
   relative to Incarnation, 27.
   taught in O. T., 58.
   the actual source of pardon, 169.
   relative to forgiveness of sins, 143.
   inferred from development of ethnic religions, 52.
   and His transcendence, bearing upon the organisation of the Church, 108.
   and Eternal Life, 273.
   relation to the Church, 132.
   relative to Holiness of Church, 111, 114.
   the true Philosophy of History, 56.
   relation to Unity of Church, 108.
   of the Word, 54.
Immanence of Holy Trinity, rational basis, 55.
Immanence *versus* the world an illusion, 55.
Immolation of the divine Victim in Christian Ceremonies, 154. See Victim.
Immortality, 276, n. 2.
   conditional, 196.
   conditional in Hinduism, 252.
   innate, not Biblical doctrine, 268.
Imperialism, a survival, 17.
   of Rome, effect upon the Church, the Church, 87, 99.
Incarnation, its essential significance, 48.
   and mediation, 181.
   Tennyson's statement, 47.
Independents. See Congregationals.
Indulgences, origin of the doctrine of, 266.
Infallibility, 23, 37.
   of Roman Church, 114, n. 1.
   a sign of Catholicity?, 117.
   origin of idea of, 85.
Infallible Church, a comprehensive definition, 116.
Irenæus, St., on Apostolic succession, 119.
   on Eternal Life, 281.
   on forgiveness of sins, 173.
   on conditional immortality, 220, 280.
   not orthodox on doctrine of Christ's natures, 11, n. 3.
   theory of the Church, 96, 99.
   on Resurrection, 220, 221.
Islam, degeneracy of, 41.
Izdubar Epic on "outer darkness," 263.
   a myth of pain and human progress, 162.

J.

Jesus, purpose of, 20.
    secret of, 45, 46.
    mediation of, 183.
    unselfish love, 40.
    misunderstood, 8.
    doctrine slowly accepted, 11.
    doctrine of the Church, 89 ff.
    doctrine of the Absolution, 169 ff.
    doctrine of the Resurrection, 200 ff.
    doctrine of the Heaven, 268 ff.
Jewish theory of Resurrection, 223.
Jews, Polish, their curious burial custom, 225.
John of Damascus, St., on divine Immanence, 66.
Justice, love, and mercy identical in the theology of the LXX., 185, n. 2.
Justification, doctrine of, 23, 111, 182, n. 3, 276, n. 1.
Justin Martyr, St., 12.
    on Forgiveness of Sins, 173.
    on Resurrection, 219.
    on identity of the Word and reason, 50.
Justinian, Emperor, 12.

K.

Karens' notion of future life, 257.
Karma, attempt to revive the theory of, 238, 240.
Karl the Great, proselytism of, 10.
Kenosis of Jesus, 182, n. 3, 102, 201.
Kenosis, Church a kenosis of Holy Ghost, 102.
    of the Holy Ghost, 63.
Kingdom of God, at first known in person of Jesus only, 90.
Kingdom of God, in parables, 90, 91.
    in relation to sociology, 91, 93.
Kingdom of God and the Church, 93, 98.
Kings, origin of theory of divine right of, 85.

L.

Lamb of God, 155, 165, 166.
Landor, W. S., quoted, 2.
Leaven, of parable is God Himself, 217.
Legal theology not saving, 278.
Legends, Christian, origin of, 11.
Leibnitz and preëstablished harmony, 68, n. 2.
Lia Fail, 16. See Stone Worship and Altar.
Liddon, Canon, denies theory of an arbitrary God, 148.
Limbo, 262.
Life, its nature, desire, 183.
    Eternal. See Eternal.
    self-retributive, 277.
    victorious over death in nature, Swinburne's opinion, 243.
    omnipresent, in poetry, 34, 35, 43, 56.
    omnipresent, in theology, 35.
Logos. See Word of God, Incarnation.
Lotze, 19.
    on resurrection of flesh, 208.
Love, divine, 47, 50, 61.
    essentially sacrificial of self, 167.
    fundamental Idea of God, 47.
    the basis of theology and religion, 26.
Love divine, Lucretius and Euripides on, 48.
Lowell, J. R., on dead souls, 272.

INDEX.

Luck, as a religious concept, 34, n. 1.
Lucretius, his idea of divine love, 48.
Luz, the bone, 223.

M.

Magic, its origin, 34, 112.
    survival among Christians, 84, 228.
    and the divine name, 112.
    influence on Christian Theology, 84, 112.
    surviving in theories of forgiveness, 145.
Magical theory of Holy Baptism, 114.
Mahomet, attempt to proclaim him God incarnate, 41.
Maimonides on soul of the dead, 233.
Manes worship, and cultus of saints, 38.
Marcus Aurelius, Emperor, on the true motive of righteousness, 283.
Marlowe, Christopher, on heaven, 247.
Martyrdom of Man, Swinburne, Æschylus, and the Gospels on, 162.
Matheson, A., on basis of the religion of humanity, 23.
Materialism in Theology, 69, 119, 163.
Mediator, Jesus Christ in His humanity, 183.
    primitive notion of, 72.
Menhirs, 14–16.
Merits, origin of the doctrine of, 264.
Metanoia, definition of, 94, n. 1.

Metempsychosis. See Transmigration.
Method of theological study, 22.
Methodism, its distinctive truth, 132.
Methodist Episcopal, theory of Episcopate, its early form, 100.
Millennial doctrines, origin, 260, 223.
Milton, on the Fall, 177.
    his abandonment of Christianity, 43.
Monotheism, pure, negates itself, 43.
    not result of evolution, 41.
    its truth, 60.
    its weakness, 61.
Monism, 19.
Moore, Rev. Aubrey L., on place in theology of sin doctrines, 26.
Mormonism, 63.
Mountains, sacred, 37.
Montanism, 9.
Mythos, how different from myth, 162.
Myths, invention of, 17.
    survivals of, 71.
Mystics of fourteenth century, 13.
Mysteries, Eleusinian, mythos of, 86.
Mystery, Paul's use of word, 47, notes.

N.

Navajo myth of a redeemer, 162.
Necromancy, 256, 258.
Nibelungenlied, 11.
Neoplatonism and Christian beliefs, 12.
Nirvana, 251.
Noble, J. A., on sin and pardon, 139.

Norse folk-faith concerning the dead, 227.
  myth of a redeemer, 161.
Notes of the Church, goal of Church's progress, 102, 109, 130. See Church.

O.

Ordination of primitive priesthood, 86.
Organisation of Church, 105.
Origen, 12.
  on resurrection body, 226.
  on Divine Immanence, 66.
  on Forgiveness of Sins, 173.
Original sin, 178.
Omar Khayyám on immortality, 233.
"Outer darkness" in Semitic folk-faith, 263.
Orthodoxy, 51.

P.

Paganism, 70, 71. See Survivals.
Pater, Walter, on peace of the Church, 12.
Pain, its use, 164.
  problem, Von Hartmann's solution, 213.
  problem of, Browning's solution, 139.
  problem of, in relation to Forgiveness of Sins, 181.
  in relation to Resurrection, 212, 243.
  a compensation for sin, influence of this theory on Christian doctrine, 264.
Pantheism, its truth, 60.
  its logical and historical evolution, 44.
Pantheism in poetry, 35.
  in folk-lore, 35.
Papacy, claims of, 105, n. 1.
Pardon and natural law, 138, 188.
  its relation to immanence of God, 169.
Parousia. See Presence.
Parson, origin of the idea of, 85.
Particular predestination. See Predestination.
Passion, the, of the universe, 214.
Passion plays, the Greek, 162.
Paul, St., on Cosmic passion, 216.
  on the problem of pain, 58.
Paul's, St., answer to pessimism, 181.
Pauline psychology of Resurrection, 208.
Penalty, relation to sin, 179.
Pessimism, 179.
Petrine Claims, 105, n. 1.
Perfection, 32.
Person, a theological term, 64, n. 2.
Pillar saints, a survival of stone worship, 16.
Plato on souls and stars, 238.
Platonism and Christian theology, 12.
  and St. Augustine, 177.
Plotinus, his last words, 74.
Polytheism, 37.
  its truth, 60.
  survivals of, 39, 72.
Pontifex Maximus, survival of, 87.
Pope, origin of the notion of, 37.
Potter, the divine, Hodge, Shedd, Carlyle, and Browning on, 150.
  the divine, in Egypt, 149.
Power, spiritual and temporal united, a concept of folk-faith, 37.

Prayer, Book of Common, 19.
Predestination, particular, doctrine, a survival from early folk-faith, 149.
Precious Blood doctrine, 203.
Priesthood, its true place in Christian Church, 92.
Presbyterians', distinctive truth, 132.
Presbyterial organisation, 107.
Presence of Christ in the world, 53.
Propitiatory sacrifices, primitive, 36, 39.
 sacrifice, basis of idea of, 60.
Protestant Episcopal Church, its actual organic condition, 108.
Prothesis, Order of, in Eastern Church, 154.
Psychology of primitive men, 250.
of Sts. Paul and Peter, 206–209.
Purgatory in folk-faith, 164, n.

R.

Ransom, 170, n. 2. See Theophylact.
Rawes, H. A., on immanence of the Triune God, 76.
Receptiveness relative to true doctrine, 9.
of mankind, 3.
Redemptive process of life, 214.
Redemption, Jeremy Taylor on, 151.
commercial theory of, 146. See Scapegoat.
Regeneration, 145.
in Holy Baptism, 112.
Reincarnation. See Transmigration.
Relics, cultus of, its origin magical, 232.

Religion, comparative, Study of, 17, 18.
primitive, 34 ff.
of Christ, in visible and corporate form, 92.
Renan, cited, 45.
Rephaim, 258.
Resurrection of Jesus, 199–204.
of the dead, in Creed, 199.
doctrine peculiar to Christianity, 195, 196.
begins in the present, 209.
a change to a higher state, 195.
in nature, Swinburne's thought, 243.
theology of, not yet highly developed in Christian theology, 218.
different from resuscitation, 207, 208 n. 1.
of the wicked, 207, n. 2.
a moral process in the world, 195.
in patristic theology, 218–223.
in Talmud, 225.
dependent on preservation of corpse, 229–233.
in Greek folk-lore, 238.
Retribution, 277.
future, subjective, 149.
theory, influence of, on art, poetry, and drama, 282.
Revelation of God in human progress, 52.
and God, 31.
Rewards and penalties according to Omar Khayyám, 149.
and punishments, influence of theology of, in development of Christendom, 282.
and punishments in folk-faith, 268.

314 INDEX.

Rewards and punishments, why a popular element of religious teaching, 277, 282.
Reynaud on heaven, 286.
Right, no arbitrary standard of, 42, n. 1, 148.
Ritual, dramatic, a survival, 104.
   and religion, 16, 84.
Rossetti, D. G., on progress of soul after death, 285.
Rothe, R., on forgiveness of sin, 139.
Roman law and doctrine of forgiveness of sins, 175.
Rufinus against resurrection of the flesh, 196.

S.

Sacerdotalism, origin of, 37.
   a survival of Shamanism, 84, 99.
Sacraments, materialistic theory of, 119.
   and magic, 84, 112.
Sacramental Absolution, its power, 190.
Sacred Heart, Symbol of Cultus, 224, n. 1.
Sacrifice, origin of custom, 34, 39.
   propitiatory, 259 n. 2.
   propiatory, origin, 39.
   of Jesus a revealment, 49.
Sacrificial system of Israel, 36, 167, n. 1.
Saining torch, 158.
Saint John's day, 11.
Saints, cultus of, 38, 70, 72.
   merits of, 264.
Saint-worship in Islam, 41.
Salvation outside Church impossible, 100.

Sanctification, immediate, a survival, 39.
Satisfaction, origin of doctrine, 153.
   first appearance in Christian theology, 174.
Saviour God, Jesus a revealment of, 89.
Sinew which shrank, why not eaten, 226.
Scapegoat, human, 85.
   in India, 157.
   among the Hebrews, 158.
   in Thibetan Buddhism, 158.
   in Athens, 159.
   Rome, 159.
   Babylon, 159.
   Mexico, 159.
   theory responsible for death of Jesus, 160.
   theory in Ante-Nicene theology, 161, 172-173.
Self-interest no part of religion of Jesus, 284, 287.
   and the Church idea, 133.
Self-sacrifice of Izdubar, 162.
Shakspere on God's forgiveness, 187.
Shamanism and revivals, 279.
   survival in hierarchial systems, 127.
Schopenhauer, how his theory differs from teaching of Jesus, 180.
Shelley on human receptiveness, 50.
   on Immanence of God, 45.
Sill, E. R., on evil of Sins of Ignorance, 191.
Sin-bearer. See Scapegoat.
   bearing and witchcraft, 157.
   eating, 155.

Sin-bearer in Hebrew rites, 156.
    doctrine, misplaced by theologians, 26.
    Christian doctrine of, not derived from folk-faith, 164.
    what it is, 183.
    place of doctrine of, in Theology, 33.
    transference of, 156, 157.
    is positive, 182, n. 1.
    and pain confused, survival of primitive notion, 163.
Social problems and Holy Communion, 113.
    and the Church, 133.
    and the Resurrection, 243.
Sociology and Forgiveness of sins, 144.
Soma, 14. See Transubstantiation.
Spinoza on Facultative Immortality, 288.
Spiridion, St., dead hand of, 228.
Spirit, guidance of Holy, did not cease with Anti-Nicene epoch, 117.
Spiritism, 70.
Shields, Professor of Princeton, on Episcopacy, the ground of Church unity, 128.
Soul's sleep in death, 237.
Stations of the Cross, origin of, 9.
Stoic sects, relative to Church organisation, 83.
Stoicheia, 71.
Stones, sacred, 14, 15.
Strauss, David, mythical theory of the Passion, 163.
Stylites, 16.
Substitutionary death, origin of custom, 153, 159.
Substitution, doctrine, of its origin, 153.

Substitutionary sacrifice, in Æschylus' drama, 161.
Sufism in Islam, 41.
Sun-myth in Church ceremonies, 226.
Survival of folk-faith in theories of atonement, 176.
    of polytheism in Christian Theology, 67.
Survivals of paganism in theology of the Resurrection, 220, 234.
    of Shamanism, 85, 127.
    of magic, 112, 146.
    of primitive materialism, 253.
    of fire worship, 14.
    of fetishism, 120, 232.
    of dualism, 37, 73, 267.
    in theories of the Church, 99.
    of eternal life, 281.
Symbols, pagan, of Christian ideas, 9.
Synagogue did not suggest the form of Church organisation, 84.

T.

Tactual Succession not the doctrine of Clement of Rome, 119.
    of the ministry, not a Roman Catholic theory, 125.
    not an Anglican theory, 125, 126.
Talmud on State of the Dead, 232.
    on Resurrection of body, 225.
Tatian on Resurrection, 219.
Taylor, Jeremy, on Divine Immanence and Incarnation, 27.
    on Comprehensiveness as basis of Unity, 131.
    on Eternal Life, 246.
    on pardon, 138.
    on true Catholicity, 2.
Telesterion at Eleusis, 83.

316 INDEX.

Tennyson, Lord, on moral evolution of man, 217.
   on Pantheism, 44.
Tertullian, non-sacerdotal theory of the Church, 78.
   gross theory of Resurrection, 221.
Testament of Jesus not His last will, 167, n. 1.
Theodore, St., and Romulus, 70.
Theologica Germanica, 13.
Theology of Church heterogeneous, 3.
   progression in, 22–24.
   consistency in, 22, 23.
   study, 7.
   new methods, 6.
Theophilus on Conditional Immortality, 196.
   on Resurrection, 221.
Theophylact, on Ransom of Christ, 168.
Thommasin on Immanence of God, 32, n. 1.
Transcendence and Immanence both true, 59.
   bare, a survival, 68.
Transmigration, survival of idea in Christian legends, 253.
   not taught by Jesus, 253.
   of souls in folk-faith, 249–251.
   in Talmud, 238.
   purpose of the doctrine, 254, 355.
Transubstantiation and fetishism, 120. See Soma.
Trinity, doctrine of, 26, 53, 59, 60, 62, 69, 70.
   doctrine of, safeguard against Agnosticism, 65.
Truth, reality, 54.

U.

Uniformity, Hooker on, 117.
   in belief and worship impracticable, 20.
Unitarianism unreasonable, 43.
Unitarians, their true principle, 131.
Unity, basis of, 104, 105.
   of Church, how signified, 103.
   of Church, a *terminus ad quem*, 109.
   of Christendom, 134.
Universalism based upon wrong idea of the nature of Eternal Life, 262.
Unselfishness, the doctrine of, 113.

V.

Valhalla, the Norse heaven, 262.
Vampirism, Babylonian origin, 234.
Vedas, theory of heaven, 263.
   their doctrine, 14.
   on efficacy of penance, 252.
Vestis Angelica, or monastic habit for a death robe, 262.
Vicar of God, in primitive folk-faith, 85.
Vicarious suffering not vicarious satisfaction in Ante-Nicene Fathers, 153.
Victim, slaying of the, Bp. Butler's criticism of this element in Christian doctrine, 176.
   in Christian theology, 163, 171, 174, 264.
   in Assyrian epic, 162.
   in Eastern liturgy, 154.
   in Greek drama, 163.

Victim in Norse mythology, 161.
   in folk-faith, 163.
   in the Gospels, 160.
Virgin, cultus of, 64–74.

W.

Watson, William, on Divine Immanence, 56.
Weregeld, influence on Christian doctrine, 175.
Wheel of Life, 210.
Word, Eternal Generation of, a practical truth, 60.
   Immanence of, a Johanine doctrine, 54.
Word of God and reason one. See St. Justin Martyr.
   St. Athanasius on, 66.
   the life of the Universe, 271.
Word-made-Flesh, significance of, 48, 52.

Wordsworth, protest against notion of bare transcendence, 73.
Works, efficacy of, 74.
Wrath principle human, 266.
Wrath of God, 283.
   Anti-Nicene doctrine of, 173.
   influence of the idea in Christian Art, 72.
   denied by Bp. Taylor, 151.

Y.

Yezidee's idea of God and of evil, 152.
Younttoo, 232.

Z.

Zeitgeist idea, 116.
Zohar, nihilism of, 43.
   its doctrine of God, 43.

January 1893

A Catalogue

of

Theological Works

published by

Macmillan & Co.

Bedford Street, Strand, London

CONTENTS

THE BIBLE—

    History of the Bible

    Biblical History

    The Old Testament

    The New Testament

HISTORY OF THE CHRISTIAN CHURCH

THE CHURCH OF ENGLAND

DEVOTIONAL BOOKS

THE FATHERS

HYMNOLOGY

SERMONS, LECTURES, ADDRESSES, AND THEOLOGICAL ESSAYS

January 1893.

MACMILLAN AND CO.'S THEOLOGICAL CATALOGUE

The Bible

HISTORY OF THE BIBLE

THE ENGLISH BIBLE: An External and Critical History of the various English Translations of Scripture. By Prof. JOHN EADIE. 2 vols. 8vo. 28s.

THE BIBLE IN THE CHURCH. By Right Rev. Bishop WESTCOTT. 10th Edition. 18mo. 4s. 6d.

BIBLICAL HISTORY

BIBLE LESSONS. By Rev. E. A. ABBOTT. Crown 8vo. 4s. 6d.

SIDE-LIGHTS UPON BIBLE HISTORY. By Mrs. SYDNEY BUXTON. Illustrated. Crown 8vo. 5s.

STORIES FROM THE BIBLE. By Rev. A. J. CHURCH. Illustrated. Two Series. Crown 8vo. 3s. 6d. each.

BIBLE READINGS SELECTED FROM THE PENTATEUCH AND THE BOOK OF JOSHUA. By Rev. J. A. CROSS. 2nd Edition. Globe 8vo. 2s. 6d.

CHILDREN'S TREASURY OF BIBLE STORIES. By Mrs. H. GASKOIN. 18mo. 1s. each. Part I. Old Testament; II. New Testament; III. Three Apostles.

A CLASS-BOOK OF OLD TESTAMENT HISTORY. By Rev. Canon MACLEAR. With Four Maps. 18mo. 4s. 6d.

A CLASS-BOOK OF NEW TESTAMENT HISTORY. Including the connection of the Old and New Testament. By the same. 18mo. 5s. 6d.

A SHILLING BOOK OF OLD TESTAMENT HISTORY. By the same. 18mo. 1s.

A SHILLING BOOK OF NEW TESTAMENT HISTORY. By the same. 18mo. 1s.

THE OLD TESTAMENT

SCRIPTURE READINGS FOR SCHOOLS AND FAMILIES. By C. M. YONGE. Globe 8vo. 1s. 6d. each; also with comments, 3s. 6d. each.—First Series: GENESIS TO DEUTERONOMY.—Second Series: JOSHUA TO SOLOMON.—Third Series: KINGS AND THE PROPHETS.—Fourth Series: THE GOSPEL TIMES.—Fifth Series: APOSTOLIC TIMES.

The Old Testament—*continued.*

WARBURTONIAN LECTURES ON THE MINOR PROPHETS. By Rev. A. F. KIRKPATRICK, B.D. Crown 8vo. [*In the Press.*

THE PATRIARCHS AND LAWGIVERS OF THE OLD TESTAMENT. By FREDERICK DENISON MAURICE. New Edition. Crown 8vo. 3s. 6d.

THE PROPHETS AND KINGS OF THE OLD TESTAMENT. By the same. New Edition. Crown 8vo. 3s. 6d.

THE CANON OF THE OLD TESTAMENT. An Essay on the Growth and Formation of the Hebrew Canon of Scripture. By Rev. Prof. H. E. RYLE. Crown 8vo. 6s.

THE EARLY NARRATIVES OF GENESIS. By Rev. Prof. H. E. RYLE. Cr. 8vo. 3s. net.

The Pentateuch—

AN HISTORICO-CRITICAL INQUIRY INTO THE ORIGIN AND COMPOSITION OF THE HEXATEUCH (PENTATEUCH AND BOOK OF JOSHUA). By Prof. A. KUENEN. Translated by PHILIP H. WICKSTEED, M.A. 8vo. 14s.

The Psalms—

THE PSALMS CHRONOLOGICALLY ARRANGED. An Amended Version, with Historical Introductions and Explanatory Notes. By Four Friends. New Edition. Crown 8vo. 5s. net.

GOLDEN TREASURY PSALTER. The Student's Edition. Being an Edition with briefer Notes of "The Psalms Chronologically Arranged by Four Friends." 18mo. 3s. 6d.

THE PSALMS. With Introductions and Critical Notes. By A. C. JENNINGS, M.A., and W. H. LOWE, M.A. In 2 vols. 2nd Edition. Crown 8vo. 10s. 6d. each.

INTRODUCTION TO THE STUDY AND USE OF THE PSALMS. By Rev. J. F. THRUPP. 2nd Edition. 2 vols. 8vo. 21s.

Isaiah—

ISAIAH XL.—LXVI. With the Shorter Prophecies allied to it. By MATTHEW ARNOLD. With Notes. Crown 8vo. 5s.

ISAIAH OF JERUSALEM. In the Authorised English Version, with Introduction, Corrections, and Notes. By the same. Cr. 8vo. 4s. 6d.

A BIBLE-READING FOR SCHOOLS. The Great Prophecy of Israel's Restoration (Isaiah xl.-lxvi.) Arranged and Edited for Young Learners. By the same. 4th Edition. 18mo. 1s.

COMMENTARY ON THE BOOK OF ISAIAH, Critical, Historical, and Prophetical; including a Revised English Translation. By T. R. BIRKS. 2nd Edition. 8vo. 12s. 6d.

THE BOOK OF ISAIAH CHRONOLOGICALLY ARRANGED. By T. K. CHEYNE. Crown 8vo. 7s. 6d.

Zechariah—

THE HEBREW STUDENT'S COMMENTARY ON ZECHARIAH, Hebrew and LXX. By W. H. LOWE, M.A. 8vo. 10s. 6d.

THE NEW TESTAMENT

APOCRYPHAL GOSPEL OF PETER. The Greek Text of the Newly-Discovered Fragment. 8vo. Sewed. 1s.

THE NEW TESTAMENT. Essay on the Right Estimation of MS. Evidence in the Text of the New Testament. By T. R. BIRKS. Crown 8vo. 3s. 6d.

THE SOTERIOLOGY OF THE NEW TESTAMENT. By W. P. DU BOSE, M.A. Crown 8vo. 7s. 6d.

THE MESSAGES OF THE BOOKS. Being Discourses and Notes on the Books of the New Testament. By Ven. Archdeacon FARRAR. 8vo. 14s.

THE CLASSICAL ELEMENT IN THE NEW TESTAMENT. Considered as a Proof of its Genuineness, with an Appendix on the Oldest Authorities used in the Formation of the Canon. By C. H. HOOLE. 8vo. 10s. 6d.

ON A FRESH REVISION OF THE ENGLISH NEW TESTAMENT. With an Appendix on the last Petition of the Lord's Prayer. By Bishop LIGHTFOOT. Crown 8vo. 7s. 6d.

DISSERTATIONS ON THE APOSTOLIC AGE. By Bishop LIGHTFOOT. 8vo. 14s.

THE UNITY OF THE NEW TESTAMENT. By F. D. MAURICE. 2nd Edition. 2 vols. Crown 8vo. 12s.

A COMPANION TO THE GREEK TESTAMENT AND THE ENGLISH VERSION. By PHILIP SCHAFF, D.D. Cr. 8vo. 12s.

A GENERAL SURVEY OF THE HISTORY OF THE CANON OF THE NEW TESTAMENT DURING THE FIRST FOUR CENTURIES. By Right Rev. Bishop WESTCOTT. 6th Edition. Crown 8vo. 10s. 6d.

THE NEW TESTAMENT IN THE ORIGINAL GREEK. The Text revised by Bishop WESTCOTT, D.D., and Prof. F. J. A. HORT, D.D. 2 vols. Crown 8vo. 10s. 6d. each.—Vol. I. Text; II. Introduction and Appendix.

THE NEW TESTAMENT IN THE ORIGINAL GREEK, for Schools. The Text revised by Bishop WESTCOTT, D.D., and F. J. A. HORT, D.D. 12mo, cloth, 4s. 6d.; 18mo, roan, red edges, 5s. 6d.; morocco, gilt edges, 6s. 6d.

THE GOSPELS—

THE COMMON TRADITION OF THE SYNOPTIC GOSPELS, in the Text of the Revised Version. By Rev. E. A. ABBOTT and W. G. RUSHBROOKE. Crown 8vo. 3s. 6d.

SYNOPTICON: An Exposition of the Common Matter of the Synoptic Gospels. By W. G. RUSHBROOKE. Printed in Colours. In Six Parts, and Appendix. 4to.—Part I. 3s. 6d. Parts II. and III. 7s. Parts IV. V. and VI. with Indices, 10s. 6d. Appendices, 10s. 6d. Complete in 1 vol., 35s. Indispensable to a Theological Student.

INTRODUCTION TO THE STUDY OF THE FOUR GOSPELS. By Right Rev. Bishop WESTCOTT. 7th Ed. Cr. 8vo. 10s. 6d.

THE COMPOSITION OF THE FOUR GOSPELS. By Rev. ARTHUR WRIGHT. Crown 8vo. 5s.

Gospel of St. Matthew—
　THE GOSPEL ACCORDING TO ST. MATTHEW. Greek Text as Revised by Bishop WESTCOTT and Dr. HORT. With Introduction and Notes by Rev. A. SLOMAN, M.A. Fcap. 8vo. 2s. 6d.
　CHOICE NOTES ON ST. MATTHEW, drawn from Old and New Sources. Crown 8vo. 4s. 6d. (St. Matthew and St. Mark in 1 vol. 9s.)

Gospel of St. Mark—
　SCHOOL READINGS IN THE GREEK TESTAMENT. Being the Outlines of the Life of our Lord as given by St. Mark, with additions from the Text of the other Evangelists. Edited, with Notes and Vocabulary, by Rev. A. CALVERT, M.A. Fcap. 8vo. 2s. 6d.
　CHOICE NOTES ON ST. MARK, drawn from Old and New Sources. Cr. 8vo. 4s. 6d. (St. Matthew and St. Mark in 1 vol. 9s.)

Gospel of St. Luke—
　THE GOSPEL ACCORDING TO ST. LUKE. The Greek Text as Revised by Bishop WESTCOTT and Dr. HORT. With Introduction and Notes by Rev. J. BOND, M.A. Fcap. 8vo. 2s. 6d.
　CHOICE NOTES ON ST. LUKE, drawn from Old and New Sources. Crown 8vo. 4s. 6d.
　THE GOSPEL OF THE KINGDOM OF HEAVEN. A Course of Lectures on the Gospel of St. Luke. By F. D. MAURICE. 3rd Edition. Crown 8vo. 6s.

Gospel of St. John—
　THE CENTRAL TEACHING OF CHRIST. Being a Study and Exposition of St. John, Chapters XIII. to XVII. By Rev. CANON BERNARD, M.A. Crown 8vo. 7s. 6d.
　THE GOSPEL OF ST. JOHN. By F. D. MAURICE. 8th Ed. Cr. 8vo. 6s.
　CHOICE NOTES ON ST. JOHN, drawn from Old and New Sources. Crown 8vo. 4s. 6d.

THE ACTS OF THE APOSTLES—
　THE ACTS OF THE APOSTLES. Being the Greek Text as Revised by Bishop WESTCOTT and Dr. HORT. With Explanatory Notes by T. E. PAGE, M.A. Fcap. 8vo. 3s. 6d.
　THE CHURCH OF THE FIRST DAYS. THE CHURCH OF JERUSALEM. THE CHURCH OF THE GENTILES. THE CHURCH OF THE WORLD. Lectures on the Acts of the Apostles. By Very Rev. C. J. VAUGHAN. Crown 8vo. 10s. 6d.

THE EPISTLES of St. Paul—
　ST. PAUL'S EPISTLE TO THE ROMANS. The Greek Text, with English Notes. By Very Rev. C. J. VAUGHAN. 7th Edition. Crown 8vo. 7s. 6d.
　A COMMENTARY ON ST. PAUL'S TWO EPISTLES TO THE CORINTHIANS. Greek Text, with Commentary. By Rev. W. KAY. 8vo. 9s.

Of St. Paul—*continued.*

ST. PAUL'S EPISTLE TO THE GALATIANS. A Revised Text, with Introduction, Notes, and Dissertations. By Bishop LIGHTFOOT. 10th Edition. 8vo. 12s.

ST. PAUL'S EPISTLE TO THE PHILIPPIANS. A Revised Text, with Introduction, Notes, and Dissertations. By the same. 9th Edition. 8vo. 12s.

ST. PAUL'S EPISTLE TO THE PHILIPPIANS. With translation, Paraphrase, and Notes for English Readers. By Very Rev. C. J. VAUGHAN. Crown 8vo. 5s.

ST. PAUL'S EPISTLES TO THE COLOSSIANS AND TO PHILEMON. A Revised Text, with Introductions, etc. By Bishop LIGHTFOOT. 9th Edition. 8vo. 12s.

THE EPISTLES OF ST. PAUL TO THE EPHESIANS, THE COLOSSIANS, AND PHILEMON. With Introductions and Notes. By Rev. J. LL. DAVIES. 2nd Edition. 8vo. 7s. 6d.

THE EPISTLES OF ST. PAUL. For English Readers. Part I. containing the First Epistle to the Thessalonians. By Very Rev. C. J. VAUGHAN. 2nd Edition. 8vo. Sewed. 1s. 6d.

ST. PAUL'S EPISTLES TO THE THESSALONIANS, COMMENTARY ON THE GREEK TEXT. By Prof. JOHN EADIE. 8vo. 12s.

The Epistle of St. James—

THE EPISTLE OF ST. JAMES. The Greek Text, with Introduction and Notes. By Rev. JOSEPH MAYOR, M.A. 8vo. 14s.

The Epistles of St. John—

THE EPISTLES OF ST. JOHN. By F. D. MAURICE. 4th Edition. Crown 8vo. 6s.

THE EPISTLES OF ST. JOHN. The Greek Text, with Notes. By Right Rev. Bishop WESTCOTT. 3rd Edition. 8vo. 12s. 6d.

The Epistle to the Hebrews—

THE EPISTLE TO THE HEBREWS IN GREEK AND ENGLISH. With Notes. By Rev. FREDERIC RENDALL. Crown 8vo. 6s.

THE EPISTLE TO THE HEBREWS. English Text, with Commentary. By the same. Crown 8vo. 7s. 6d.

THE EPISTLE TO THE HEBREWS. With Notes. By Very Rev. C. J. VAUGHAN. Crown 8vo. 7s. 6d.

THE EPISTLE TO THE HEBREWS. The Greek Text, with Notes and Essays. By Right Rev. Bishop WESTCOTT. 8vo. 14s.

REVELATION—

LECTURES ON THE APOCALYPSE. By F. D. MAURICE. 2nd Edition. Crown 8vo. 6s.

LECTURES ON THE APOCALYPSE. By Rev. Prof. W. MILLIGAN. Crown 8vo. 5s.

THE REVELATION OF ST. JOHN. By Rev. Prof. W. MILLIGAN. 2nd Edition. Crown 8vo. 7s. 6d.

REVELATION—*continued.*
   LECTURES ON THE REVELATION OF ST. JOHN. By Very Rev. C. J. VAUGHAN. 5th Edition. Crown 8vo. 10s. 6d.

   THE BIBLE WORD-BOOK. By W. ALDIS WRIGHT. 2nd Edition. Crown 8vo. 7s. 6d.

Christian Church, History of the

Church (Dean).—THE OXFORD MOVEMENT. Twelve Years, 1833-45. Globe 8vo. 5s.
Cunningham (Rev. John).—THE GROWTH OF THE CHURCH IN ITS ORGANISATION AND INSTITUTIONS. 8vo. 9s.
Dale (A. W. W.)—THE SYNOD OF ELVIRA, AND CHRISTIAN LIFE IN THE FOURTH CENTURY. Cr. 8vo. 10s. 6d.
Hardwick (Archdeacon).—A HISTORY OF THE CHRISTIAN CHURCH. Middle Age. Ed. by Bishop STUBBS. Cr. 8vo. 10s. 6d.
   A HISTORY OF THE CHRISTIAN CHURCH DURING THE REFORMATION. Revised by Bishop STUBBS. Cr. 8vo. 10s. 6d.
Hort (Dr. F. J. A.)—TWO DISSERTATIONS. I. On ΜΟΝΟΓΕΝΗΣ ΘΕΟΣ in Scripture and Tradition. II. On the "Constantinopolitan" Creed and other Eastern Creeds of the Fourth Century. 8vo. 7s. 6d.
Killen (W. D.)—ECCLESIASTICAL HISTORY OF IRELAND, FROM THE EARLIEST DATE TO THE PRESENT TIME. 2 vols. 8vo. 25s.
Simpson (W.)—AN EPITOME OF THE HISTORY OF THE CHRISTIAN CHURCH. Fcap. 8vo. 3s. 6d.
Vaughan (Very Rev. C. J., Dean of Llandaff).—THE CHURCH OF THE FIRST DAYS. THE CHURCH OF JERUSALEM. THE CHURCH OF THE GENTILES. THE CHURCH OF THE WORLD. Crown 8vo. 10s. 6d.
Ward (W.)—WILLIAM GEORGE WARD AND THE OXFORD MOVEMENT. Portrait. 8vo. 14s.

The Church of England

Catechism of—
   A CLASS-BOOK OF THE CATECHISM OF THE CHURCH OF ENGLAND. By Rev. Canon MACLEAR. 18mo. 1s. 6d.
   A FIRST CLASS-BOOK OF THE CATECHISM OF THE CHURCH OF ENGLAND, with Scripture Proofs for Junior Classes and Schools. By the same. 18mo. 6d.
   THE ORDER OF CONFIRMATION, with Prayers and Devotions. By the Rev. Canon MACLEAR. 32mo. 6d.

Collects—
  COLLECTS OF THE CHURCH OF ENGLAND. With a Coloured Floral Design to each Collect. Crown 8vo. 12s.

Disestablishment—
  DISESTABLISHMENT AND DISENDOWMENT. What are they? By Prof. E. A. FREEMAN. 4th Edition. Crown 8vo. 1s.
  DISESTABLISHMENT: or, A Defence of the Principle of a National Church. By GEORGE HARWOOD. 8vo. 12s.
  A DEFENCE OF THE CHURCH OF ENGLAND AGAINST DISESTABLISHMENT. By ROUNDELL, EARL OF SELBORNE. Crown 8vo. 2s. 6d.
  ANCIENT FACTS & FICTIONS CONCERNING CHURCHES AND TITHES. By the same. 2nd Edition. Crown 8vo. 7s. 6d.

Dissent in its Relation to—
  DISSENT IN ITS RELATION TO THE CHURCH OF ENGLAND. By Rev. G. H. CURTEIS. Bampton Lectures for 1871. Crown 8vo. 7s. 6d.

Holy Communion—
  THE COMMUNION SERVICE FROM THE BOOK OF COMMON PRAYER, with Select Readings from the Writings of the Rev. F. D. MAURICE. Edited by Bishop COLENSO. 6th Edition. 16mo. 2s. 6d.
  BEFORE THE TABLE: An Inquiry, Historical and Theological, into the Meaning of the Consecration Rubric in the Communion Service of the Church of England. By Very Rev. J. S. HOWSON. 8vo. 7s. 6d.
  FIRST COMMUNION, with Prayers and Devotions for the newly Confirmed. By Rev. Canon MACLEAR. 32mo. 6d.
  A MANUAL OF INSTRUCTION FOR CONFIRMATION AND FIRST COMMUNION, with Prayers and Devotions. By the same. 32mo. 2s.

Liturgy—
  A COMPANION TO THE LECTIONARY. By Rev. W. BENHAM, B.D. Crown 8vo. 4s. 6d.
  AN INTRODUCTION TO THE CREEDS. By Rev. Canon MACLEAR. 18mo. 3s. 6d.
  AN INTRODUCTION TO THE THIRTY-NINE ARTICLES. By the same. 18mo. [*In the Press.*
  A HISTORY OF THE BOOK OF COMMON PRAYER. By Rev. F. PROCTER. 18th Edition. Crown 8vo. 10s. 6d.
  AN ELEMENTARY INTRODUCTION TO THE BOOK OF COMMON PRAYER. By Rev. F. PROCTER and Rev. Canon MACLEAR. 18mo. 2s. 6d.
  TWELVE DISCOURSES ON SUBJECTS CONNECTED WITH THE LITURGY AND WORSHIP OF THE CHURCH OF ENGLAND. By Very Rev. C. J. VAUGHAN. 4th Edition. Fcap. 8vo. 6s.

Devotional Books

Brooke (S. A.)—FORM OF MORNING AND EVENING PRAYER, and for the Administration of the Lord's Supper, together with the Baptismal and Marriage Services, Bedford Chapel, Bloomsbury. Fcap. 8vo. 1s. net.

Eastlake (Lady).—FELLOWSHIP: LETTERS ADDRESSED TO MY SISTER-MOURNERS. Crown 8vo. 2s. 6d.

IMITATIO CHRISTI, LIBRI IV. Printed in Borders after Holbein, Dürer, and other old Masters, containing Dances of Death, Acts of Mercy, Emblems, etc. Crown 8vo. 7s. 6d.

Kingsley (Charles).—OUT OF THE DEEP: WORDS FOR THE SORROWFUL. From the writings of CHARLES KINGSLEY. Extra fcap. 8vo. 3s. 6d.

DAILY THOUGHTS. Selected from the Writings of CHARLES KINGSLEY. By his Wife. Crown 8vo. 6s.

FROM DEATH TO LIFE. Fragments of Teaching to a Village Congregation. With Letters on the "Life after Death." Edited by his Wife. Fcap. 8vo. 2s. 6d.

Maclear (Rev. Canon).—A MANUAL OF INSTRUCTION FOR CONFIRMATION AND FIRST COMMUNION, WITH PRAYERS AND DEVOTIONS. 32mo. 2s.

THE HOUR OF SORROW; OR, THE OFFICE FOR THE BURIAL OF THE DEAD. 32mo. 2s.

Maurice (Frederick Denison).—LESSONS OF HOPE. Readings from the Works of F. D. MAURICE. Selected by Rev. J. LL. DAVIES, M.A. Crown 8vo. 5s.

RAYS OF SUNLIGHT FOR DARK DAYS. With a Preface by Very Rev. C. J. VAUGHAN, D.D. New Edition. 18mo. 3s. 6d.

Service (Rev. John).—PRAYERS FOR PUBLIC WORSHIP. Crown 8vo. 4s. 6d.

THE WORSHIP OF GOD, AND FELLOWSHIP AMONG MEN. By FREDERICK DENISON MAURICE and others. Fcap. 8vo. 3s. 6d.

Welby-Gregory (The Hon. Lady).—LINKS AND CLUES. 2nd Edition. Crown 8vo. 6s.

Westcott (Rt. Rev. B. F., Bishop of Durham).—THOUGHTS ON REVELATION AND LIFE. Selections from the Writings of Bishop WESTCOTT. Edited by Rev. S. PHILLIPS. Crown 8vo. 6s.

Wilbraham (Frances M.)—IN THE SERE AND YELLOW LEAF: THOUGHTS AND RECOLLECTIONS FOR OLD AND YOUNG. Globe 8vo. 3s. 6d.

The Fathers

Cunningham (Rev. W.)—THE EPISTLE OF ST. BARNABAS. A Dissertation, including a Discussion of its Date and Authorship. Together with the Greek Text, the Latin Version, and a New English Translation and Commentary. Crown 8vo. 7s. 6d.

Donaldson (Prof. James).—THE APOSTOLICAL FATHERS. A Critical Account of their Genuine Writings, and of their Doctrines. 2nd Edition. Crown 8vo. 7s. 6d.

Lightfoot (Bishop).—THE APOSTOLIC FATHERS. Part I. ST. CLEMENT OF ROME. Revised Texts, with Introductions, Notes, Dissertations, and Translations. 2 vols. 8vo. 32s.

THE APOSTOLIC FATHERS. Part II. ST. IGNATIUS to ST. POLYCARP. Revised Texts, with Introductions, Notes, Dissertations, and Translations. 3 vols. 2nd Edition. Demy 8vo. 48s.

THE APOSTOLIC FATHERS. Abridged Edition. With Short Introductions, Greek Text, and English Translation. 8vo. 16s.

Hymnology

Brooke (S. A.)—CHRISTIAN HYMNS. Edited and arranged. Fcap. 8vo. 2s. net.
This may also be had bound up with the Form of Service at Bedford Chapel, Bloomsbury. Price complete, 3s. net.

Palgrave (Prof. F. T.)—ORIGINAL HYMNS. 18mo. 1s. 6d.

Selborne (Roundell, Earl of)—
THE BOOK OF PRAISE. From the best English Hymn Writers. 18mo. 2s. 6d. net.
A HYMNAL. Chiefly from *The Book of Praise*. In various sizes.—A. Royal 32mo. 6d.—B. Small 18mo, larger type. 1s.—C. Same Edition, fine paper. 1s. 6d.—An Edition with Music, Selected, Harmonised, and Composed by JOHN HULLAH. Square 18mo. 3s. 6d.

Woods (M. A.)—HYMNS FOR SCHOOL WORSHIP. Compiled by M. A. WOODS. 18mo. 1s. 6d.

Sermons, Lectures, Addresses, and Theological Essays

(*See also* 'Bible,' 'Church of England,' 'Fathers.')

Abbot (Francis)—
SCIENTIFIC THEISM. Crown 8vo. 7s. 6d.
THE WAY OUT OF AGNOSTICISM : or, The Philosophy of Free Religion. Crown 8vo. 4s. 6d.

Abbott (Rev. E. A.)—
CAMBRIDGE SERMONS. 8vo. 6s.
OXFORD SERMONS. 8vo. 7s. 6d.
PHILOMYTHUS. An Antidote against Credulity. A discussion of Cardinal Newman's Essay on Ecclesiastical Miracles. 2nd Edition. Crown 8vo. 3s. 6d.
NEWMANIANISM. A Reply. Crown 8vo. Sewed, 1s. net.

Ainger (Rev. Alfred, Canon of Bristol).—SERMONS PREACHED IN THE TEMPLE CHURCH. Extra fcap. 8vo. 6s.

Alexander (W., Bishop of Derry and Raphoe).—THE LEADING IDEAS OF THE GOSPELS. New Edition, Revised and Enlarged. Crown 8vo. 6s.

Baines (Rev. Edward).—SERMONS. With a Preface and Memoir, by A. BARRY, D.D., late Bishop of Sydney. Crown 8vo. 6s.

Bather (Archdeacon).—ON SOME MINISTERIAL DUTIES, CATECHISING, PREACHING, ETC. Edited, with a Preface, by Very Rev. C. J. VAUGHAN, D.D. Fcap. 8vo. 4s. 6d.

Binnie (Rev. William).—SERMONS. Crown 8vo. 6s.

Birks (Thomas Rawson)—
THE DIFFICULTIES OF BELIEF IN CONNECTION WITH THE CREATION AND THE FALL, REDEMPTION, AND JUDGMENT. 2nd Edition. Crown 8vo. 5s.
JUSTIFICATION AND IMPUTED RIGHTEOUSNESS. Being a Review of Ten Sermons on the Nature and Effects of Faith, by JAMES THOMAS O'BRIEN, D.D., late Bishop of Ossory, Ferns, and Leighlin. Crown 8vo. 6s.
SUPERNATURAL REVELATION : or, First Principles of Moral Theology. 8vo. 8s.

Brooke (Rev. Stopford A.)—SHORT SERMONS. Cr. 8vo. 6s.

Brooks (Phillips, Bishop of Massachusetts)—
THE CANDLE OF THE LORD, and other Sermons. Crown 8vo. 6s.
SERMONS PREACHED IN ENGLISH CHURCHES. Crown 8vo. 6s.
TWENTY SERMONS. Crown 8vo. 6s.
TOLERANCE. Crown 8vo. 2s. 6d.
THE LIGHT OF THE WORLD. Crown 8vo. 3s. 6d.

Brunton (T. Lauder).—THE BIBLE AND SCIENCE. With Illustrations. Crown 8vo. 10s. 6d.

Butler (Rev. George).—SERMONS PREACHED IN CHELTENHAM COLLEGE CHAPEL. 8vo. 7s. 6d.

Butler (W. Archer)—
SERMONS, DOCTRINAL AND PRACTICAL. 11th Edition. 8vo. 8s.
SECOND SERIES OF SERMONS. 8vo. 7s.

Campbell (Dr. John M'Leod)—
THE NATURE OF THE ATONEMENT. 6th Ed. Cr. 8vo. 6s.
REMINISCENCES AND REFLECTIONS. Edited with an Introductory Narrative, by his Son, DONALD CAMPBELL, M.A. Crown 8vo. 7s. 6d.
THOUGHTS ON REVELATION. 2nd Edition. Crown 8vo. 5s.
RESPONSIBILITY FOR THE GIFT OF ETERNAL LIFE. Compiled from Sermons preached at Row, in the years 1829-31. Crown 8vo. 5s.

Canterbury (Edward White, Archbishop of)—
  BOY-LIFE: its Trial, its Strength, its Fulness. Sundays in Wellington College, 1859-73. 4th Edition. Crown 8vo. 6s.
  THE SEVEN GIFTS. Addressed to the Diocese of Canterbury in his Primary Visitation. 2nd Edition. Crown 8vo. 6s.
  CHRIST AND HIS TIMES. Addressed to the Diocese of Canterbury in his Second Visitation. Crown 8vo. 6s.

Carpenter (W. Boyd, Bishop of Ripon)—
  TRUTH IN TALE. Addresses, chiefly to Children. Crown 8vo. 4s. 6d.
  THE PERMANENT ELEMENTS OF RELIGION: Bampton Lectures, 1887. 2nd Edition. Crown 8vo. 6s.

Cazenove (J. Gibson).—CONCERNING THE BEING AND ATTRIBUTES OF GOD. 8vo. 5s.

Church (Dean)—
  HUMAN LIFE AND ITS CONDITIONS. Crown 8vo. 6s.
  THE GIFTS OF CIVILISATION, and other Sermons and Lectures. 2nd Edition. Crown 8vo. 7s. 6d.
  DISCIPLINE OF THE CHRISTIAN CHARACTER, and other Sermons. Crown 8vo. 4s. 6d.
  ADVENT SERMONS. 1885. Crown 8vo. 4s. 6d.
  VILLAGE SERMONS. Crown 8vo. 6s.
  CATHEDRAL AND UNIVERSITY SERMONS. Crown 8vo. 6s.
  CLERGYMAN'S SELF-EXAMINATION CONCERNING THE APOSTLES' CREED. Extra fcap. 8vo. 1s. 6d.

Congreve (Rev. John).—HIGH HOPES AND PLEADINGS FOR A REASONABLE FAITH, NOBLER THOUGHTS, LARGER CHARITY. Crown 8vo. 5s.

Cooke (Josiah P., Jun.)—RELIGION AND CHEMISTRY. Crown 8vo. 7s. 6d.

Cotton (Bishop).—SERMONS PREACHED TO ENGLISH CONGREGATIONS IN INDIA. Crown 8vo. 7s. 6d.

Cunningham (Rev. W.)—CHRISTIAN CIVILISATION, WITH SPECIAL REFERENCE TO INDIA. Cr. 8vo. 5s.

Curteis (Rev. G. H.)—THE SCIENTIFIC OBSTACLES TO CHRISTIAN BELIEF. The Boyle Lectures, 1884. Cr. 8vo. 6s.

Davies (Rev. J. Llewelyn)—
  THE GOSPEL AND MODERN LIFE. 2nd Edition, to which is added Morality according to the Sacrament of the Lord's Supper. Extra fcap. 8vo. 6s.
  SOCIAL QUESTIONS FROM THE POINT OF VIEW OF CHRISTIAN THEOLOGY. 2nd Edition. Crown 8vo. 6s.
  WARNINGS AGAINST SUPERSTITION. Extra fcap. 8vo. 2s. 6d.
  THE CHRISTIAN CALLING. Extra fcap. 8vo. 6s.
  ORDER AND GROWTH AS INVOLVED IN THE SPIRITUAL CONSTITUTION OF HUMAN SOCIETY. Crown 8vo. 3s. 6d.

Davies (Rev. J. Llewelyn)—*continued.*
  BAPTISM, CONFIRMATION, AND THE LORD'S SUPPER, as interpreted by their Outward Signs. Three Addresses. New Edition. 18mo. 1s.

Diggle (Rev. J. W.)—GODLINESS AND MANLINESS. A Miscellany of Brief Papers touching the Relation of Religion to Life. Crown 8vo. 6s.

Drummond (Prof. James).—INTRODUCTION TO THE STUDY OF THEOLOGY. Crown 8vo. 5s.

ECCE HOMO. A Survey of the Life and Work of Jesus Christ. 20th Edition. Globe 8vo. 6s.

Ellerton (Rev. John).—THE HOLIEST MANHOOD, AND ITS LESSONS FOR BUSY LIVES. Crown 8vo. 6s.

FAITH AND CONDUCT : An Essay on Verifiable Religion. Crown 8vo. 7s. 6d.

Farrar (Ven. F. W., Archdeacon of Westminster)—
  THE HISTORY OF INTERPRETATION. Being the Bampton Lectures, 1885. 8vo. 16s.
  Collected Edition of the Sermons, etc. Crown 8vo. 3s. 6d. each.
  SEEKERS AFTER GOD.
  ETERNAL HOPE. Sermons Preached in Westminster Abbey.
  THE FALL OF MAN, and other Sermons.
  THE WITNESS OF HISTORY TO CHRIST. Hulsean Lectures.
  THE SILENCE AND VOICES OF GOD.
  IN THE DAYS OF THY YOUTH. Sermons on Practical Subjects.
  SAINTLY WORKERS. Five Lenten Lectures.
  EPHPHATHA : or, The Amelioration of the World.
  MERCY AND JUDGMENT. A few last words on Christian Eschatology.
  SERMONS AND ADDRESSES delivered in America.

Fiske (John).—MAN'S DESTINY VIEWED IN THE LIGHT OF HIS ORIGIN. Crown 8vo. 3s. 6d.

Forbes (Rev. Granville).—THE VOICE OF GOD IN THE PSALMS. Crown 8vo. 6s. 6d.

Fowle (Rev. T. W.)—A NEW ANALOGY BETWEEN REVEALED RELIGION AND THE COURSE AND CONSTITUTION OF NATURE. Crown 8vo. 6s.

Fraser (Bishop).—SERMONS. Edited by Rev. JOHN W. DIGGLE. 2 vols. Crown 8vo. 6s. each.

Hamilton (John)—
  ON TRUTH AND ERROR. Crown 8vo. 5s.
  ARTHUR'S SEAT : or, The Church of the Banned. Crown 8vo. 6s.
  ABOVE AND AROUND : Thoughts on God and Man. 12mo. 2s. 6d.

Hardwick (Archdeacon).—CHRIST AND OTHER MASTERS. 6th Edition. Crown 8vo. 10s. 6d.

Hare (Julius Charles)—
 THE MISSION OF THE COMFORTER. New Edition. Edited by Dean PLUMPTRE. Crown 8vo. 7s. 6d.
 THE VICTORY OF FAITH. Edited by Dean PLUMPTRE, with Introductory Notices by Prof. MAURICE and Dean STANLEY. Crown 8vo. 6s. 6d.

Harper (Father Thomas, S.J.)—THE METAPHYSICS OF THE SCHOOL. In 5 vols. Vols. I. and II. 8vo. 18s. each. Vol. III. Part I. 12s.

Harris (Rev. G. C.)—SERMONS. With a Memoir by CHARLOTTE M. YONGE, and Portrait. Extra fcap. 8vo. 6s.

Hutton (R. H.)—
 ESSAYS ON SOME OF THE MODERN GUIDES OF ENGLISH THOUGHT IN MATTERS OF FAITH. Globe 8vo. 6s.
 THEOLOGICAL ESSAYS. Globe 8vo. 6s.

Illingworth (Rev. J. R.)—SERMONS PREACHED IN A COLLEGE CHAPEL. Crown 8vo. 5s.
 UNIVERSITY AND CATHEDRAL SERMONS. Crown 8vo. [*In the Press.*

Jacob (Rev. J. A.)—BUILDING IN SILENCE, and other Sermons. Extra fcap. 8vo. 6s.

James (Rev. Herbert).—THE COUNTRY CLERGYMAN AND HIS WORK. Crown 8vo. 6s.

Jeans (Rev. G. E.)—HAILEYBURY CHAPEL, and other Sermons. Fcap. 8vo. 3s. 6d.

Jellett (Rev. Dr.)—
 THE ELDER SON, and other Sermons. Crown 8vo. 6s.
 THE EFFICACY OF PRAYER. 3rd Edition. Crown 8vo. 5s.

Kellogg (Rev. S. H.)—THE LIGHT OF ASIA AND THE LIGHT OF THE WORLD. Crown 8vo. 7s. 6d.
 THE GENESIS AND GROWTH OF RELIGION. Cr. 8vo. 6s.

Kingsley (Charles)—
 VILLAGE AND TOWN AND COUNTRY SERMONS. Crown 8vo. 3s. 6d.
 THE WATER OF LIFE, and other Sermons. Crown 8vo. 3s. 6d.
 SERMONS ON NATIONAL SUBJECTS, AND THE KING OF THE EARTH. Crown 8vo. 3s. 6d.
 SERMONS FOR THE TIMES. Crown 8vo. 3s. 6d.
 GOOD NEWS OF GOD. Crown 8vo. 3s. 6d.
 THE GOSPEL OF THE PENTATEUCH, AND DAVID. Crown 8vo. 3s. 6d.
 DISCIPLINE, and other Sermons. Crown 8vo. 3s. 6d.
 WESTMINSTER SERMONS. Crown 8vo. 3s. 6d.
 ALL SAINTS' DAY, and other Sermons. Crown 8vo. 3s. 6d.

Kirkpatrick (Prof. A. F.)—THE DIVINE LIBRARY OF THE OLD TESTAMENT. Its Origin, Preservation, Inspiration, and Permanent Value. Crown 8vo. 3s. net.

Kirkpatrick (Prof. A. F.)—*continued.*
   THE DOCTRINE OF THE PROPHETS. Warburtonian Lectures 1886-1890. Crown 8vo. 6s.

Kynaston (Rev. Herbert, D.D.)—SERMONS PREACHED IN THE COLLEGE CHAPEL, CHELTENHAM. Crown 8vo. 6s.

Lightfoot (Bishop)—
   LEADERS IN THE NORTHERN CHURCH: Sermons Preached in the Diocese of Durham. 2nd Edition. Crown 8vo. 6s.
   ORDINATION ADDRESSES AND COUNSELS TO CLERGY. Crown 8vo. 6s.
   CAMBRIDGE SERMONS. Crown 8vo. 6s.
   SERMONS PREACHED IN ST. PAUL'S CATHEDRAL. Crown 8vo. 6s.
   SERMONS PREACHED ON SPECIAL OCCASIONS. Crown 8vo. 6s.
   A CHARGE DELIVERED TO THE CLERGY OF THE DIOCESE OF DURHAM, 25th Nov. 1886. Demy 8vo. 2s.
   ESSAYS ON THE WORK ENTITLED "Supernatural Religion." 8vo. 10s. 6d.
   DISSERTATIONS ON THE APOSTOLIC AGE. 8vo. 14s.
   BIBLICAL MISCELLANIES. 8vo. [*In the Press.*

Maclaren (Rev. Alexander)—
   SERMONS PREACHED AT MANCHESTER. 11th Edition. Fcap. 8vo. 4s. 6d.
   A SECOND SERIES OF SERMONS. 7th Ed. Fcap. 8vo. 4s. 6d.
   A THIRD SERIES. 6th Edition. Fcap. 8vo. 4s. 6d.
   WEEK-DAY EVENING ADDRESSES. 4th Ed. Fcap. 8vo. 2s. 6d.
   THE SECRET OF POWER, AND OTHER SERMONS. Fcap. 8vo. 4s. 6d.

Macmillan (Rev. Hugh)—
   BIBLE TEACHINGS IN NATURE. 15th Ed. Globe 8vo. 6s.
   THE TRUE VINE; OR, THE ANALOGIES OF OUR LORD'S ALLEGORY. 5th Edition. Globe 8vo. 6s.
   THE MINISTRY OF NATURE. 8th Edition. Globe 8vo. 6s.
   THE SABBATH OF THE FIELDS. 6th Edition. Globe 8vo. 6s.
   THE MARRIAGE IN CANA. Globe 8vo. 6s.
   TWO WORLDS ARE OURS. 3rd Edition. Globe 8vo. 6s.
   THE OLIVE LEAF. Globe 8vo. 6s.
   THE GATE BEAUTIFUL AND OTHER BIBLE TEACHINGS FOR THE YOUNG. Crown 8vo. 3s. 6d.

Mahaffy (Rev. Prof.)—THE DECAY OF MODERN PREACHING: AN ESSAY. Crown 8vo. 3s. 6d.

Maturin (Rev. W.)—THE BLESSEDNESS OF THE DEAD IN CHRIST. Crown 8vo. 7s. 6d.

Maurice (Frederick Denison)—
   THE KINGDOM OF CHRIST. 3rd Ed. 2 Vols. Cr. 8vo. 12s.
   EXPOSITORY SERMONS ON THE PRAYER-BOOK; AND ON THE LORD'S PRAYER. New Edition. Crown 8vo. 6s.

Maurice (Frederick Denison)—*continued*.
  SERMONS PREACHED IN COUNTRY CHURCHES. 2nd Edition. Crown 8vo. 6s.
  THE CONSCIENCE. Lectures on Casuistry. 3rd Ed. Cr. 8vo. 4s. 6d.
  DIALOGUES ON FAMILY WORSHIP. Crown 8vo. 4s. 6d.
  THE DOCTRINE OF SACRIFICE DEDUCED FROM THE SCRIPTURES. 2nd Edition. Crown 8vo. 6s.
  THE RELIGIONS OF THE WORLD. 6th Edition. Cr. 8vo. 4s. 6d.
  ON THE SABBATH DAY; THE CHARACTER OF THE WARRIOR; AND ON THE INTERPRETATION OF HISTORY. Fcap. 8vo. 2s. 6d.
  LEARNING AND WORKING. Crown 8vo. 4s. 6d.
  THE LORD'S PRAYER, THE CREED, AND THE COMMANDMENTS. 18mo. 1s.
  SERMONS PREACHED IN LINCOLN'S INN CHAPEL. In Six Volumes. Crown 8vo. 3s. 6d. each.

  Collected Works. Monthly Volumes from October 1892. Crown 8vo. 3s. 6d. each.
  CHRISTMAS DAY AND OTHER SERMONS.
  THEOLOGICAL ESSAYS.
  PROPHETS AND KINGS.
  PATRIARCHS AND LAWGIVERS.
  THE GOSPEL OF THE KINGDOM OF HEAVEN.
  GOSPEL OF ST. JOHN.
  EPISTLE OF ST. JOHN.
  LECTURES ON THE APOCALYPSE.
  FRIENDSHIP OF BOOKS.
  SOCIAL MORALITY.
  PRAYER BOOK AND LORD'S PRAYER.
  THE DOCTRINE OF SACRIFICE.

Milligan (Rev. Prof. W.)—THE RESURRECTION OF OUR LORD. Fourth Thousand. Crown 8vo. 5s.
  THE ASCENSION AND HEAVENLY PRIESTHOOD OF OUR LORD. *Baird Lectures*, 1891. Crown 8vo. 7s. 6d.

Moorhouse (J., Bishop of Manchester)—
  JACOB: Three Sermons. Extra fcap. 8vo. 3s. 6d.
  THE TEACHING OF CHRIST. Its Conditions, Secret, and Results. Crown 8vo. 3s. net.

Mylne (L. G., Bishop of Bombay).—SERMONS PREACHED IN ST. THOMAS'S CATHEDRAL, BOMBAY. Crown 8vo. 6s.

NATURAL RELIGION. By the author of "Ecce Homo." 3rd Edition. Globe 8vo. 6s.

Pattison (Mark).—SERMONS. Crown 8vo. 6s.

PAUL OF TARSUS. 8vo. 10s. 6d.

PHILOCHRISTUS. Memoirs of a Disciple of the Lord. 3rd Ed. 8vo. 12s.

Plumptre (Dean).—MOVEMENTS IN RELIGIOUS THOUGHT. Fcap. 8vo. 3s. 6d.

Potter (R.)—THE RELATION OF ETHICS TO RELIGION. Crown 8vo. 2s. 6d.

REASONABLE FAITH: A Short Religious Essay for the Times. By "Three Friends." Crown 8vo. 1s.

Reichel (C. P., Bishop of Meath)—
THE LORD'S PRAYER, and other Sermons. Crown 8vo. 7s. 6d.
CATHEDRAL AND UNIVERSITY SERMONS. Crown 8vo. 6s.

Rendall (Rev. F.)—THE THEOLOGY OF THE HEBREW CHRISTIANS. Crown 8vo. 5s.

Reynolds (H. R.)—NOTES OF THE CHRISTIAN LIFE. Crown 8vo. 7s. 6d.

Robinson (Prebendary H. G.)—MAN IN THE IMAGE OF GOD, and other Sermons. Crown 8vo. 7s. 6d.

Russell (Dean).—THE LIGHT THAT LIGHTETH EVERY MAN: Sermons. With an introduction by Dean PLUMPTRE, D.D. Crown 8vo. 6s.

Salmon (Rev. Prof. George)—
NON-MIRACULOUS CHRISTIANITY, and other Sermons. 2nd Edition. Crown 8vo. 6s.
GNOSTICISM AND AGNOSTICISM, and other Sermons. Crown 8vo. 7s. 6d.

Sandford (C. W., Bishop of Gibraltar).—COUNSEL TO ENGLISH CHURCHMEN ABROAD. Crown 8vo. 6s.

SCOTCH SERMONS, 1880. By Principal CAIRD and others. 3rd Edition. 8vo. 10s. 6d.

Service (Rev. John).—SERMONS. With Portrait. Crown 8vo. 6s.

Shirley (W. N.)—ELIJAH: Four University Sermons. Fcap. 8vo. 2s. 6d.

Smith (Rev. Travers).—MAN'S KNOWLEDGE OF MAN AND OF GOD. Crown 8vo. 6s.

Smith (W. Saumarez).—THE BLOOD OF THE NEW COVENANT: A Theological Essay. Crown 8vo. 2s. 6d.

Stanley (Dean)—
THE NATIONAL THANKSGIVING. Sermons preached in Westminster Abbey. 2nd Edition. Crown 8vo. 2s. 6d.
ADDRESSES AND SERMONS delivered during a visit to the United States and Canada in 1878. Crown 8vo. 6s.

Stewart (Prof. Balfour) and **Tait** (Prof. P. G.)—THE UNSEEN UNIVERSE; OR, PHYSICAL SPECULATIONS ON A FUTURE STATE. 15th Edition. Crown 8vo. 6s.
PARADOXICAL PHILOSOPHY: A Sequel to "The Unseen Universe." Crown 8vo. 7s. 6d.

Stubbs (Rev. C. W.)—FOR CHRIST AND CITY. Sermons and Addresses. Crown 8vo. 6s.

Tait (Archbishop)—
  THE PRESENT POSITION OF THE CHURCH OF ENGLAND. Being the Charge delivered at his Primary Visitation. 8vo. 3s. 6d.
  DUTIES OF THE CHURCH OF ENGLAND. Being seven Addresses delivered at his Second Visitation. 8vo. 4s. 6d.
  THE CHURCH OF THE FUTURE. Charges delivered at his Third Quadrennial Visitation. 2nd Edition. Crown 8vo. 3s. 6d.

Taylor (Isaac).—THE RESTORATION OF BELIEF. Crown 8vo. 8s. 6d.

Temple (Frederick, Bishop of London)—
  SERMONS PREACHED IN THE CHAPEL OF RUGBY SCHOOL. SECOND SERIES. 3rd Edition. Extra fcap. 8vo. 6s.
  THIRD SERIES. 4th Edition. Extra fcap. 8vo. 6s.
  THE RELATIONS BETWEEN RELIGION AND SCIENCE. Bampton Lectures, 1884. 7th and Cheaper Ed. Cr. 8vo. 6s.

Trench (Archbishop).—HULSEAN LECTURES. 8vo. 7s. 6d.

Tulloch (Principal).—THE CHRIST OF THE GOSPELS AND THE CHRIST OF MODERN CRITICISM. Extra fcap. 8vo. 4s. 6d.

Vaughan (C. J., Dean of Llandaff)—
  MEMORIALS OF HARROW SUNDAYS. 5th Edition. Crown 8vo. 10s. 6d.
  EPIPHANY, LENT, AND EASTER. 3rd Ed. Cr. 8vo. 10s. 6d.
  HEROES OF FAITH. 2nd Edition. Crown 8vo. 6s.
  LIFE'S WORK AND GOD'S DISCIPLINE. 3rd Edition. Extra fcap. 8vo. 2s. 6d.
  THE WHOLESOME WORDS OF JESUS CHRIST. 2nd Edition. Fcap. 8vo. 3s. 6d.
  FOES OF FAITH. 2nd Edition. Fcap. 8vo. 3s. 6d.
  CHRIST SATISFYING THE INSTINCTS OF HUMANITY. 2nd Edition. Extra fcap. 8vo. 3s. 6d.
  COUNSELS FOR YOUNG STUDENTS. Fcap. 8vo. 2s. 6d.
  THE TWO GREAT TEMPTATIONS. 2nd Ed. Fcap. 8vo. 3s. 6d.
  ADDRESSES FOR YOUNG CLERGYMEN. Extra fcap. 8vo. 4s. 6d.
  "MY SON, GIVE ME THINE HEART." Extra fcap. 8vo. 5s.
  REST AWHILE. Addresses to Toilers in the Ministry. Extra fcap. 8vo. 5s.
  TEMPLE SERMONS. Crown 8vo. 10s. 6d.
  AUTHORISED OR REVISED? Sermons on some of the Texts in which the Revised Version differs from the Authorised. Crown 8vo. 7s. 6d.
  LESSONS OF THE CROSS AND PASSION. WORDS FROM THE CROSS. THE REIGN OF SIN. THE LORD'S PRAYER. Four Courses of Lent Lectures. Crown 8vo. 10s. 6d.
  UNIVERSITY SERMONS. NEW AND OLD. Cr. 8vo. 10s. 6d.

Vaughan (C. J., Dean of Llandaff)—*continued.*
 NOTES FOR LECTURES ON CONFIRMATION. Fcap. 8vo. 1s. 6d.
 THE PRAYERS OF JESUS CHRIST: a closing volume of Lent Lectures delivered in the Temple Church. Globe 8vo. 3s. 6d.
 DONCASTER SERMONS. Lessons of Life and Godliness, and Words from the Gospels. Cr. 8vo. 10s. 6d.
 RESTFUL THOUGHTS IN RESTLESS TIMES. Crown 8vo.
   [*In the Press.*

Vaughan (Rev. D. J.)—THE PRESENT TRIAL OF FAITH. Crown 8vo. 9s.

Vaughan (Rev. E. T.)—SOME REASONS OF OUR CHRISTIAN HOPE. Hulsean Lectures for 1875. Crown 8vo. 6s. 6d.

Vaughan (Rev. Robert).—STONES FROM THE QUARRY. Sermons. Crown 8vo. 5s.

Venn (Rev. John).—ON SOME CHARACTERISTICS OF BELIEF, SCIENTIFIC AND RELIGIOUS. 8vo. 6s. 6d.

Warington (G.)—THE WEEK OF CREATION. Cr. 8vo. 4s. 6d.

Welldon (Rev. J. E. C.)—THE SPIRITUAL LIFE, and other Sermons. Crown 8vo. 6s.

Westcott (B. F., Bishop of Durham)—
 ON THE RELIGIOUS OFFICE OF THE UNIVERSITIES. Sermons. Crown 8vo. 4s. 6d.
 GIFTS FOR MINISTRY. Addresses to Candidates for Ordination. Crown 8vo. 1s. 6d.
 THE VICTORY OF THE CROSS. Sermons preached during Holy Week, 1888, in Hereford Cathedral. Crown 8vo. 3s. 6d.
 FROM STRENGTH TO STRENGTH. Three Sermons (In Memoriam J. B. D.) Crown 8vo. 2s.
 THE REVELATION OF THE RISEN LORD. Cr. 8vo. 6s.
 THE HISTORIC FAITH. 3rd Edition. Crown 8vo. 6s.
 THE GOSPEL OF THE RESURRECTION. 6th Ed. Cr. 8vo. 6s.
 THE REVELATION OF THE FATHER. Crown 8vo. 6s.
 CHRISTUS CONSUMMATOR. 2nd Edition. Crown 8vo. 6s.
 SOME THOUGHTS FROM THE ORDINAL. Cr. 8vo. 1s. 6d.
 SOCIAL ASPECTS OF CHRISTIANITY. Crown 8vo. 6s.
 ESSAYS IN THE HISTORY OF RELIGIOUS THOUGHT IN THE WEST. Globe 8vo. 6s.
 THE GOSPEL OF LIFE. Cr. 8vo. 6s.

Wickham (Rev. E. C.)—WELLINGTON COLLEGE SERMONS. Crown 8vo. 6s.

Wilkins (Prof. A. S.)—THE LIGHT OF THE WORLD: an Essay. 2nd Edition. Crown 8vo. 3s. 6d.

Wilson (J. M., Archdeacon of Manchester)—
 SERMONS PREACHED IN CLIFTON COLLEGE CHAPEL. Second Series. 1888-90. Crown 8vo. 6s.
 ESSAYS AND ADDRESSES. Crown 8vo. 4s. 6d.
 SOME CONTRIBUTIONS TO THE RELIGIOUS THOUGHT OF OUR TIME. Crown 8vo. 6s.

Printed by R. & R. CLARK, *Edinburgh*